Preface

Robert Frost and George Seferis, two poets who lived at about the same time, wrote in different languages and knew little or nothing of one another's work. This study suggests that we can profitably read the two poets in relation to one another nevertheless. It examines the way both men use a few recurrent images taken from landscape to express their sense not only of place but also of the past, the unknown, and the problems of language.

The idea of juxtaposing Frost and Seferis began with my pleasure in both their voices, together with a vague sense that those voices were somehow kindred. It began, also, with my affectionate familiarity with New England and Greece, the respective locales of their most characteristic work. As well as the inception of this study, such pleasure may well be where it ends. I do not claim to have forged an indissoluble link of influence between the two poets, or even to have revealed any likeness which bonds the two writers so strongly that neither can henceforth be read alone. Indeed, my discussion of each man's work could be read separately.

Nevertheless, between the initial attraction to the poets and the final satisfaction of a deeper understanding of two oeuvres, my study represents a series of discoveries. These touch on each poet's work, on analogies between the two oeuvres, and on the nature of poetry itself. Thus this work can be approached in various ways: as a comparative examination of how two poets write about landscape or use imagery; as an exploration of how each comes to terms with his poetic heritage; as a discussion of the workings of poetic imagery, in particular synecdoche; and finally, as an essay in painstaking reading. However the study is regarded, the images which are its chief focus are not only a topic in themselves but also a peg on which to hang recurring concerns with the nature of poetic thought and the capabilities of language.

All such concerns are derived from my examination of three

7

image clusters which I have found to be common to the work of
Frost and Seferis. The two poets' voices had struck me as akin
long before I compared the ways in which they approached their
subject matter. That subject matter is clearly much involved with
a sense of place—with love for and deep familiarity with a certain landscape. (This fact is a critical commonplace in the case of
one poet, not the other.) Since both poets write constantly about
locales they know, generally out of doors, certain images persis-
tently crop up in their work. Wall, stone, sea, tree, light . . . the
ubiquity of such images is inseparable from the marked simplicity of each poet's mature voice. What I had begun by sensing as
similarity in the voices resolved itself into something more precisely definable in terms of images.

(Before attempting to define "image" as I use the word, I
should note, in connection with the similarity of voices, that
despite their writing in different languages Frost and Seferis
markedly share certain stylistic qualities and goals. Neither is a
radical innovator, yet each seeks to modify the excesses of his
predecessors, to come closer to the sound of a speaking voice.
These shared concerns are of interest from the point of view of
literary history; they also seem to show that Frost and Seferis
were at work along parallel paths in other matters than the use of
images. This matter is further explored in the Introduction.)

If the chief similarity between the two poets' voices cannot be
a matter of actual words used, wherein does it lie? In a shared
habit of husbandry, a similar restraint in the way each takes his
language from the world. In contrast to certain of their contemporaries (Stevens, Pound, and Crane come to mind in English,
Sikelianos above all in Greek), neither Frost nor Seferis is very
inventive or extravagant, idiosyncratic or even fanciful. Both
are comparatively sober and (despite Seferis's occasional ob-
scurity) simple—with a simplicity that accommodates considerable depth.

Both poets were aware of their limitations, to judge from
Frost's remark that he was "pretty nearly an anti-vocabularian"
and Seferis's declaration that he (Seferis) was a "monotonous
and obstinate sort of man who has gone on saying the same
things over and over again." Rather than either dismissing such
deprecations as untrue (both happen to contain a measure of
truth) or else reproaching the poets with being monotonous, I
have made these very limitations and repetitions my subject. I

have looked long and hard at the major images in each poet's work.

An image might be defined as what stands between voice and landscape. A poet's voice is what we hear behind or through the words on the page; landscape, what we see behind or through the words. An image makes use of both aural and visual imagination: it is what the voice, or poetic style, makes of the landscape, or poetic subject. Many perusals have convinced me that Frost's and Seferis's more important images (they might also be called—have been called—emblems or symbols, but I prefer the more neutral term) have in common a remarkable quality—one which can finally be perceived as a whole but can only be described in stages.

To begin with, Frost's and Seferis's images are readily identifiable from a world of virtually universal experience. Few of us have actually seen Stevens's "Arabian in my room, / With his damned hoobla-hoobla-hoobla-how, / Inscribe a primitive astronomy," but most of us have seen stones, trees, sunlight. Stare at an image in Frost or Seferis: the old farmhouse, the battered marble column are recognizable, familiar. Ponder them further: they begin to radiate feeling—the personal meaning of walls in a life, the human tragedy in broken stones, the hopes that accompany putting in a garden. Continue to contemplate the image: the corona of emotion gives way to something that, while still subjective, is less personal, more abstract, finally universal in its scope; something eloquent of limits, cycles, history. Carried to their extremes of evocation, these major images seem to be proposing the major ways in which people accommodate themselves to time, for they limn time as linear or cyclical and perceive what is beyond time as a vast oscillation between opposing poles.

The final suggestion may be of the limits of language. By the time Frost and Seferis have done with an image, little remains to be said. The reader is left to construe, and a silence falls—vibrant with possibilities, but still a silence. It comes as a confirmation of these poets' kinship that near the end of their lives both approach the end of words, not so much in a Poundian repudiation of utterance as in simply admitting more empty space into utterance than either had ever allowed before.

The working of these images as I have tried to convey it may very well not be restricted to these two poets. It may be that *any* poetic image can be read to operate in this way. True; but I have never felt the same combination of outwardly radiating associative energy with a spare surface in quite the same way elsewhere, particularly in the poetry of this century. The uncluttered quality of Frost's and Seferis's work, together with its adherence to the familiar features of our world, makes their relatively sparse images easy to isolate and to gauge.

Moreover, I would defend my choice of this particular pair of poets by the fact that Frost and Seferis not only put images to similar uses; almost startlingly, they use many of *the same images.* If not identical, the important clusters of images in their work are strikingly analogous. Frost's three main groups are walls and by extension houses; growing things, especially trees but also gardens; and stars. In another triple cluster, Seferis returns again and again to stones; to the sea; and to the sun and generally light. The similarities I have traced between the two poets' uses of each image group have determined the way this study is presented. Chapter I explores walls and stones, Chapter II discusses gardens and the sea, and Chapter III is devoted to stars and light. Each chapter attempts to summarize the kinds of meaning derived from each image group—meaning which, as I have suggested, continually radiates outward from small things to large, from the familiar to the cosmic.

My critical approach is synecdoche-like in its attempt consistently to derive a maximum of suggestiveness for the whole from the parts. Frost once said on this subject, "All an artist needs is samples. Enough success to know what money is like; enough love to know what women are like. . . . Imagery and after-imagery are about all there is to poetry. Synecdoche and synecdoche—my motto is that something must be left to God."

Though I have gathered many different "samples" of the major images mentioned above, I have also tried to respect the principle of leaving something to God. That is, the images discussed here are not the only ones that could conceivably be found in the work of these two poets; the study could perhaps be expanded to include more poets; and my analysis is selective, not exhaustive, in its choice of poems. The principle of selection has been my assumption throughout that for these two poets, at any rate, the relevant unit of poetic thought is an image. Its very incompleteness is stimulating, for an image is always part of some larger whole which it becomes the reader's challenging task to reconstruct.

A critic who calls Frost's "literalness" an asset has maintained that imagery is not argument.* For Frost and Seferis I believe the opposite is true. Their prose as well as their poetry amply shows both writers to be preoccupied from first to last with the ability of poetry to communicate; with the importance of metaphor to thought. Hence both frequently employ imagery as argument—not argument as dogma or debate, to be sure, but in the sense that the ideas and associations incessantly radiating from the central core of images give to each poet's work much of its continuity and substance. Both poets are able to use images as word-paintings, to make us see beauty; but both want to do more than that with language. Their images prod us to connect, extend, recall, apply, compare—in other words, to think.

Looked at one way, the relatively restricted number of major images in their work confirms the "anti-vocabularian" side of Frost or the "monotonous and obstinate" side of Seferis. But the reverse truth has at least an equal claim on us. Mining a wealth of meaning from a limited number of images is an example of poetic resourcefulness, a way of making the most out of the givens of language. Frost wrote:

> The very words of the dictionary are a restriction to make the best of or stay out of and be silent. Coining new words isn't encouraged. We play the words as we find them. We make them do. Form in language is such a lot of old broken pieces it seems almost as nonexistent as spirit till the two meet in the sky.

Images, in other words, are the nouns and verbs and adjectives in the vocabulary constituted by an entire oeuvre. In Frost and Seferis, walls and stones, trees and sea, stars and light are made to "do" a great deal.

It is interesting to observe that within the larger landscapes of the poetry of their time, both poets managed to strike a balance between public and private worlds, both in the subjects of their art and in its tones. Although references to the opposing extremes of war and love can certainly be detected in their work, both Frost and Seferis steer pretty clear of political statement on the one hand or confessional outcry on the other. To an extent rare in this century, each writes of the public life in tones that are

*Reginald L. Cook, *The Dimensions of Robert Frost* (1958).

quiet enough to be private and of the private life in ways accessible enough to be public. In fact, "public" and "private" become misleading terms for these poets, who hold with surprising tenacity to a characteristic mean.

The balance between inner and outer worlds in each poet's work is reflected in the two lives. Frost, originally a loner who resisted institutions, ended his career as a kind of maverick public monument, even enjoying an unofficial cultural ambassadorship to the Soviet Union. Seferis worked for the Greek government as a professional diplomat for most of his life; constantly bemoaning the yoke of officialdom, he somehow never chose to give it up. Each man surely used his art to achieve some crucial private balance, however precarious, between worlds.

Both poets were deeply familiar with the poetry of the past; neither, understandably, was enamored of the twentieth century. Yet unlike some of their contemporaries, neither tried to turn back time to arrive at an impossible past. Perhaps this refusal of nostalgia was owing to both the American and the Greek poets' keen awareness of the ways in which the past was present, whether in stones underfoot or in the languages they wrote in. The sense of the solidity of the past beneath their feet provides a counterweight to the transcendent yearnings both poets express late in their work. Despite such longings, both Frost and Seferis keep their feet, Antaeus-like, on their own soil. Without ever quite leaving earth, they both end by attaining cosmic voices through sheer persistence in contemplating earthly vistas in such a way that they can still glimpse infinities.

Note on the Text

Edward Connery Lathem's *The Poetry of Robert Frost* (New York: Holt, Rinehart and Winston, 1977) is the only full collection of Frost's poems currently in print. My preference, however, is for the earlier edition; thus wherever in this study I have quoted from Robert Frost's poems, the text I have used has been the *Complete Poems of Robert Frost* (New York: Holt, Rinehart and Winston, 19th printing, 1967). For a discussion of the different editions of Frost's poems, see Donald Hall, "Robert Frost Corrupted," in Hall's collection of essays, *The Weather for Poetry: Essays, Reviews, and Notes on Poetry, 1970–76* (Ann Arbor: University of Michigan Press, 1982). A shorter version of the essay appeared in *Atlantic Monthly* (March 1982).

Note on Sources

Quotations from Frost poems are from *The Complete Poems of Robert Frost* (New York: Holt, Rinehart & Winston, 19th printing, 1967).

Quotations from Seferis poems are from *George Seferis: Collected Poems* (expanded edition), translated, edited, and introduced by Edmund Keeley and Philip Sherrard (Princeton, N.J.: Princeton University Press, 1981).

If no translator is given for quotations from Greek, the translator should be assumed to be myself. Titles of books in Greek have also been translated by me.

Acknowledgments

One summer day in 1971, I was lying on a pebbly beach on the southern shore of the island of Samos. I was, incidentally, sunbathing; chiefly I was reading *The Prelude*. A shadow on the book made me lift my head. A neighboring child named Ariadne was asking if she could borrow my flippers. The moment went later into a poem called "Island Noons":

> I put the poet down and plunge away,
> the secret greenwood seared and quenched
> and hissing in salt water.

That hissing as one element met another must, I think, have signaled the start of this study. English poetry did not carry that day, but I never really put the poet down. As I floated in the Aegean, lines of Shakespeare or Tennyson would rise in my head. Speaking Greek, reading and writing poetry in English, I used to be at a loss when the Samians asked if maybe I hadn't forgotten my native language by now.

A few years later, living in Vermont, I rediscovered green and trees, but wanted ocean too. Again, a poem expresses the moment best (I am a poet first and any other kind of writer second):

> Green, green:
> now in the treeland I want sea again.

This study, then, is my attempt to eat my cake and have it too. The stuff of which it is made is not only the words of Frost and Seferis but also the accumulation of mornings and afternoons, seasons and weathers, that I lived through in Samos and Vermont. My literary and personal acknowledgments are few, for my primary debt in the writing of these pages is to two dear remembered parts of the earth's surface.

The study began as a doctoral thesis; and my advisers, Robert Fagles and Edmund Keeley, have my warm thanks. Each in his

15

own way, they both provided me with confidence when I lacked it and discriminating suggestions when I needed them. Their enthusiastic yet discerning guidance was a fact I could always count on, but I am especially grateful that they had enough faith in me to leave me pretty much alone with two tough old men.

Elizabeth Chamberlayne Hadas helped make me into a lover and memorizer of poetry, and helped make me. Stavros Kondilis brought me to his island. Barbara Waxenberg helped me to see that mountains are not utterly forbidding, especially mountains of my own construction.

Finally, my husband, George Edwards, has seen me through the writing of this study from beginning to end. He has always given me the kinds of space I needed; even more, he has continually shown me what it means to have belief in, and to be true to, one's work. To him, my loving thanks.

Short References

These frequently cited works are, after their first mention in the Notes following each chapter, abbreviated as follows.

Aspects of Death	*Aspects of Death in Early Greek Art and Poetry* by Emily Vermeule
Constellations	*The Poetry of Robert Frost: Constellations of Intention* by Reuben Brower
Fire and Ice	*Fire and Ice: The Art and Thought of Robert Frost* by Lawrance Thompson
Interviews	*Interviews with Robert Frost* edited by Edward Connery Lathem
Lentricchia	"Robert Frost and Modern Literary Theory" by Frank Lentricchia
Major Themes	*The Major Themes of Robert Frost* by Radcliffe Squires
My Brother GS	*My Brother George Seferis* by Ioanna Tsatsou
On the Greek Style	*Seferis on the Greek Style* edited by Rex Warner
Poet and Dancer	*The Poet and the Dancer* by Nasos Vayenas
Poetics of Space	*The Poetics of Space* by Gaston Bachelard
Profile	*Profile of Robert Frost* edited by Lewis Simpson
RF: The Individual & Society	*Robert Frost: The Individual and Society* by Peter J. Stanlis
RF on Writing	*Robert Frost on Writing* edited by Elaine Barry

Three Secret Poems   *Three Secret Poems of George Seferis* translated by Walter Kaiser

Work of Knowing   *Robert Frost: The Work of Knowing* by Richard Poirier

Form,
Cycle,
Infinity

Introduction

The purpose of this introduction is twofold. First, it furnishes some material on Frost's and Seferis's literary backgrounds, and on each poet's attitude toward his own heritage. For the Greekless reader, such facts about Seferis are not easy to come by. Frost's relation to literary tradition, by contrast, is of course well known. Nevertheless, juxtaposing the two accounts enables us to discern some striking parallels.

Having taken such material into account, the introduction then considers the fact that both Frost and Seferis notoriously resist easy categorization as members of poetic movements or schools. Indeed, the relation of the two poets to one another might be traced from their shared rejection of the abrupt, "vertical" mode of modernist poetics. Both Frost and Seferis, I suggest, use what might be termed a horizontal mode of constructing poetic landscapes—landscapes, as the body of this work shows, of striking continuity. Frost's and Seferis's two landscapes differ, naturally—that is, in nature, for one poet imaginatively appropriates the natural features of New England, the other those of Greece. Each, however, composes his world in a manner not only coherent within itself but remarkably continuous, if we trouble to make the connections, with the other poet's landscape.

1. Backgrounds and Attitudes

For the reader who is motivated to explore the traditions and influences which Frost and Seferis had assimilated (or reacted against) when they began to write, it is a piece of good fortune that both poets were interviewed—in their old age—for the *Paris Review Writers at Work* series. Not coincidentally, the interviewer in each case was one of the most discerning critics of the poet in question, or was later to become so: Richard Poirier of Frost, Edmund Keeley of Seferis.

Asked the usual question about influences on their work, both poets gave replies that were illuminating and evasive. Frost, asked by Poirier whether he read much in the Romantic poets, Wordsworth in particular, answered "No, you couldn't pin me there."[1] Later he added "Oh, I read all sorts of things." The interviewer persisted: "When you began to write, was there any writer you especially admired?" Frost: "I was the enemy of that theory . . . that you should play the sedulous ape to anybody." Poirier made one more attempt: "Did you ever feel any affinity between your work and any other poet's?" Frost: "I'll leave that for somebody else to tell me. I wouldn't know."

Seferis's tone, as always, is more formally decorous than Frost's; and in keeping with this decorum, Keeley put the question of tradition and influence in the third person. "How about the relation of the Greek poet to his particular historical tradition?" Seferis was equally cautious when he replied: ". . . Greece is a continuous process. In English the expression 'ancient Greece' includes the meaning of 'finished,' whereas for us Greece goes on living, for better or worse. . . ."[2] Asked about the development of his style, Seferis again referred to the presentness of the Greek past—a theme we will see is ubiquitous in his work. "In my youth I worked very much over the Greek language. Glossaries, old texts, medieval texts, and things of that kind. But the difficulty wasn't only in studying them; the difficulty was to forget them and be natural."

What these responses share is an understandable caviling at the assumption that a poet's literary genealogy is so clear that he either could or would recite his own pedigree. Beyond this, however, the poets' evasiveness masks an embarrassment of riches. For both Frost and Seferis, bonds to the broader concept of tradition are more crucial than the influence of this or that particular writer—perhaps a paradoxical state of affairs, but an important one for any poet who wishes, as Seferis put it, to forget [models] and be natural. It is not that influences do not exist; but, in the phrase of Valéry that Seferis was fond of quoting, "le lion est fait de mouton assimilé." Quoting this phrase, Seferis adds, "I believe there is no parthenogenesis in art."[3] Similarly, a beautiful passage using figures from the natural world constitutes a tacit admission on the part of Frost that influence, while never clear and simple, certainly does exist:

No one given to looking underground in spring can have failed to notice how a bean starts its growth from the seed.

Now the manner of a poet's germination is less like that of a bean in the ground than of a water-spout at sea. He has to begin as a cloud of all the other poets he ever read. That can't be helped. And first the cloud reaches down toward the water from above and then the water reaches up toward the cloud from below and finally cloud and water join together to roll as one pillar between heaven and earth. The base of water he picks up from below is of course all the life he ever lived outside of books. . . .[4]

A quick glance at the books the two young poets had read, and the lives they had led outside books, shows a not unexpected divergence. Frost began by hearing Bible stories and fairy tales from his poetry-loving, Scots-born mother. Later (still at home) he heard Scots ballads and Romantic poetry read aloud; and at the not very precocious age of fourteen or so began to read books to himself for pleasure. During his short sojourns at Dartmouth and later Harvard, Frost became acquainted with the works of Emerson, Thoreau, William James, and Santayana. In addition, it should be emphasized that his background in Greek and especially Latin was a very solid one, perhaps more thorough than his reading in English literature. Other than the classics of antiquity, Frost was little acquainted with foreign languages or literatures.[5]

Seferis represents an altogether more cosmopolitan mode. Born in Smyrna, he was brought to Athens at fourteen, studied law in Paris, and later as a diplomat lived in Turkey, South Africa, and London. Seferis was bilingual in Greek and French from an early age; moreover, there were deep divisions within his native language, of which Vayenas gives an illuminating brief account.

Until the age of fourteen Seferis lived in Smyrna, a seat of greater Hellenism whose language naturally lacked the homogeneity of that of the national center. Aside from the "tidied-up *koine,*" as Seferis calls it, which was the official language of the bourgeoisie, there was the folk language of the people—a kind of *koine* of the islands, related to the language of Crete—and the commercial language, an idiom of the customs and mercantile offices, with many foreign words and characteristic alterations in print, which were used by the Fench colonies. French was in common use. Seferis studied at a Helleno-Gallic school where some lessons were given in French. In addition, he also had French tutors in Smyrna as well as, later, in Athens. When in 1914 he arrived in Athens,

Seferis felt that his speech sounded different from that of the capital: "When I went to high school in Athens," he writes, "from the startled or suspicious faces of my fellow students when I spoke to them, I understood that my language—very close to that of the *Erotocritos*—was not correct."[6]

Such internal cleavages were perhaps less important for Seferis the poet than the agonizing problem of which language to write in—a dilemma reflecting the discontinuity Seferis felt all his life between his official diplomatic persona and his private self as a poet. The sense of displacement begins with language but does not end there. "Always the same agony, the same hopelessness looking at my situation: a man of another race rooted in French culture—this creates a host of problems which become mixed up together and tyrannize over me."[7] Seferis's journal of about this time reveals that even his dreams were sometimes divided between Greek and French.

Frost never completed his formal education, but seems always to have had a circle of loyal mentors, critics, and friends, from his mother and his wife Elinor (herself a poet) and friend Carl Hubell to Susan Hayes Ward, the editor who first accepted a poem of Frost's for publication and proved an encouraging and sympathetic correspondent. In England there was the Georgian poet Edward Thomas; in America, students like John Bartlett, to whom Frost wrote many of his thoughts on prosody, and friends like Louis Untermeyer, to whom he wrote about almost everything.[8]

By contrast, Seferis at first confided his thoughts on poetry only to his journals and in letters to his sister; during much of his life he thirsted for congenial literary peers, who were apparently in short supply either in the literary circles of Athens or in diplomatic posts in Ankara or Albania. Moreover, although Seferis spent what seemed to him interminable years as a student (about the equivalent of college and graduate school today, and thus far more years than Frost submitted to schools), he repeatedly refers to himself in the journals as an autodidact. At first this looks like disingenuousness or excessive modesty: well read in the French symbolists and, later, poetry in English as well as the whole range of Greek literature, Seferis was hardly culturally impoverished. If anything, he was a lion confronted with a bewildering variety of meats to assimilate. But as Vayenas points out, it was the comparison of the Greek tradition with the foreign which made Seferis repeat that he had no teachers. The lack of unbroken literary tradition in Greece made him feel that in relation to the French or English [poet], the Greek poet is self-taught. By teachers he naturally means poets of his own language, who would normally transmit their craft to younger men.[9]

Vayenas goes on to observe that Seferis did indeed find mentors in the Greek tradition; but that with the exceptions of Cavafy and Sikelianos, he had to go far back in time in order to do so. Such masters were Cornaros, author of the masterpiece of the Cretan Renaissance, *Erotocritos;* the nineteenth-century memoirist Makriyannis (a true autodidact); and the poets Solomos and Calvos. These writers are for Seferis masters of demotic expression; they should not be thought of as somewhat recherché discoveries in poetic taste, like the Metaphysicals or Jacobean drama for Eliot. In Solomos, Calvos, and Cavafy, writes Vayenas, "Seferis will find the lack of rhetoric he sought, and they will become the chief counterbalance for his apprenticeship in foreign literatures. At the heart of the problem is a demand which for Seferis was always one of the chief principles of his poetic: the demand for purity of vision and accuracy of expression."[10]

It might seem, then, that Frost and Seferis were far apart not only in respect to their literary antecedents but in their relations to those forebears. Frost is secure in English; Seferis has to choose between French and Greek—or even one among various forms of Greek. Frost rejects the academy and wants independence, yet has the support of a widening circle of sympathetic critics (even before his monumental fame); Seferis, a young student in a cosmopolitan city, regrets the isolation of his position. Perhaps all the two young men had in common was that each wanted to write and to be read. Neither always wrote with great facility, but writing was as preferable to farming for Frost as it was, for Seferis, to law and diplomacy.

And write they both did. But the parallels are in fact much greater than this bare fact suggests. Even early in their careers (and *A Boy's Will* and *Turning Point* are not books which have attained the poets' mature voices), Frost and Seferis are aiming for related goals. In his quest for a true voice, each is dissatisfied with the prissy, elaborate, or artificial language of late nineteenth-century poetry. Each, in his own poetic language, might be said to favor demotic over katharevousa.[11]

Long before Frost promulgated his theory of the "sound of sense" (in the 22 February 1914 letter to Bartlett), he was extraordinarily sensitive to the way things sounded. We have noted that he was not an early reader; poetry first came to him through the ear, not the eye. Reuben Brower adduces an almost Keatsian sensibility in a very early letter:

> For several weeks now when not teaching I have spent my time lying around either consciously sleeping or unconsciously waking and in both cases irresponsibly iratable [*sic*] to the last degree. It is due to my nerves—they are so suceptible [*sic*] to sound. . . .[12]

But despite such sensitivity, Frost always emphatically separated the kind of verbal sound to which the letter refers and to which his ear responded from pure sound, or music. When Frost began to make more confident pronouncements about poetry, his concern was to maintain clear categories of poetry and music, not to abolish them in the fashionable Symbolist manner. A letter to Untermeyer in 1915 indicates Frost's irritation at any blurring of these two separate art forms.

> Tell me, Louis . . . while it is uppermost in my mind what, when you are doing the high critical, do you mean by "overtones" in poetry.

At Untermeyer's presumably reassuring reply that it meant nothing, Frost's relief is obvious:

> It's all right then. . . . It's just one of those bad analogies that obliterates the distinction between poetry and music.[13]

It was not just that Frost objected to "bad analogies"; he saw that it was time to work in a different direction.

> You see the great successes in recent poetry [he wrote Bartlett in 1913] have been made on the assumption that the music of words was a matter of harmonised vowels and consonants. Both Swinburne and Tennyson arrived largely at effects in assonation. But they were on the wrong track or at any rate on a short track. They went the length of it. Any one else who

goes that way must go after them. And that's where most are going.[14]

It is interesting that Frost had a balanced view of "effects in assonation," since he also faulted the Imagists for paying insufficient attention to sound in their eagerness for "eye images."[15]

The poems of Swinburne and Tennyson that Frost presumably had in mind were shorter lyrics where "assonation" carries the whole poem. The poems that most appealed to Frost, on the other hand, were less purely lyrical and more dramatic; he tended to agree with Emerson's dictum that "not metres but a metre-making argument" are of chief poetic importance. Action, conflict, event, above all the human voice speaking intelligibly— these seem to have been the qualities to which Frost responded in his reading before he sought them in his writing. By the time he wrote the above-cited letters to Untermeyer and Bartlett, Frost had completed *North of Boston* (publication date 1914, but many of the poems were written much earlier), a book which masterfully combines the lyric and dramatic modes within poems.

Some of Frost's most famous and memorable statements about poetry are more intelligible when we bear in mind his very specific objection to a poetry which leans too heavily on sound without paying enough attention to sense. The craggily *ex cathedra* tone of some Frostian pronouncements can obscure the fact that the poet was living in a particular moment and had definite disapprovals and resentments rather than speaking straight from Parnassus. This is not to undercut the magnificent expressiveness and often the shrewdness of such declarations as the following:

. . . The sound is the gold in the ore. Then we will have the sound out alone and dispense with the inessential. We do till we make the discovery that the object in writing poetry is to make all poems sound as different as possible from each other, and the resources for that of vowels, consonants, punctuation, syntax, words, sentences, meter are not enough. We need the help of context—meaning—subject matter. That is the greatest help toward variety. All that can be done with words is soon told. . . .[16]

If Frost objected to the musical-poetic mist in which the fol-
lowers of Tennyson and Swinburne had become blurred and
confused, then his clearest analogue among nineteenth-century
poets is Wordsworth. Although (or because) Frost dodged
Poirier's inquiry about Wordsworthian influence, nevertheless
Wordsworth is probably the poet who most frequently comes to
mind as one reads Frost. The association of "humble and rustic
life" with purity of feeling expressed in "a plainer and more
emphatic language" which Wordsworth makes in his *Preface to
Lyrical Ballads* is closely akin to Frost's preferred subject matter (ordinary and rustic people) and unadorned manner. Still we
must remember that Frost was born more than a century after
Wordsworth. In the words of Lawrance Thompson,

> There is a striking difference between Wordsworth's insis-
> tence on "plainer and more emphatic language" and Frost's
> theory of the sound of sense. Each poet set out in revolt
> against entirely different traditions of the past. The artificiality
> of poetic diction which Wordsworth deplored was that of mo-
> notonous eighteenth-century restraint, while the artificiality of
> diction which Frost deplored was the lush exuberance of
> nineteenth-century artifice.[17]

Not only do Frost's and Wordsworth's diction necessarily differ,
but chronology also dictates an interesting gulf between their
respective views of their rural subjects.

> [Frost] has said that his "country neighbors" whether formally
> educated or not, were "all much the same," that "a certain
> level up there in Vermont or New Hampshire" stays about the
> same. He could never speak as Wordsworth does of "humble
> and rustic life." The historical reasons for the difference be-
> tween English and American country life are familiar enough.
> For one thing, the peasantry did not survive transplantation to
> America. For another, the New England farmer, schooled by
> congregational and town meetings in theological and political
> debate, had acquired very different intellectual habits from his
> old world counterpart. But poetic style did not catch up surely
> with this difference in mind and speech before Frost. . . .
> Frost—not to be confused with the farmers he writes about—
> has realized that their idiom, though awkward sounding to
> urban ears, is often used to compress meaning and over-
> meaning in ways that bring them nearer to Falstaff than to
> Peter Bell.[18]

Since much of Frost's prose—brief, gnarled, figurative, evocative rather than discursive—tends toward examples rather than exegesis of poetic practice, there is in Frost's writings no one manifesto comparable to Wordsworth's celebrated *Preface*. But one statement shows well enough Frost's true kinship to Wordsworth, his aims in using the kind of diction he used—and provides a link with Seferis.

> There are two kinds of language: the spoken language and the written language—our every day speech which we call the vernacular; and a more literary, sophisticated, artificial, elegant language that belongs to books. We often hear it said that a man talks like a book in this second way. We object to anybody's talking in this literary, artificial English; we don't object to anybody's writing in it; we rather expect people to write in a literary, somewhat artificial style. I, myself, could get along very well without this bookish language altogether.[19]

Now this distinction between the written and spoken forms of a language is more precisely and formally true of Greek in its demotic and katharevousa forms than it is of English, where such distinctions can be relatively blurred. The last sentence in the above passage might very well have come from the Greek poet Solomos's *Dialogue* on the subject of the virtues of demotic Greek; or it might have come from Seferis.

It is not that Seferis was the first poet writing in modern Greek to use demotic. We have seen that his spoken Greek was related to that of the *Erotocritos*—a Cretan version of demotic and one of Seferis's stylistic models. Other poetic antecedents using demotic are Greek folk songs and the works of Solomos, to some degree Calvos and Cavafy, and closer to Seferis's own time Palamas, Sikelianos, and Caryotakis. The battle of choosing the living language rather than the artificial and ungainly constructed one had essentially been won, at least for poets, by the time Seferis began to write. But Seferis's goal—to use demotic to create the sound of a living voice—had been neither achieved nor, probably, even conceived by Palamas and Sikelianos with their rhetorical effusions or Cavafy with his highly idiosyncratic and ironic style. Without sacrificing the complexity of his themes, Seferis wished to achieve a cleaner, purer, simpler voice.

A key to such ambitions is Seferis's lifelong devotion to the *Memoirs* of General Makriyannis; the essay on the *Memoirs,* as well as being one of Seferis's most original, penetrating, and sympathetic, casts light on the poet's struggles and aims. Makriyannis, poor and uneducated, was so far from being an accomplished writer that he had to teach himself to write (after a fashion) in order to set down his opinions and experiences. The resulting prose is thus paradoxical: free of formal embellishments yet imbued with tradition. For Seferis, always nostalgic for an elusive idea of Greece, bilingual, well-read, yet feeling a sense of alienation from both the cultures he knew, this paradoxical combination is style in the truest sense. Something of Makriyannis's unabashed authenticity, as Seferis gives us an account of it, may recall Frost's respect for his country neighbors' way with language.[20]

> Obviously Makriyannis would like to have had the means to become educated. But this fact does not make him a lesser man, does not, as we say, give him an inferiority complex. He feels, and makes us feel with him, that he is a man on whom God has conferred the gift of speech, a gift which no one has the right to take away from him. Wherever he may be, whether in a palace or in a cottage, he speaks his mind and he speaks with confidence. And because he has this innate confidence in his power of expression, he can speak with color, with a wide spectrum of varying shades, with tonality and with rhythm. I have the impression that any philologist of Makriyannis' text should be careful first of all to base his work on his own ability to hear the spoken word.[21]

It is this spoken word, as rendered on paper by a nonwriter, that so appeals to Seferis in Makriyannis. In the same essay, Seferis argues that the apparent victory of demotic over katharevousa as a literary language is not, by itself, sufficient to produce good writing (an opinion which the intervening years have amply justified).

> If . . . the language problem seems to have been liquidated, we should not forget that there can be no writer of stature who is not a "lord" of the language and that he will acquire this quality not through dictionaries and syntax but through that real living nature which comes to him every moment in the breathing of his race.[22]

A final excerpt from the Makriyannis essay reveals Seferis's strong but nearly inarticulate sense (a sense recurring also in the journals) of the inherent difficulty of expressing feeling truly through language—of the agonistic nature of style.

> Meaning, language; the meaning that wants to be expressed and the language which must give a form, a positive existence to the meaning and so allow it to escape from obscurity. This force and this counterforce, unified in the end, create the style. These two conflicting forces are the difficulties of a writer. Out of these a style—a "voice," as the ancients called it— . . . takes on shape. The word is made articulate. This is why through language alone, however well we may know it, we can only create fine phrases, like "chaff on the threshing floor," as the song says, but without the resistance and the weight of the matter which we have to articulate, we shall never achieve style. Style is the difficulty encountered when a man tries to express himself; style is the human effort; "style is the very man," as the wise saying goes. That is why Makriyannis's style is so real. . . .[23]

This emphasis on "the weight of the matter which we have to articulate" is a good description of the unique and authoritative voice which Seferis eventually developed, a voice whose characteristic timbre can be heard through the various modes that (especially early in his career) tinge Seferis's style. An avid reader of French poetry during his student years in Paris, Seferis for a time regarded Laforgue as a spiritual elder brother and used to go to the Bibliothèque Nationale in order to copy down Valèry's verse.[24] But it was not long before Seferis felt that the Symbolists' goal of *poésie pure* and his own strivings for a personal voice were strange bedfellows. Indeed, the general critical reception of *Turning Point,* his first volume of verse, as a Greek version of *poésie pure* was acceptable to Seferis only if the phrase were understood as referring to technical perfection. With a Makriyannesque intolerance for lofty abstractions, he wrote, "There is no such thing as pure poetry for the artist. Poetry exists or does not exist. . . . The whole meaning of *poésie pure* (if there is such a thing) would be to bring back poetry to its original source, to return it to the level of the craftsman who is making a chair."[25]

Other than French poetry, Seferis's great non-Greek influence was T. S. Eliot. Although Seferis shared with Eliot a taste for such poets as Laforgue, what drew him to Eliot was not so much Eliot's indebtedness to the Symbolists as the importance of the

said of this passage, "But that's a real island. I was there in 1946."

Seferis's sense of what Poirier calls "decorum about the limits of poetry" clearly involves a willed spareness, partly temperamental, partly perhaps mimetic of the Greek landscape's quality of spareness. In the poetry, such spareness takes the form of a few key images' repeated recurrence—a recurrence that combines with the natural gravity of Seferis's voice to endow these images with a cumulatively portentous significance. We return to Seferis's words on Makriyannis about "the weight of the matter which we have to articulate" with a fresh sense of the importance of such weightiness in the poetry. One critic has described Seferis's poetic voice as marked by "a complicated purity . . . that depends on his language always being quite genuine; everything in the poems, and *the increasing weight of context* that bears on each fresh line as you hear it, rings completely true."[29] (Italics mine.)

Without making any violent ruptures with their respective literary heritages, Frost and Seferis both achieved, over the course of long careers, characteristically weighty, personal, pure voices, versions of English and Greek whose strength and simplicity are in keeping with "the weightiness of the matter which we have to articulate." Since that matter is now more weighty and now less, it follows that the voices are also flexible. But they are both poetic voices with a very recognizable style. Their gravity and craggy strength measure what Seferis calls, writing of Makriyannis, the difficulty encountered when a man tries to express himself.

2. Vertical and Horizontal: Continuity and the Idea of a Poetic Landscape

In connection with Frost's and Seferis's resistance to critical categorizing—a resistance we saw in the *Paris Review* interviews—it is illuminating to note the plethora of labels applied to Frost between about 1910 and the poet's death. This list is cited by Reginald Cook in his essay "Robert Frost and the Critics":

In 1926 Gorham Munson, Frost's first biographer, labelled Frost a classical poet, and over thirty years later reiterated his position. Mark Van Doren called him a symbolist (but not in

Arthur Symons' sense). John Lynen interpreted his poetry in the pastoral tradition. Reuben Brower thought this view an overemphasis. Localist (Amy Lowell), revisionist (Louis Untermeyer), ordinary man (Sidney Cox), Emersonian Romantic (Yvor Winters), glorified neighbor (G. R. Elliott), bard (John Ciardi), diversionist (R. L. Cook), each interpreted the poet differently, and Frost, a willing player of this game, has called himself a sensibilitist, an environmentalist [a prophetic note!], a realmist, a synecdochist, a lone striker, one acquainted with the night, a watcher of the void, a lover who has quarreled with the world, and even an Old Slow Coach![30]

Such a proliferation of labels represents a series of attempts to define something hard to capture—the quality of a poetic voice, the nature of a poetic world. But by making an oeuvre apparently more controllable, easier to grasp and summarize, categorizations have the unfortunate effect of reducing it. Seferis's stature is less if he is shown to be merely a Greek version of T. S. Eliot or leader of the Generation of the Thirties; Frost is far less formidable as a good gray poet, old neighbor, and so on. In the case of Frost, for example, such a conception insidiously relieves readers of the responsibilities of attention and alertness that they would bring to a poet with the reputation of being learned or obscure. When Frost is acknowledged—as he now generally is—to be a complex poet, the process of reading him becomes more multi-layered, complex, and rewarding.

With Seferis, critical preconceptions and their accompanying distortions are almost the opposite of those we find about Frost. Seferis is said to be notoriously difficult and allusive; at the same time, he is rarely given credit for much originality but is often said (either in praise or blame) to be rewriting other poets. What these conceptions of each poet ignore is the balanced quality of both oeuvres. Frost's undoubted accessibility is enriched by concealed learning, references often below the surface of the language. Seferis's apparently hermetic language is eased by the consistent, cogent quality of his allusions, which are not at all arbitrary but appear and reappear with the force almost of a refrain. In fact, each poet is original without being radical; each manages to be learned, to have access to the past, without sacrificing the sound of his own language, spoken as it was in his own time. To capture that immediacy of sound was, as we have seen, a primary (though not a sole) aim of each poet in his work.

As we saw earlier in this introduction, as well as the classics in which both poets are well versed, there are more contemporary sources for the youthful work of Frost and Seferis. Some of the poems in *A Boy's Will* sound like de la Mare or Dante Gabriel Rossetti; Seferis in *Turning Point* sounds now like Laforgue or Corbière, now like Valéry. This is hardly surprising; Eliot too was enchanted by Laforgue and Corbière, Pound by the Pre-Raphaelites. But what soon distinguishes Frost and Seferis from many of their contemporaries, and what we can perceive as a bond between them, is also what makes them hard to classify in the way Cook's passage shows. It is this: when they outgrow their most obvious influences and begin to sound like their mature selves, both these poets reject only superficial mannerisms; each holds firmly to essentials. Neither, in other words, thinks of himself primarily as having a mission to discard outmoded styles or smash rigid formal canons. Rather than breaking new ground or old rules, their sense of the poet's task is closer to what Robert Graves, writing of Frost, has called staying put and working patiently at the problem.

Neither poet literally stayed put, since Frost went to England at a crucial time in his career while Seferis, first as a student and then as a professional diplomat, was constantly away from Greece. But actual whereabouts hardly matter. For both men, staying put was a matter of listening with passionate attention to the sounds of their native languages. When Frost notes every inflection of Derry farm speech and records it in *North of Boston;* when Seferis reads Makriyannis and attempts to capture a true demotic in the speech of the Stratis Thalassinos poems, they are not rejecting but consolidating, preserving, and renewing.

The first portion of this introduction has examined in more detail some of the processes and sources in Frost's and Seferis's searches for what were to become their true voices. My purpose here is to understand those voices in the context of their time—a time of revolt against the poetic norms of the nineteenth century. An important element of poetic practice in the first decades of this century was rejection of what many poets perceived as outworn styles or themes. The poetic revolt against the past is broadly referred to as modernism—so broadly and so automatically, indeed, that poets working after a certain time find themselves labeled postmodern. But how good are the claims of modernism to utter newness—to be a true alternative to the much-condemned practices of Romanticism and its Victorian aftermath?

In a passage written forty years ago and still germane, Randall Jarrell explained why what was dubbed modernism in poetry, despite its clamorous proclamations of newness, was in many ways an outgrowth of the movement from which it claimed so radically to differ. Jarrell calls modernist poetry an extension; his figure is that of a vector.

> Modernist poetry . . . appears to be and is generally considered to be a violent break with romanticism; it is actually . . . an extension of romanticism, an end product in which most of the tendencies of romanticism have been carried to their limits. Romanticism—whether considered as the product of a whole culture, or, in isolation, as a purely literary phenomenon—is necessarily a process of extension, a vector; it presupposes a constant experimentalism, the indefinite attainment of "originality," generation after generation, primarily by the novel extrapolation of previously exploited processes. . . . All these romantic tendencies are exploited to their limits; and the movement which carries out this final exploitation, apparently so different from earlier stages of the same process, is what we call modernism.
>
> Both modern and conventional critics have been unable to see the fundamental similarities between modernist and romantic poetry because they were unwilling to see anything but differences; these were to the former a final recommendation, to the latter a final condemnation.[31]

Jarrell goes on to catalogue the underlying points of similarity between modernistic and romantic poetic practice, citing such shared features as experimentalism, lack of restraint or proportion, and emphasis on detail—on parts, not wholes.

Two points in particular stand out as marking Frost and Seferis different from this vector movement: its penchant for experimentalism and its concentration on the part rather than the whole. We have said that Frost and Seferis prefer to conserve and maintain and renew rather than to experiment and reject. This is one point; the other is that both poets are notably concerned with creating poems which are coherent wholes. Their work, in its individual poems and as total oeuvres, is quite free of the forward-pressing haste which is Jarrell's apt metaphor for such modern poetry. Not only does their work not approach the limits of what is technically or theoretically feasible; but the desire to make it new—to attain, as Jarrell says, an indefinite originality—is neither a very important motive for either poet nor a major motif in the work.

Frost's poetry is saturated, albeit subtly, with the poetry of the past—not by means of a collage of references, but because classical poetry is so often woven into the very fabric of his language. When Frost writes of poems "holding each other apart in their places as the stars do," and of "getting among" these poems, he is referring to a wide range of literary tradition, a range to which he had constant and comfortable access, while respecting the demands of privacy and space ("holding each other *apart*"). The kind of circulation to which Helen Bacon refers in an article on Frost is a wholly different kind of poetic motion from the ambitious headlong zoom of modernism:

> What is not generally recognized, even when his familiarity with classical literature is acknowledged, is how often Frost circulates, and wishes us to circulate, among the poems of classical antiquity. . . . Frost was particularly grumpy about the fact that Pound and Eliot with their direct quotations in dead languages, their footnotes and learned allusions, were acclaimed as learned and scholarly, while his less obtrusive and more complex use of classical material went unnoticed.[32]

A very similar circulation among classical poems characterizes the work of Seferis. It is true that Seferis's use of such material is not so unobtrusive as Frost's. Seferis quite often quotes words or lines in a "dead" language; he can make use, as Nasos Vayenas has shown of *Thrush,* of a most complex brew of mixed allusions. But by far the greater number of Seferis's literary references are Greek—ranging from Homer through tragedy and Plato to the New Testament to poems of the Cretan Renaissance and ballads of the eighteenth and nineteenth centuries, and finally to Makriyannis, Solomos, and Calvos. The effect of strangeness and foreignness is thus considerably reduced, for the poet and his audience, by the all-important common denominator of Hellenism—a fact not clearly understood by critics who are overly anxious to associate Seferis with Eliot.

Seferis is uninterested in the shock of newness, the speed of modernism; he wants to write good clear Greek, contemporary Greek, and also to get his point across as well and tightly as possible. If Makriyannis has found the best way of phrasing an idea, then Seferis does not hesitate to use the older writer's words—but, as Helen Bacon says of Frostian borrowings, "perfectly fitted into a new context." One example of this practice is a line from Seferis's "Last Stop":

> or simply bad habits, fraud and deceit.

Two words are taken verbatim from Makryannis's *Memoirs,* so there is an added richness of application if we pause to compare the Greek War of Independence with Seferis's principal theme in "Last Stop," the Second World War. But the use of the quote is hardly puzzling or obtrusive; if we do not recognize it, our understanding will not be diminished.

Another example, to be discussed in detail in Chapter II, is the various uses to which Seferis puts his beloved line from Aeschylus's *Agamemnon* about the inexhaustibility of the sea. Seferis's different uses of this line, all appropriate in their respective contexts, also all bring out new shades of meaning in the Aeschylean line. If the poet's desire had been to parade classical learning or to puzzle the reader by discontinuity, Seferis could have used scores of different lines from dozens of tragedies. In fact, his uses of this single line are so perfectly dovetailed into their several contexts in different poems that, like many Frostian allusions, they are undetectable if one is not familiar with the classical reference in the first place. And even in the absence of such familiarity, the poem remains luminous, generous, comprehensible.

Such skillful dovetailing of the old with the new makes it possible for Seferis and Frost to maintain a remarkable homogeneity of diction—or perhaps we could pose the matter the other way and say that only a confident and consistent diction could allow for such precise blendings and insertions. In either case, the smoothness and coherence that inform both poets' styles make the experience of reading their work a distinctive one. Trying to define this special quality in Seferis, Peter Levi has written of the authority of the poet's voice; and the same, I find, is true for Frost (and notably lacking in the numerous imitators of each poet). Authority of voice means that a poem's language is internally consistent; it also means that each individual poem partakes of a larger scheme, fits into the broader design or tone of the oeuvre. Here again Frost and Seferis fail to meet the criterion of the romantic-modernist continuum: what

Jarrell calls preoccupation with detail at the expense of wholeness.

The idea of the poem as an inseparable whole, words and thought complementing each other, in some ways recalls the Imagist ideal of the identity of meaning and function in a poem. An important difference exists, though. Such an equivalence was often achieved, in Imagist lyrics, through isolated bursts and flashes of brief utterance. One critic sums up the experience of reading a good deal of early twentieth-century poetry when he refers to lyrics "crowded with intense moments that reverberate with complex associations, but the moments are isolated from each other."[33] Even with the long poems of this time, the effect is often one of isolation or patchiness, a collagelike discontinuity where the reader's task is to arrange the shards or guide the thread into a discernible pattern.

Reading Frost or Seferis presents a different kind of challenge, since the design of each poet's work is cumulative in its effect. The more one reads and rereads the discrete, fairly short poems which comprise the bulk of both oeuvres, the stronger is the sense that all these separate (and independent) utterances build or can be built into an overall argument—not necessarily a narrative line, but nonetheless a *meaning,* a comprehensible structure. Frost himself articulated something of this sense of cumulative eloquence when he considered his own work near the end of his life. Frost spoke of

> looking backward over the accumulation of years to see how many poems I could find toward some one meaning it might seem absurd to have had in advance, but it would be all right to accept from fate after the fact. The interest, the pastime was to learn if there had been any divinity shaping my ends and I had been building better than I knew. In other words could anything of larger design, even the roughest, any broken or dotted fragment of a figure be discovered among the apparently random lesser designs of the several poems?[34]

There is thus a basic contrast between the sporadic, isolated linguistic texture of many modernist poems and the more homogeneous and undramatic diction favored by Frost and Seferis—a diction that calls far less attention to itself as linguistic surface or event.

Perhaps a new kind of spatial metaphor is now in order. We

find it in the work of a critic who had most probably read neither Frost nor Seferis, but who was pondering what he called classical language in modern poetry—or the lack of such language. In *Is There Any Poetic Writing?* Roland Barthes makes a vivid distinction between the continuous flow of "classical language" and the abrupt "verticality" of language/syntax in much modern poetry. Classical language, says Barthes, is full of connections which

> lead the word on, and at once carry it toward a meaning which is an ever-deferred project. . . . Classical language is always reducible to a persuasive continuum, it postulates the possibility of dialogue, it establishes a universe in which men are not alone, where words never have the terrible weight of things, where speech is always a meeting with the other. . . . On the contrary modern poetry destroyed relationships in language and reduced discourse to words as static things. This implies a reversal in our knowledge of Nature. The interrupted flow of the new poetic language initiates a discontinuous Nature, which is revealed only piecemeal . . . Modern poetry is a poetry of the object. In it, Nature becomes a fragmented space, made of objects solitary and terrible, because the links between them are only potential. . . . The bursting upon us of the poetic word then institutes an absolute object; Nature becomes a succession of verticalities, of objects, suddenly standing erect, and filled with all their possibilities: one of these can only be a landmark in an unfulfilled, and thereby terrible, world. . . .[35]

Barthes's rendering of modernist discontinuity as vertical has interesting echoes and applications in both the work of and critical notices about Frost and Seferis. Frost's implicit expectation of a design, a structure in his oeuvre is in contrast with Barthes's image of a succession of steep, discontinuous fragments, whether the fragments are poems or parts of poems. Moreover, a critic has used the following terms to emphasize the continuous nature of Frost's world—as it were, its horizontality: "[Frost's] country horizon expands into the total human horizon where all perspectives . . . are available."[36]

And in a similar rejection of the discontinuous, vertical version of the world—more particularly, the world of literary tradition—Seferis emphasizes the synchronicity and horizontality/continuity of what he perceives as the Greek tradition:

. . . the Greek tradition, the whole tradition, indivisible as it is.
For this tradition is not, as some see it, an affair of isolated
promontories [compare Barthes's "verticalities"], some great
names, some illuminating texts; instead it is like what others
of us see and feel in the little mosaics of a humble Byzantine
church—the Ionian philosophers, the popular verses of the
period of the Comneni, the epigrams of the Anthology, Greek
folk song, Aeschylus, Palamas, Solomos, Sikelianos, Calvos,
Cavafy, the Parthenon, Homer [and, he does not add, Seferis],
all living in a moment of time. . . .[37]

The expansion of a country horizon into the total human horizon in Frost's work; Seferis's containment of tradition in humble
as well as majestic cultural emblems—these are examples of
synecdoche, surely the most important poetic trope for both
men's work. "I never tire," said Frost, "of being shown how the
limited can make snug in the limitless."[38] He might equally well
have said that he never tired of showing how the limitless could
be contained in a small compass. Seferis's carved remains,
Frost's abandoned houses radiate a significance beyond, and
larger than, themselves, at the same time that they fit with per-
fect tact and appropriateness into a particular, even a "realistic"
scene. The "persuasive continuum" to which Barthes refers
when writing about classical language is a poetic scheme which
accommodates the particular on the way to the general. In Frost
and Seferis, significance seems to accumulate en route from the
one to the other—on the way to that "meaning which is an ever-
deferred project." Not that meaning is far to seek; rather, there is
always a little more of it than any one reading can encompass.
The importance of synecdoche in the thought and poetic practice of these poets is crucial to the aptness of the landscape
metaphor for their work—a metaphor which shapes this study. It
is not just that they take much of their subject matter from the
natural world—many poets do. But Frost and Seferis compose
the perceived materials of their worlds into arrangements that
are both familiar and intelligible, orderly and suggestive, and
endlessly evocative—not a common poetic achievement in their,
or indeed in any, time.
A phenomenological critic writes:

The world is no conglomeration of mere objects to be described in the language of physical science. The world is our
home, our habitat, the materialization of our subjectivity. Who

wants to become acquainted with man, should listen to the language spoken by the things in his existence. Who wants to describe man should make an analysis of the "landscape" within which he demonstrates, explains, and reveals himself. "Landscape" suggests both a configuration of objects really there in nature and the phenomenological notion that any particular landscape is coherent because the mind of the artist makes it so. . . . The special qualities of coherence and the peculiar dominance of this or that object in the landscape are reflections of the artist's subjectivity, his deepest inclination. . . . "Landscapes" are clues to the essential expression of the poet.[39]

But in modernist poetic practice, the world which is here so aptly called the materialization of our subjectivity *is* frequently expressed as nothing other than a "conglomeration of mere objects." Recall Roland Barthes's phrase: "Modern poetry is a poetry of the object."

It is true that the term *landscape* in literary parlance has a double meaning: a landscape consists first of objects there in nature and secondly of what the poet makes of them. Nevertheless, the term is surely more appropriate for poets like Frost and Seferis than for writers who deliberately set out to shatter and disconnect the givens of the senses. If every poetic oeuvre without distinction is said to constitute some landscape or other, the term *landscape* loses every vestige of its metaphorical point and shrinks to a pretentious synonym for "oeuvre"; thus every poetic world, no matter how discontinuous and "vertical," would be automatically dubbed a landscape. But if we retain some of the force of the word, then Frost's and Seferis's "materializations of subjectivity" have more claim to be called landscapes than do those of most of their contemporaries. These poets give their subjectivities a local habitation and a name; more, they endow them with shapes we can recognize and delight in, pore over and return to.

This study shows how Frost and Seferis build up their landscapes by the repeated, though varied, use of a few images. Such image clusters as stone or light or trees or the sea provide clues to what Van Den Berg, quoted above, calls the essential expression of our poets. Beyond this, such features of the landscape furnish indications, should we be seeking them, of where Frost and Seferis belong in any larger scheme of the poetics of their time; this is true because, as I hope to show, the meaning of each image extends beyond mere "expression" to poetics. Although Frost and Seferis were both generally reluctant to make theoretical pronouncements about poetry, their images do the talking for them. If we are attentive, we shall probably find that studying their major images tells us what we want to know about such poetic choices as form, the poet's relation to the past, or the matter of personal voice. That an image can be so richly packed with meaning is evidence as to these poets' mastery of synecdoche.

Notes

1. This and all other quotes from the *Paris Review* Writers at Work Series interview with Frost is from *Writers at Work: The Paris Review Interviews,* Second Series, "Robert Frost" (New York: Viking, 1963), 9–34.

2. "The Art of Poetry: George Seferis," interview conducted by Edmund Keeley, *Paris Review,* no. 50 (Fall 1970): 57–93.

3. Seferis, "Letter to a Foreign Friend," trans. Nanos Valaoritis and amended by Edmund Keeley, in Rex Warner, ed. and trans., *Seferis on the Greek Style* (London: Bodley Head, 1966), 175.

4. Frost, "Introduction to *Dartmouth Verse*" (Portland, Maine, 1925), quoted by Lawrance Thompson in *Fire and Ice: The Art and Thought of Robert Frost* (New York: Russell and Russell, 1961), 94.

5. On Frost's early reading, see Thompson, *Robert Frost: The Early Years, 1874–1915* (New York: Holt, Rinehart & Winston, 1966), 20, 23, 35, 69, 85, and passim.

6. Nasos Vayenas, *The Poet and the Dancer* (Athens: Kedros, 1979), 109.

7. Seferis, *Meres* (Journal), entry for 19 March 1926, vol. I, 1925–1931 (Athens: Ikaros, 1975), 47.

8. See Thompson, ed., *Selected Letters of Robert Frost* (New York: Holt, Rinehart & Winston, 1964); *The Letters of Robert Frost to Louis Untermeyer* (New York: Holt, Rinehart & Winston, 1963); and Margaret Bartlett Anderson, *Robert Frost and John Bartlett: The Record of a Friendship* (New York: Holt, Rinehart & Winston, 1963).

9. *Poet and Dancer,* 110.

10. *Poet and Dancer,* 110.

11. *Demotic:* the vernacular form of spoken Greek which developed from the post classical period through the Middle Ages, the Cretan Renaissance, the eighteenth- and nineteenth-century popular songs to become the language used in writing (as well as the universal form of speech) by such Greek writers as Solomos and Makriyannis at the beginning of the nineteenth century. Demotic contains a great many loan words (especially from Turkish) and in it the classical declensions and conjugations are considerably modified and eroded. See Robert Browning, *Medieval and Modern Greek* (London: Hutchinson University Library, 1969). *Katharevousa:* the "clean" or learned tongue, based on Attic and *koine* but with many neologisms and artificial archaisms. Katharevousa ignored all words of non-Greek origin. Used in official documents, government newspapers, and by a literary school; taught in schools under rightist governments, most recently the 1967–74 junta. The split between demotic and katharevousa, or language question, has been a subject of intellectual and political debate in Greece (also, periodically, of bloodshed) ever since the liberation from the Turks in 1821.

12. Reuben Brower quotes this 1894 letter of Frost to Susan Hayes Ward in *The Poetry of Robert Frost: Constellations of Intention* (New York: Oxford University Press, 1963), 4.

13. Quoted in Elaine Barry, ed., *Robert Frost on Writing* (New Brunswick, N.J.: Rutgers University Press, 1973), 11.

14. Barry, *RF on Writing,* 110.

15. See an undated letter of Frost to his daughter Lesley Frost Francis, in Arnold Grade, ed., *Family Letters of Robert and Elinor Frost* (Albany: State University of New York Press, 1972), 162:

> An Imagist is simply one who insists on clearer sharper less muddled half realized images (chiefly eye images) than the common run of small poets. Thats certainly good as far as it goes. Strange with all their modernity and psychology they didnt have more to say about ear images and other images—even kinesthetic.

16. From Frost, "The Figure a Poem Makes," 1939, used as a preface to the first and succeeding editions of Robert Frost's collected poems and quoted also in Barry, *RF on Writing,* 125.

17. Thompson, *Fire and Ice,* 43.

18. Brower, *Constellations,* 80–81.

19. *RF on Writing,* 13.

20. On Frost's respect for and eventual imitation of his country neighbors' speech-ways, see Thompson, *Robert Frost: The Early Years,* 284ff. (on Derry) and also the essay by Peter Davison in *Robert Frost: Lectures on the Centennial of His Birth,* published by the Library of Congress, 1975.

21. Seferis's essay "Makriyannis" in *On the Greek Style,* 33.

22. *On the Greek Style,* 60.

23. *On the Greek Style,* 61.

24. *Poet and Dancer,* 112–14.

25. Quoted in Vayenas, 115. See also Vayenas, 19: ". . . the contradiction which [Seferis] must have noticed between the view that the work of art is an autonomous world and his own conviction that art is a medium of communication."

26. "The Art of Poetry," 61.

27. Robert Frost, quoted in Helen Bacon, "Dialogue of Poets: *Mens Animi* and the Renewal of Words," *Massachusetts Review* 19, no. 2 (Summer 1978): 324.

28. "The Art of Poetry," 61.

29. Peter Levi, S.J., "Seferis' Tone of Voice," in Edmund Keeley and Peter Bien, eds., *Modern Greek Writers* (Princeton, N.J.: Princeton University Press, 1982), 185.

30. Reginald L. Cook, "Robert Frost and the Critics," in Committee on the Frost Centennial of the University of Southern Mississippi, comp., *Frost, Centennial Essays* (Jackson: University Press of Mississippi, 1974), 18.

31. Randall Jarrell, "The End of the Line," *Nation,* 21 February 1942, reprinted in *Kipling, Auden & Co.* (New York: Farrar, Straus & Giroux 1980), 78.

32. Bacon, "Dialogue of Poets," 323–24.

33. Kenneth Fields, Introduction to *Tribute to Freud,* by H.D. (Boston: David R. Godine Publisher, repr. 1975), xxviii.

34. Robert Frost, quoted in Brower, *Constellations,* viii.

35. Roland Barthes, "Is There any Poetic Writing?" quoted in Fields, Introduction, *Tribute to Freud.*

36. Theodore Morrison, quoted in Bacon, "Dialogue of Poets," 323.

37. Goerge Seferis, "Cavafy and Eliot—A Comparison," *On the Greek Style,* 161.

38. Robert Frost, quoted by Nancy Vogel, *Robert Frost, Teacher* (Bloomington, Ind.: Phi Delta Kappa, 1974), 12.

39. J. H. Van Den Berg, "The Phenomenological Approach to Psychiatry," quoted in Frank Lentricchia, "Robert Frost and Modern Literary Theory," *Robert Frost, Centennial Essays,* 317.

CHAPTER I

Boundary, Wall, House, Inscription: The Image of Stone

In the rocky terrain of Greece and New England, stones crop out of the ground to be gathered into piles, built into walls or shelters, carved into inscriptions, shaped into statues. It is inevitable that in the work of Frost and Seferis, poets who pay close attention to their surroundings and prefer to write about the out-of-doors, stone in its various guises should frequently appear.

Inert and silent, stones seem an unpromising poetic topic unless their very passivity is a provocation. There they sit, inanimate lumps, waiting to be interpreted, given speech. Frost and Seferis do indeed interpret stones, with reticence but also with characteristic intensity. Unlike the "old stones that cannot be deciphered" of "East Coker," stones in the worlds of Frost and Seferis are, if not finally deciphered, at least passionately perused.

If we can read its message, stone has a unique ability to tell us about the past. We might expect the American poet to concentrate on the relatively recent past of his country—the few generations since the land has been settled. By the same token, the Greek poet ought to reach back in time to the ancient world whose remnants are a part of his everyday experience. To some degree this is true. In Frost's "The Black Cottage," for example, the memories of both speakers go no further back than the Civil War, whereas in Seferis's "The King of Asine" the spectator of ruins is thinking of the *Iliad*. Yet the reverse holds too. In "The Black Cottage," the visitor to the empty house ends by envisioning a nomadic society wildly remote in time and place. In other Frost poems such as "The Census-Taker" or "A Cliff Dwelling," the sight of abandoned houses or sites sends the speaker's thoughts back thousands of years. In "Mending Wall" the neighbor is seen as an "old-stone savage armed"—that is, as paleolithic. On the other hand, in "The King of Asine," despite the Homeric point of reference, the ancient remains bring to mind *contemporary* sorrow; and at the close of the first section of Seferis's long sequence *Mythical History,* relics are apparently transported from the past to the present time and place: "We brought back / these carved reliefs of a humble art."

Like any image, stone means several things at once. In Frost and Seferis it is a fragment of the past that can be read historically; a symbolic reference that can send the mind leaping away from the present; and an image of the raw material of art. Both poets seem extraordinarily alert to the symbolic possibilities of stone, and in both oeuvres a progression can be traced between stone as it occurs in nature and stone as shaped by and to human purposes. For in contrast to images taken from nature such as flowers and the sea (which we shall examine in the next chapter, and which are beautiful objects of contemplation that undergo change independent of human will), stone is a picture of potential, amenable to metamorphosis by human hands. As such it has obvious affinities with art.

It is striking that both Frost and Seferis refer to their writing as if it were the craft of a sculptor. Frost may well have read William James's statement in *Principles of Psychology* that "the mind . . . works on the data it receives very much as a sculptor works on his block of stone."[1] This metaphor for the creative act is certainly discernible in Frost's prose. "My object is true form—is and always will be. . . . I fight to be allowed to sit cross-legged on the old flint pile and flake a lump into an artifact."[2] "I thank the lord," he wrote elsewhere, "for crudity which is rawness, which is raw material. . . . A real artist delights in roughness for what he can do to it. He's the brute who can knock the corners off the marble block . . ."[3] And in a less direct use of the scriptural metaphor which emphasizes the participation of the reader or beholder in apprehending the meaning of art, "Every poem, almost, that I write is figurative in two senses. It will have figures in it, of course; but it is also a figure in itself— a figure for something, and it's made so that you can get more than one figure out of it, I suppose."[4]

In Seferis the metaphoric bonding between writing and sculpture (including carving and inscriptions) is a deep and lasting one. Seferis's essay on Makriyannis, of major importance in this connection, has been mentioned in the Introduction and will also be discussed in this chapter; but some relevant passages from journals and letters can be adduced here. In her memoir of her brother, Ioanna Tsatsou compares his slow, devoted practice of his art or craft *(téchni)* to that of a woodcarver. She also quotes a letter in which Seferis speaks of "This obstinate and painful thing that so-called art is—in other words to have your very own self for material and to chip away at it here and there until it speaks. You must make an effort and not make an effort, you must be burning up all over, oh, the hell with it."[5]

To the roles of the sculptor whose material is himself and of the woodcarver, we may add the equally painstaking personae of an archaeologist and Sisyphus (from two journal entries):

> The way I'm writing now, I make desperate motions in the void and express nothing. . . . In order to say what you want to say, you must contrive another language and cherish it for years and years with whatever you loved, whatever you lost, whatever you will never find again . . . I know languages, I know how to read a few hieroglyphics. But I'm deaf and dumb.

> Late at night: harder to complete a line of poetry than to lift a stone.[6]

For both poets, clearly, the practice of art is a strenuous process, a gouging of a figure from some resistant substance—whether that substance is the actual rocky landscape familiar to both, or language, or the self, or some tough alloy of the three.

This chapter traces the major uses Frost and Seferis in turn make of the image of stone. The connections are now overt, now submerged, but I believe they hold. In Frost the stone functions first simply as a boundary marker, a division between inside and outside and thus generally as any achievement of form in a formless world. A sense of boundary, of territory was always personally vital to Frost, and we shall see the poetic implications of this sense in a poem such as "Mending Wall," which must be read in terms of both personal space and poetic form. Boundaries, after all, are walls. Walls combine to make larger structures, houses; and the house is another central image for Frost, particularly the empty or abandoned house which is in the process (once people have left it) of turning into an abstract division between man and nature. The wall/house is for Frost the central human artifact and cultural symbol. From the center of the home and the shelter it provides, all else in his work may be said to follow.

For Seferis stones are first of all messages—ostrakha recovered from the past, precious relics that can be sought or carried. Exiled from home early in life, Seferis feels the house as more of an absence than a center of gravity: "the houses I had they took from me." "Carved reliefs" may endure, but houses are often reduced to their component parts, anonymous rubble, far more thoroughly than Frost's abandoned buildings. But Seferis feels keenly the actual presence of stones as a substance beneath his feet, the stuff Greece is made of: tough, but not impervious to the rhythms imposed by time, by those same forces of dissolution which Frost calls the "something" that doesn't love a wall.

For both poets, stone is a primary ingredient not only in the physical world but also in the world of their work. In many ways, what we make of stone (in both senses of the phrase) shows us what we have made of the world. It furnishes clues about our past and present, our artistic languages and the way we have arranged our lives in relation to space. Stone is an excellent touchstone (so to speak) of the ways people have crafted space—a touchstone buried sometimes deep in the past, but durable and potentially recoverable to poetic scrutiny.

1. Frost

i *Suggestions of form*

In a reminiscence Frost wrote of his years on the Derry farm, the theme most strongly sounded is that of the need for a clear demarcation between the self and the world.

> We didn't even know enough to know how hopelessly lost we must have looked *from the outside*. We never can recapture that. It was for once in a lifetime. That's roughly what *A Boy's Will* is about. Life was peremptory and threw me into confusion. I couldn't have held my own and done myself credit unless I had been a quitter. My infant industries needed the protection of a dead space around them. Everybody was too strong for me, but at least I was strong enough not to stay where they were. I'm still much the same. What's room for if it isn't to get away from minds that stop your works?[7]

Such insistence on "dead space" means an exacerbated awareness of boundaries, protections for those "infant industries" in need of space and privacy. Such boundaries are the subject of several poems of Frost which, without focusing on a wall or a house, nevertheless organize themselves around some breach, locating their figures on one side or the other of a crucial division. In various ways "The Figure in the Doorway," "A Mood Apart," and "Trespass" define the experiences of being on the inside or the outside.

"The Figure in the Doorway" is a man both as he is glimpsed and as he is further imagined by people passing on a train.

> His great gaunt figure filled his cabin door,
> And had he fallen inward on the floor,
> He must have measured to the further wall,
> But we who passed were not to see him fall.

The moment of passage affords the observers just enough time to note the salient outer details of a life: "He had a hen, he had a pig in sight, / He had a well, he had the rain to catch. / He had a ten-by-twenty garden patch." But this recital of vital statistics is interrupted, only a stanza from the end of the poem, when the viewpoint swivels and the observers become (at least potentially) the observed. The polysyllabic rhyme seems to signal the comic possibilities of such abrupt reversal:

> Nor did he lack for common entertainment.
> That I assume was what our passing train meant.
> He could look at us in our diner eating,
> And if so moved uncurl a hand in greeting.

The poem allows no time to learn whether or not the figure *will* be "so moved."

The central image in "The Figure in the Doorway" is charged with a mysterious glow of brief intensity against an anonymous background ("as through the monotony we ran, / We came to where there was a living man."). Ordinary though he is, the man stands out from the undifferentiated nature which surrounds him; it is above all his inaccessibility that makes him special. The figure (a painterly word) is out of reach. To the viewer it has a picturesque, framed quality; the man stands in the doorway like a portrait in an oblong frame. Unlike a painted figure, however, "He could look at us in our diner eating." Framedness turns out to be reciprocal; "we" are framed by the lighted train window as "he" by the door. Two tableaux meet and pass. ("Meeting and Passing," an early love poem which comes to mind here, traces another such inscrutable chiasmus; "A Passing Glimpse," another train-window poem, equates the brevity of time for seeing with the preciousness of the thing seen: "Heaven gives its glimpses only to those / Not in position to look too close.")

In all these poems, partitions are enhancements, even if also hindrances, of perception. But it is characteristic of Frost's dialectical imagination that not only does he turn the tables of viewer/viewed within one poem, but also has entire poems which express the feeling of the person who is being perceived, or rather spied on. "A Mood Apart" and "Trespass," for example, use the first person to express moods of violation, definite resentment of being watched or impinged on at all. The activity which engages the speaker of the first-named poem is connected with creation and reproduction (compare a similar posture in "Putting in the Seed," Chapter II); hence the boys' interruption is tinged with a hint of voyeurism.

> Once down on my knees to growing plants
> I prodded the earth with a lazy tool
> In time with a medley of sotto chants;
> But becoming aware of some boys from school
> Who had stopped outside the fence to spy,
> I stopped my song and almost heart.
> For any eye is an evil eye
> That looks in on to a mood apart.

In "Trespass" no such intimate activity is going on, but boundaries are nonetheless important. The tone is stubborn, a bit defensive, but convinced:

> No, I had set no prohibiting sign,
> And yes, my land was hardly fenced.
> Nevertheless the land was mine:
> I was being trespassed on and against.

Both these poems erect strong resistances to intrusion from the outside—more defensive barriers than the niche found by the

young lovers in the earlier "In Neglect." In that poem the pair
"*try* if we cannot feel forsaken"; but what was then a luxury of
solitude seems to have become a habit, if not a necessity.

Other poems that deal more or less centrally with barriers and
breaches include "A Time to Talk," "The Cow in Apple Time,"
and "A Drumlin Woodchuck" ("Mending Wall" will have a separate section devoted to it). The first of these poems transforms
the rebarbative solitude of the singer/planter or landowner above
into a guarded gregariousness. "A Time to Talk" depicts social
intercourse as valuable and appropriate within limits—the limits
both of space (the wall in the poem is a buffer against intrusion)
and of time (*a* time, not all time, to talk) and generally also of
convention. It is convention that prevents the speaker from mis-
taking his friend's signs of sociability for need.

> When a friend calls to me from the road
> And slows his horse to a meaning walk,
> I don't stand still and look around
> On all the hills I haven't hoed,
> And shout from where I am, "What is it?"
> No, not as there is a time to talk.
> I thrust my hoe in the mellow ground,
> Blade-end up and five feet tall,
> And plod: I go up to the stone wall
> For a friendly visit.

As both men engage in a deliberate ballet of both verbal and
nonverbal gestures, the wall remains between them. Its mediat-
ing function and limiting presence are as crucial as the space a
pair of speakers maintains between themselves at a crowded
party.

Another pithy treatment of appropriate limits is "The Cow in
Apple Time." If walls are useful boundaries for the two talkers,
they are ignored and transgressed by the cow. ("Something in-
spires the only cow of late, / To make no more of a wall than an
open gate, / And think no more of wall-builders than fools.")
This cameo portrait of transgression has the sting of parody,
since the transgressor, though not a human being, hews to an
archetypal female image of apple-eater and rule-breaker. In the
end, the joke seems to be on the cow. The triple rhyme in the
poem's final lines (after four rhymed couplets) nails home the
lesson that the fool is not the wall-builder but the poor cow:

> She leaves them bitten when she has to fly.
> She bellows on a knoll against the sky.
> Her udder shrivels and the milk goes dry.

The young couple in "In Neglect" or in the passage about the years in Derry *look* lost but are snug and secure; here the cow, having wholly disregarded boundaries, is truly lost.

"A Drumlin Woodchuck" also ponders boundaries in the form of an animal fable. The woodchuck respects walls as much as the cow scorns them; indeed, he builds walls, tunneling into the earth for greater safety. Whereas the cow is tempted to eat forbidden fruit and violate set boundaries, the woodchuck is wary of being lured out even for food. His use of the first person plural (the class of "all . . . who prefer to live") opposes a tribally conservative pluralism to the cow's rash individuality:

> All we who prefer to live
> Have a little whistle we give,
> And flash, at the least alarm
> We dive down under the farm.
>
> We allow some time for guile
> And don't come out for a while
> Either to eat or drink.
> We take occasion to think.

The poem concludes

> If I can with confidence say
> That still for another day,
> Or even another year,
> I will be there for you, my dear,
>
> It will be because, though small
> As measured against the All,
> I have been so instinctively thorough
> About my crevice and burrow.

These poems repeatedly make connections between limitations and safety, boundaries and prudence. To clarify this connection, it is helpful to look at a prose passage written at about the same time as "A Drumlin Woodchuck" and which again emphasizes a

link (moral and aesthetic as well as ethical) between strength and
a form of restriction. In "Letter to the *Amherst Student*," Frost
is discussing poetic form in terms that are clearly not confined to
poetry:

> We people are thrust forward out of the suggestions of form
> in the rolling clouds of nature. . . . When in doubt there is
> always form to go with. Anyone who has achieved the least
> form to be sure of it, is lost to the larger excruciations. . . .
> Fortunately, too, no forms are more engrossing, gratifying,
> comforting, staying, than those lesser ones we throw off like
> vortex rings of smoke, all our individual enterprise and need-
> ing nobody's cooperation: a basket, a letter, a room, an idea, a
> picture, a poem. . . .
>
> The background is hugeness and confusion shading away
> from where we stand into black and utter chaos; and against
> the background any small man-made figure of order and con-
> centration. What pleasanter than that this should be so? Un-
> less we are novelists or economists we don't worry about this
> confusion; we *look out on it* with an instrument or tackle it to
> reduce it.[8] (Italics mine.)

The phrase I have italicized, "Look out on," recalls the woodchuck in his burrow, the figure in the doorway, the people in the
train, the man behind the fence. In all these passages, form is a
refuge *from* which we may observe "the larger excruciations"
but *within* which we are "lost to" them. We are not to envision
form as a splendid edifice in the manner of Tennyson's Palace of
Art. The forms resulting from "individual enterprise" which
Frost lists in the "Letter" are scaled to human size, often the size
of a single person. Yet how small, really, is a picture, a poem, an
idea? The words expand into eternal values. It is only "as mea-
sured against the All," we remember, that the woodchuck seems
small.

Frost's apparently small subjects allow for a considerable
scope of human possibility, just as the "small man-made figure"
in the "Letter" is the more poignant for standing out against a
scene of nonhuman monotony, wildness, and confusion. By
placing such a figure between "where we stand" and the wild
background, Frost makes the human shape itself into a kind of
boundary line.

ii   *The need for walls*

Frost's best-known poem about boundaries poses a question—whether good fences make good neighbors, whether boundaries are benevolent or not—akin to the concerns of the poems we have been discussing. But "Mending Wall" is more social in its method than the other poems, dealing as it does with two points of view. Appropriately, then, it uses a dialectic as well as an emblematic strategy for posing its problem. Rather than narrating or depicting a particular action or moment (the cow's meandering, the woodchuck's retreat, the farmer's plodding up to chat), "Mending Wall" mimics a meditative discussion. Although there is only one speaker, the views he presents seem to be those of two neighbors who must devise a way to manage their common boundary, the wall. This sharedness is crucial; without the neighbor, "Mending Wall" would lose much of its edge. In the *"Amherst Student* Letter" Frost speaks of such "forms of individual enterprise" as a basket, letter, garden, or room, saying "For those we haven't to get a team together before we can play." Although sharply individualistic, the game in "Mending Wall" *does* involve more than one player.

True to the teasing spirit of some games, "Mending Wall" hardly seems to make a serious attempt at resolving the ambiguities inherent in the notion of limit. The matter of the wall is worried over by the speaker before the neighbor enters the poem; after that there is a disagreement as to the need for fences. The centrality of the wall ("we keep the wall between us as we go") suggests a reciprocity or equity in the debate, but in fact the discourse is far from symmetrical. The speaker breaks the rules of a game which calls for "one on a side." Instead of staying within the limits of his own side, he trespasses (both *stay* and *trespass* are important Frostian verbs) by trying to read the other's mind, by wondering "if I could put a notion in his head," and in general by straddling the wall (one thinks of the phrase "sitting on a fence"). In fact he is of two minds about walls.

Critics have been of two minds about the poem as well. Frost once said that the poet is entitled to everything the reader can find in the poem, and many have found in "Mending Wall" easy and attractive allegory against separation, for brotherhood. But Frost (who can nearly always be quoted against himself) also said that the heart sinks when robbed of the chance to see for itself what a poem is all about. Reading is more than extracting plums of meaning from the pastry of form, though Frost would doubtless lay claim to all the juiciest plums.

Recall that the speaker in "Mending Wall" questions his neighbor's stolid assumption that "good fences make good neighbors." What he objects to is not so much the sentiment itself as the unwillingness or inability of the other to think for himself, to "go beyond his father's saying." Just so; we must try to get behind the apophthegm-like opening line of "Mending Wall," testing carefully for gradations of tone as we proceed. Is it the proverblike authority of "something there is . . ." that makes it so natural to equate "something" with the speaker? Once this equation has been made, the reader joins the speaker in sympathizing with this mysterious "something" and hence in opposing the neighbor's unthinking defense of walls.

Frost rings subtly drastic changes on the sound of a phrase like "good fences make good neighbors." By the time the poem ends, this line has acquired some of the pat stupidity of a slogan. Similar turns of the screw affect the opening line, when to it is added the darker phrase "that wants it down" and again when the speaker refuses to name the antiwall "something." "Elves" is the closest he gets, yet "It's not elves exactly, and I'd rather / He said it for himself." Elves may mean not willowy things out of Tolkien but darker forces of the wood, for the next image is one of darkness. The neighbor is viewed as subtly menacing, "an old-stone savage armed." Yet this man has been the one to defend boundaries. The apparently relaxed and leisurely pace of the poem has made us lower our own boundaries and forget who is on what side.

At any rate, although the speaker's ironic evasiveness undermines any confident interpretation, Poirier is surely right when he makes the following point.

> . . . it is not the neighbor . . . a man who can only dully repeat "good fences make good neighbors"— . . . it is not he who initiates the fence-making. Rather it is the far more spirited, lively, and "mischievous" speaker of the poem. While admitting that they do not need the wall, it is he who each year "lets my neighbor know beyond the hill" that it is time to do the job anyway, and who will go out alone to fill the gaps made in the wall by hunters. . . . Though the speaker may or may not think that good neighbors are made by good fences, it is abundantly clear that he likes the yearly ritual, the yearly "outdoor game"

by which fences are made. Because if fences do not make good neighbors the *making* of fences can.[9]

Part of an old-fashioned neighborliness which results from the annual wall mending is fellowship, the potential exchange of feelings and ideas. More salient still is the joint maintenance of form for its own sake, not for utility, so that wall-making also becomes "a time to talk."

At the same time, repairing the wall means renewing that structure protective of "infant industries" or "a mood apart," protective from trespass on a symbolic level, even if "My apple trees will never get across / And eat the cones under his pines." As an occasion for craft, besides being a guarantee of privacy, the wall is also crucial. Frost often compared free verse to playing tennis without the net—a remark which no one has ever interpreted as an attack on nets.

iii   *This house in one year fallen to decay*

Auden has commented that one of Frost's favorite images is that of the abandoned house; and having considered boundaries and walls, we can see that the feelings about limits reappear on a larger scale in some of the poems about houses. Houses, after all, reduce to walls; walls elaborate to form nook, cranny, burrow. A key feature of all such structures is the same. All serve as protective boundaries which interpose between us and "the sameness of the wood," the undifferentiated wild or the indifferent outside world. All are strengthened and cemented by tradition—or need to be, for all are exposed to the ravages of time. The connection with time is crucial. Walls and houses, markers constructed to divide space, end by recording time as well. Frost's preference for abandoned houses means a predilection for pondering time past, on a scale that varies from the domestic to the glacial, as we shall see in such poems as "The Black Cottage," "The Census Taker," "The Need of Being Versed in Country Things," "The Thatch," and "A Cliff Dwelling."

The first two of these poems are narratives of lengths comparable to those of better known Frostian "eclogues" such as "The Death of the Hired Man" or "The Fear." The longer the narrative span allotted to a poem, the more emphasis the poem is likely to place on the effect of time; indeed, Frost's poetic depictions of houses often offer suggestions of before and after views. There

is room in narrative for alteration of spatial as well as temporal
perspective. In virtually all the poems to be discussed, a structure is initially seen at a distance; approached more closely (or in
one case retreated from) it seems different. The changing perspectives indicate that even inanimate structures undergo a kind
of metamorphosis, either crumbling back to nature or else un-
cannily desolate, unchanged, inhospitably empty. In most of
these poems a lonely outsider confronts a scene that is the
lonelier for having once been associated with life, family, love.
More than walls, houses have a corona of domestic (social, mat-
rimonial) connotations—all institutions or structures subject to
dismemberment and decay, eloquent to the viewer of the ravages
of time.

The central portion of "The Black Cottage" consists of a reminiscence which seems to concern the cottage itself only as a
point d'appui for the speaker's thoughts. Yet the most striking
sections of the poem—its opening and closing passages—
symmetrically bracket the central part with paired and very dis-
similar images of human habitation. At the beginning, the cottage is seen as distant and picturesque—an inviolable vignette
which recalls the framedness of vision in "A Passing Glimpse" or
"The Figure in the Doorway." The house may be looked at but is
essentially untouchable.

> We chanced in passing by that afternoon
> To catch it in a sort of special picture
> Among tar-banded ancient cherry trees,
> Set well back from the road in rank lodged grass,
> The little cottage we were speaking of,
> A front with just a door between two windows,
> Fresh painted by the shower a velvet black.
> We paused, the minister and I, to look.
> He made as if to hold it at arm's length
> Or put the leaves aside that framed it in.
> "Pretty," he said. "Come in. No one will care."
> The path was a vague parting in the grass
> That led us to a weathered window-sill.
> We pressed our faces to the pane.

The cottage is presented with theatrical artfulness. Like a stage
set, it is like "a front with just a door between two windows."
The syntax contributes to the effect of studied suspense, delay-
ing until lines 5–8 the apposition which completes the meaning of

"it," object of the sentence's main verb, in line 2. Just as the cottage is "set well back from the road," the arrangement of words enhances the effect of inaccessibility.

The minister then describes at some length the character of an old lady who was the last person to live in the cottage. The sketch of a stubborn, conservative, yet engaging personality is no more than a development of the framed, tight, distant effect of the first glimpse of the lady's cottage. People die, places endure; in visiting her house the two men are visiting her, or rather peering through her windows to get an elusive glimpse.

So far "The Black Cottage" is a skillful, pervasively mild evocation of a place and person not unusual in *North of Boston*. But in the course of the minister's talk, something without parallel in that book happens to the language of the poem. As in the beginning, a place, rather than a person, is being described—a metaphorical place whose evocation grows out of further musing on the old lady. The minister remarks that her staunch conservatism had prevented him from ever altering the wording of the Creed at Sunday service. Sympathetic to her ritual feeling for liturgy, he is " 'just as glad she made me keep my hands off' " (as if the Creed were a tightly shuttered, untouchable place), " 'For, dear me, why abandon a belief / Merely because it ceases to be true.' " The mildly coy teasing and folksiness of these lines probably recall the actual words that have passed between the two; the dip in diction is typical of Frost's delicate ear for human speech, particularly in *North of Boston*. But after this mild mimesis, as the speaker pursues his train of thought, the unobtrusive diction and imagery of the passage gather weight, force, and a majestic impetus. The quiet anecdote is transformed into a stately but wild glimpse of another world, in a unique passage worth quoting.

> "For, dear me, why abandon a belief
> Merely because it ceases to be true.
> Cling to it long enough, and not a doubt
> It will turn true again, for so it goes.
> Most of the change we think we see in life
> Is due to truths being in and out of favor.
> As I sit here, and oftentimes, I wish
> I could be monarch of a desert land
> I could devote and dedicate forever
> To the truths we keep coming back and back to.
> So desert it would have to be, so walled

> By mountain ranges half in summer snow,
> No one would covet it or think it worth
> The pains of conquering to force change on.
> Scattered oases where men dwelt, but mostly
> Sand dunes held loosely in tamarisk
> Blown over and over themselves in idleness.
> Sand grains should sugar in the natal dew
> The babe born in the desert, the sand-storm
> Retard mid-waste my cowering caravans—
> There are bees in this wall."

The most remarkable thing about this eloquent evocation of a visionary dreariness (the phrase from the *Prelude* seems entirely appropriate) is the crescendoing splendor of language and idea, both beginning with truisms and building to remote, severe, yet extravagant extremes. One critic has dubbed this passage "a curiously ironic Utopia." The actual flight of fancy is perhaps whimsical, but all the irony seems to me to lie in the linguistic jolt we (and the minister's hearer and probably also the speaker himself) experience as the tone, having billowed to the utmost, abruptly lurches back to reality, out of majestic iambics to something like anapests: "There are bees in this wall." The downward bump in diction signals a transition from an imagined world of splendid desolation to a much more pedestrian form of abandonment, the bee-infested wall of the same cottage. We are back to the inscrutable little house which has been—circuitously—the occasion of the flight of fancy.

> "There are bees in this wall." He struck the clapboards.
> Fierce heads looked out; small bodies pivoted.
> We rose to go. Sunset blazed on the windows.

The fierce bees pose a more practical threat than imaginary sandstorms. In their inhospitality, the bees demonstrate the truth of the minister's earlier remark about the desolation of the place:

> But what I'm getting to is how forsaken
> A little cottage this has always seemed;
> Since she went more than ever, but before—
> . . . I mean by the world's having passed it by—
> As we almost got by this afternoon.

"The Black Cottage" is in fact a study of a personality in terms of shelter. The desert world of sand dunes and cowering caravans is a world without houses, without walls except mountain ranges, probably without private property altogether. Its desolation echoes that of the cottage, but the old lady was no nomad; her staunch refusal to change or even move is somehow embodied in the belated and gratuitous hostility of the bees. Warily protecting their turf, they usher the visitors out and effectively seal off the house at the close of the poem, just as it was sealed off at the start. An added touch of closure is the sunset blazing on the windows—a hellish, glorious, or merely valedictory light which seems to indicate several simultaneous kinds of ending. The old lady's life and way of thought; the house's habitability; a man's daydream; a visit by two intruders; a day; and a poem, all come to an end.

This remarkable meditation on habitation, abandonment, and the translation of personality into place is also a study of imaginative movement. By giving its readers the same data as those that contribute to the minister's reverie, "The Black Cottage" equips us all for visions uniquely our own yet rooted in a single image of place. As Gaston Bachelard notes in *The Poetics of Space,* "images are incapable of repose. Poetic revery, unlike somnolent revery, never falls asleep. Starting with the simplest of images, it must always set the waves of the imagination radiating. But however cosmic the isolated house lighted by the star of its lamp may become, it will always symbolize solitude."[10]

"The Census-Taker" also explores connections between departed people and surviving houses. But whereas the minister and his companion never actually enter the black cottage and are finally driven even from the porch by a kind of tutelary spirit, the house in "The Census-Taker" is almost obscenely open to all comers. Its nakedness and emptiness reflect the wasted landscape through which the poem moves before coming upon the house. More accurately, the house is mentioned almost at once ("I came an errand one cloud-blowing evening / To a slab-built, black-paper-covered house") and then backed off from again with a motion characteristic of what one critic has called Frost's cinematic genius.

> I came as census-taker to the waste
> To count the people in it and found none,
> None in the hundred miles, none in the house,
> Where I came last with some hope, but not much
> After hours' overlooking from the cliffs

> An emptiness flayed to the very stone.
> I found no people that dared show themselves,
> None not in hiding from the outward eye.

As the cliffs are "flayed," the trees are bare and rotten, "without a single leaf to spend on autumn, / Or branch to whistle after what was spent."

The house has almost none of the distinguishing marks of civilization—so little humanity that observation has to feed on fantasy. An imaginative progression from wind to tree to door to threshold to table is all that enables the census-taker actually to enter the house.

> Perhaps the wind the more without the help
> Of breathing trees said something of the time
> Of year or day the way it swung a door
> Forever off the latch, as if rude men
> Passed in and slammed it shut each one behind him
> For the next one to open for himself.
> I counted nine I had no right to count
> (But this was dreamy unofficial counting)
> Before I made the tenth across the threshold.
> Where was my supper? Where was anyone's?
> No lamp was lit. Nothing was on the table.

The desolation once inside the house further stimulates the census-taker's already "dreamy, unofficial" imaginings. Like the minister's in "The Black Cottage" but with the more fluid continuity characteristic of this poem, his thoughts turn back from the present blankness to an age before people lived in houses. The minister envisioned a nomad world of sand dunes and caravans; here, as befits the cliffs, the suggestion is of cave dwellers. Almost entirely through negatives, one passage manages to evoke an eerie sense of armed ferocity.

> The people that had loudly passed the door
> Were people to the ear but not the eye.
> They were not on the table with their elbows.
> They were not sleeping in the shelves of bunks.
> I saw no men there and no bones of men there.
> I armed myself against such bones as might be
> With the pitch-blackened stub of an ax-handle
> I picked up off the straw-dust covered floor.
> Not bones, but the ill-fitting window rattled.

The rattling has of course already been heard—in the clatter of "pitch-blackened" and "ax-handle."

The silence and emptiness of the house create a vacuum filled by fantasies extending both forward and backward in time. These fantasies encompass the decay of civilization—a process of which the house is a good emblem. At the same time as they encourage imagination, the silence and emptiness enhance the rhetorical drama which is taking place. A spate of language bursting through the speaker's thoughts finally demands utterance aloud.

> This house in one year fallen to decay
> Filled me with no less sorrow than the houses
> Fallen to ruin in ten thousand years
> Where Asia wedges Africa from Europe.
> Nothing was left to do that I could see
> Unless to find that there was no one there
> And declare to the cliffs too far for echo,
> "The place is desert and let whoso lurks
> In silence, if in this he is aggrieved,
> Break silence now or be forever silent.
> Let him say why it should not be declared so."

Like the minister's peroration in "The Black Cottage," this passage fills silence with imaginary speech, or rather real speech addressed to nebulous listeners. The movement of association in both is a ripple-like spread from an abandoned house to an entire landscape and culture, encompassing a generous span of geography and history. The house as synecdoche for humanity is beautifully encapsulated in "The Census-Taker," where the speaker feels "no less sorrow" for the single house than for aeons and continents. Sorrow on a local scale is more humanly apprehensible than catastrophe in the remote past or at a glacial pace. On the other hand, a single empty shack opens out enormous vistas to the ready imagination. Frost said "I talk about universals in terms of New England . . . I talk about the whole world in terms of New England. But that's just because I have it all around me."[11]

Both the census-taker and the minister are poets. Both feel compelled to counter the silence and inscrutability of the past with that most human of responses, language. "The Need of Being Versed in Country Things" takes the same elements—a house fallen to decay, the spectator's emotions, the capabilities of speech—and calls human response into question. What allows this mildly ironic glance at the pathetic fallacy is the role of the birds as emotional mediators between spectator and house.

> The birds that came to it through the air
> At broken windows flew out and in,
> Their murmur more like the sigh we sigh
> From too much dwelling on what has been.
>
> Yet for them the lilac renewed its leaf,
> And the aged elm, though touched with fire;
> And the dry pump flung up an awkward arm;
> And the fence post carried a strand of wire.
>
> For them there was really nothing sad.
> But though they rejoiced in the nest they kept,
> One had to be versed in country things
> Not to believe the phoebes wept.

No visitor is at hand to peer into the burnt house—no close observer except the omniscient and removed-seeming voice of the speaker. Thus the birds inherit the role of responding to ruin, and the quoted stanzas which describe their comings and goings execute a little dialectical dance around the notion of "the urban sophistication of pastoral, which lies behind the pathetic fallacy." The birds *sound* mournful, as people might well feel at a sad sight. At the same time, various kinds of renewal are quietly taking place "for them," both in nature (the lilac and elm) and in such manmade objects as the pump and fencepost. Therefore (the poem omits this logical connective) for the birds there is no cause for sadness. Yet it is tempting to believe that the phoebes really are lamenting a sadness which they may not feel but which we people do. "The Need of Being Versed" manages to have it both ways: the poem expresses grief, excusing anyone who reads grief into the landscape and birdsong; at the same time it delicately hints that such grief is nonexistent. The speaker *is* presumably "versed in country things" and does not misinterpret the phoebes' song; but the musical and affective pull of the poem is in the direction of plangency. Lyric rather than narrative or meditative, "The Need of Being Versed" is perhaps as close as Frost ever comes to pure lamentation for ruin and loss; but as we have seen, it is hardly an unadulterated or unconsidered expression of grief.

"The Thatch" also deals with the affect of a damaged dwelling place through the medium of birds rather than human beings. The source and symbol of feeling in the poem is a house, a thatched cottage which is inhabited and not abandoned. But this poem is still a variation on the theme of the empty house, for the cottage's inhabitants are struggling with chaotic emotions. As the poem begins, the speaker ("The Thatch" makes a relatively lavish use of "I") has left the house as if to escape the pain; but its emotional tug remains strong.

> Out alone in the winter rain,
> Intent on giving and taking pain.
> But never was I far out of sight
> Of a certain upper-window light.
> The light was what it was all about:
> I would not go in till the light went out,
> It would not go out till I came in.
> Well, we should see which one would win,
> We should see which one would be first to yield.

The speaker can hardly bear to refer to his intimate antagonist by so much as a personal pronoun. Thus the house, especially the lighted window, both represents the opponent and mediates between the two of them. This lighted window may recall the equally anthropomorphic but more sociable windows in "Good Hours": "I had for my evening walk / No one at all with whom to talk / But I had the cottages in a row / Up to their shining eyes in snow." But the movement here is away from the hostile house into the winter night where "the world was a black invisible field." Moving brusquely through darkness, the speaker accidentally flushes fledgling birds out of their shelter in the thatch into "mulch and mire." Is the distress he immediately feels (and makes us feel) a result of sentimentality, evidence of a pathetic fallacy–like preference for birds over human beings? Perhaps; but let Gaston Bachelard describe what nests mean to us.

> It is striking that even in our homes, where there is light, our consciousness of well-being should call for comparison with animals in their shelters. . . . well-being takes us back to the primitiveness of the refuge. Physically, the creature endowed with a sense of refuge, huddles up to itself, takes to cover, etc. . . . If we were to look among the wealth of our vocabulary for verbs that express the dynamics of retreat, we should find images based on animal movements of withdrawal. . . .

A nest, like any other image of rest and quiet, is immediately associated with the image of a simple house. When we pass from the image of a nest to the image of a house, and vice versa, it can only be in an atmosphere of simplicity. . . . Van Gogh's thatched cottages are overladen with thatch. Thick, coarsely plaited straw emphasizes the will to provide shelter by extending well beyond the walls. Indeed, in this instance, among all the shelter virtues, the roof is the dominant evidence. Under the roof's coverings the walls are of earth and stone. The openings are low. A thatched cottage is set on the ground like a nest in a field.[12]

This association of nest, refuge, roof, shelter, and well-being reads like a gloss on Frost's poem. In "The Thatch" the speaker is at a loss to explain the intensity of his remorse at his inadvertent violence or make the connection between grief and grief, violence and violence. But the connection is eloquently there in the poem.

> It grieved my soul,
> It started a grief within a grief,
> To think their case was beyond relief—
> They could not go flying about in search
> Of their nest again, nor find a perch.
> They must brood where they fell in mulch and mire,
> Trusting feathers and inward fire
> Till daylight made it safe for a flyer.
> My greater grief was by so much reduced
> As I thought of them without nest or roost.
> That was how that grief started to melt.

Without a pause or change of end-rhyme, "The Thatch" moves on to conclude with a larger grief in a protective boundary, a larger time-scale, and a sort of coda:

> They tell me the cottage where we dwelt,
> Its wind-torn thatch now goes unmended;
> Its life of hundreds of years has ended
> By letting the rain I knew outdoors
> In on to the upper chamber floors.

The sustained flow of feeling in "The Thatch" is especially striking if we consider that the focus never returns directly to the source of trouble at the start of the poem—strife between the speaker and the unnamed other waiting at the window. Rather than returning to the house, the fate of the birds arouses a cathartic tenderness that starts to "melt" the "greater" grief (and thaw the cold anger); then the scale shifts, as if the cottage were being perceived from a distance in space and time—a strategy familiar from "The Black Cottage" and "The Census-Taker."

Nabokov wrote in *Pnin:*

> I do not know if it has ever been noted before that one of the main characteristics of life is discreteness. Unless a film of flesh envelops us, we die. Man exists only insofar as he is separated from his surroundings. . . . It may be wonderful to mix with the landscape, but to do so is the end of the tender ego.[13]

It had indeed been noted before. Throughout "The Thatch," and implicitly in some of Frost's other poems about houses, violation is imaged as a breach in the protective boundaries which shelter birds, couples, families, relationships, entire civilizations. As Bachelard conceived of it, a wall is an extension of the integument necessary to the physical and psychological integrity of a life. Frost, like Van Gogh, gives walls a vulnerable and sensitive life of their own.

I conclude this section with "A Cliff Dwelling," probably the poem of Frost's which best exemplifies his tendency to consider even a faint semblance of a human habitation in terms of human time. The poem links ideas of shelter with human history, or rather prehistory:

> There sandy seems the golden sky
> And golden seems the sandy plain.
> No habitation meets the eye
> Unless in the horizon rim,
> Some halfway up the limestone wall,
> That spot of black is not a stain
> Or shadow, but a cavern hole,
> Where someone used to climb and crawl
> To rest from his besetting fears.
> I see the callus on his sole
> The disappearing last of him
> And of his race starvation slim,
> Oh, years ago—ten thousand years.

"A Cliff Dwelling" combines the visionary mode of the minister's fantasy in "The Black Cottage" with the speculative attitude—at once awed and dreamy—of so many Frostian musings over old dwelling places. But *is* this a dwelling place? Out of vacancy and at a great distance the speaker discerns a spot of black which has the look of a refuge. With this imaginative elaboration of the spot, a human figure becomes barely discernible. Almost invisible in space, "ten thousand years" ago in time (the same sum of years that occurs to the census-taker), the diminutive figure nevertheless serves as an emblem of our inveterate human need for shelter.

"A Cliff Dwelling" shares some features with the much earlier "Into My Own," the poem which introduces Frost's first volume.[14] Each poem envisages a world divided into zones of enclosure and exposure. In each case the distant prospect is evoked with so many negatives, conditionals, and hedgings that its reality is called into question by the same language that confirms the poem's imaginative authority. Beyond the evasive screen of "as if"s and negatives, the common element in the visionary realm of both poems is the way remoteness of space is linked with equally vast stretches of time. The cliff dwelling is as far as the horizon rim; the young man in "Into My Own" wishes that the trees would stretch away as far as "the edge of doom." The time scale involved is vast; yet there is also the sense that "years ago—ten thousand years" is only an instant in the annals of time. Either way, human habitation leaves traces which tell us of the past, whether that past is recent or prehistoric. Houses are not only records of the past, moreover, but centers of human meaning, without which we could not in fact be fully human. Since the house always symbolizes human existence and endeavor, response to houses means response to a humanized, acculturated nature.

Frost observes and records what he sees on an astoundingly varied scale, ranging from an entomological delicacy to great vistas of time and space (as we shall see in *Stars*). Always the house is on a human scale; empty, inaccessible, burnt-out, it still represents a possible center of human life, a place where wilderness once made room for civilization. But without the sympathetic observer, Frost's houses—like the tree falling in an empty forest—might have nothing to convey; they are in need of interpretation, like any pieces of the past.

2. Seferis

i   Carved remains

Seferis too uses stone as a central human artifact and a way to read the past. As in Frost boundaries, walls, and houses are, so to speak, developments of the same idea, in Seferis the recurring image of stone, marble, or ruins has a range of possible meanings, which need to be considered bearing in mind both the history and landscape of Greece and Seferis's sense of his own imagery. For example, a passage from his "Letter to a Foreign Friend" alerts us to the metamorphic potential in the relatively few images Seferis uses.

> You see, we are a people who have had great Church Fathers, but we are now without great mystics; we are devoted to emotions and ideas, but we like to have even the most abstract notions presented in a familiar form, which a Christian of the West would call idolatry. . . . Is it the climate? Is it the race? I can't tell. I believe it's really the light. There must surely be something about the light that makes us what we are. In Greece one is more friendly, more at one with the universe. I find this difficult to express. An idea becomes an object with surprising ease. It seems to become all but physically incarnated in the web of the sun. On the other hand, at times you cannot discern whether the mountain opposite is a stone or a gesture. The *Logos* in its disembodied form is something which transcends our powers.[15]

The point about this passage is not that Greeks are unable to abstract, but that the Greek imagination (or more accurately Seferis's imagination) tends to be strongly pictorializing. But what it pictures may well be some kind of transformation. If an image is liable to turn at any moment into something else, the result is to enrich the possible variety of language and landscape without the need for a huge vocabulary or vast topography. Stare at the mountain long enough, Seferis seems to suggest, and it may seem to become a gesture—or vice versa. (Of course the passage is somewhat disingenuous; is it not the poet who effects such transformations?) Still the idea of metamorphosis, and of idea made thing, is a useful tool when reading Seferis's work,

which can often seem at first far more abstract and difficult than
that of Frost.

Stone is an image that recurs in Seferis's poetry as frequently
as it does in the Greek countryside, whether in the form of
boulders, broken columns, statues, or in general ruins. The
stones are real enough in Greece; Seferis insisted in a *Paris
Review* interview that they originated in "a landscape I had
seen." How then do they become ideas, or what ideas do they
become? The long sequence *Mythical History* with its epigraph
from Rimbaud "Si j'ai du goût, ce n'est guères / Que pour la terre
et les pierres," is a good place to begin exploring.

Seferis's poetry moves along a line which connects unhewn
rock (the raw material of art) and wrought remains. At the end of
the continuum nearest us in time are the remains. Section I of
Mythical History ends: "We brought back / these carved reliefs
of a humble art." Far in the past (that time from which we have
brought remains back) are / were fresh and immaculate works of
art, among them words. A unique resource of modern Greek is
the luminous (because often still comprehensible) antiquity of
many of the words in the language. Edmund Keeley has said of
Greek,

> It's the oldest living tradition, the oldest language tradition
> that is still alive. . . . Any modern Greek who uses certain
> words will bring with him in those words the Byzantine tradi-
> tion and the classical tradition, and maybe the pre-classical
> tradition as well. An example of this is the word "angel." The
> word in Greek carries with it connotations of angel in the
> simplest contemporary sense—"she's an angel"—of herald in
> the Medieval sense—the kind that announces a religious expe-
> rience—and of the messenger in classical drama. At least
> those three strata of meaning are in that word, and it's a word
> that goes back to the beginnings of the Greek tradition. I don't
> think we have a parallel in our language. . . . The echoes in
> Greek go back naturally to Homer. It's a tremendous advan-
> tage to the Greek poet, a tremendous disadvantage to the
> translator of Greek poetry.[16]

An advantage to the Greek poet indeed—yet Seferis is sensitive
to the fact that over the centuries words inevitably lose some of
the gloss of newness, some of their original power. Moreover,
any one writer's ability to make any impression on so great a
mass of tradition is small. Both these ideas, which appear in

essays Seferis wrote about the Greek tradition ancient and modern, form part of the thought of his poetry, a poetry which constantly ponders old things.

The carved reliefs brought back at the end of *Mythical History 1* connect the present with the past. (Elsewhere, as in "The King of Asine," relics are sought but not necessarily found; yet the poet bridges the gap in time by combining in one famous line "the ancient monuments and the contemporary sorrow.") The whole of *Mythical History* is a quest for the past that sometimes forgets what tradition it is after. The search goes from island to island and myth to myth (for example, are the Companions Argonauts or Odysseus's shipmates or contemporary refugees from Smyrna?). "What are they after, our souls, traveling / on rotten brine-soaked timbers / from harbor to harbor?" "Shifting broken stones . . . swimming in the waters of this sea / and of that sea / without the sense of touch . . ." The search is for the ancient monuments that appear sporadically throughout the poem. Yet the nature of these monuments is paradoxical: they are, at different times, indestructible, indispensable, broken, fugitive, burdensome, or forgotten. The way the object of the quest in *Mythical History* goes in and out of focus, vanishes and reappears, is a demonstration of the incongruities and contradictions of what Seferis has called

> . . . the Greek tradition, the whole tradition, indivisible as it is. For this tradition is not, as some see it, an affair of isolated promontories, some great names, some illuminating texts; instead it is like what others of us see and feel in the little mosaics of a humble Byzantine church—the Ionian philosophers, the popular verses of the period of the Comneni, the epigrams of the Anthology, Greek folk song, Aeschylus, Palamas, Solomos, Sikelianos, Calvos, Cavafy, the Parthenon, Homer, all living in a moment of time, in this Europe of today and looking at our devastated homes.[17]

This synchronic vision is an excellent guideline for approaching *Mythical History:* the deliberate temporal blurring, the simultaneous messages of continuity, damage, and loss.

The above passage also shows Seferis's bonding of a cultural tradition and stone artifacts in a way that may throw further light on *Mythical History* in particular and on stone in Seferis's imagery in general. Before returning to the poem, it is worth pausing to glance at the fullest exposition in Seferis of the kinship

between stone and language. This occurs in an essay on the
nineteenth-century freedom fighter and memoirist Makriyannis.
The following passage from the essay describes Makriyannis's
homemade handwriting. Seferis is not merely paying tribute to
the energy of an autodidact; Makriyannis has for him heroic
stature because Seferis felt both sympathy and veneration for
the man who virtually constructed his own language, stone by
battered stone, with apparently no help from anyone. (Seferis,
by the way, often referred to himself as an autodidact.)

> . . . he did not have the means to go to a teacher. He was just
> capable of writing, and it is doubtful if he could actually read
> anything except what he wrote himself. . . . After all, his
> handwriting is a purely personal invention. "Coarse writing,"
> he calls it himself. It took Vlahoyannis seventeen months'
> work to read, or rather to decipher it and to produce an intelli-
> gible copy. And a glance at a single page of this huge manu-
> script will soon show one why. Phonetic transcriptions of the
> local Roumelia speech, bizarre improvised couplings of letters
> make the page look like an endless succession of spidery
> arabesques. There are no signs to mark a paragraph or any
> other interruption; there is not even any punctuation. Only
> occasionally does a kind of perpendicular bar mark a major
> stop. The text looks like an old wall in which, if one looks
> closely, one can trace every movement of the builder, how he
> fitted one stone to the next, how he adjusted every effort he
> made to what had gone before and was to follow after, leaving
> on the finished building the imprint of the adventures of an
> uninterrupted human action. This is the thing that so moves us
> and to which we give the name of style or rhythm. So in this
> handwriting of Makriyannis, illegible as it may appear to the
> ordinary reader, we can discern even more clearly than from
> the words themselves the abiding will of the author to paint his
> own very self upon the paper.[18]

The "style or rhythm" traceable in a text is of course an individual characteristic of each writer. But the description of the
builder adjusting his every effort to what had gone before and
was to follow after encourages us to widen our vision and perceive each separate text in a tradition as a single stone in a larger
wall (as well as each word's being a stone in the wall of a single
text). The "uninterrupted human action" then becomes not one
man's effort but the collective contribution of the living and the
dead.

The relation of stone to wall, of the present moment to the general flow of time, is germane to another theme of Makriyannis which Seferis touches on in his essay—the relation of "I" to "we." The quoted passage (Seferis here quotes the words of Makriyannis) is not only political and ethical but also inescapably literary in its purport—for Seferis if not for the original writer.

> The reason why we all fought was that we might keep this country for all of us together, so that neither the weak nor the strong should say "I." Do you know when one can say "I"? When a man struggles all by himself . . . then he may say "I." But when many people join together in the struggle and accomplish something then they should say "we." In the life which we live it is "We" and not "I."[19]

A connection may be suspected between this passage and the paucity of the pronoun "I" in Seferis's work. Long sequences like *Mythical History* shift persons constantly, but most often the movement is between "we" and "you." And many Seferic speakers who do say "I" wear the guise of another character (Odysseus, Orestes), thus attaining a composite nature.

It is clear that Makriyannis—lifting and carving stones, fitting them into place, learning hieroglyphics (his native tongue)—is for Seferis an object of worshipful identification, an emblem par excellence of heroic endeavor within a great tradition. Although there is no such central hero in *Mythical History,* it should now be clearer that the subject of the sequence is that same struggle with tradition which so preoccupied Seferis. The voyagers in *Mythical History* variously try to bring back, transport, even *find* the precious relics of a heritage—a heritage which is embodied (as Seferis says Greeks often "embody" ideas) in stone.

In *Mythical History 1* the "carved reliefs" are easily portable. In the following section, access to the past is already more difficult, a matter for nostalgic reminiscence:

> Still another well inside a cave.
> It used to be easy for us to draw up idols and ornaments . . .
>
> The ropes have broken; only the grooves on the well's lip
> remind us of our past happiness. . . .

The treasures of the past are submerged, out of reach. In the third section of *Mythical History* the burden is again more accessible, but it is emphatically a *burden*. The entire section follows.

> I woke with this marble head in my hands;
> it exhausts my elbows and I don't know where to put it
>   down.
> It was falling into the dream as I was coming out of the
>   dream
> so our life became one and it will be very difficult for it to
>   disunite again.
>
> I look at the eyes: neither open nor closed
> I speak to the mouth which keeps trying to speak
> I hold the cheeks which have broken through the skin.
> I don't have any more strength
>
> My hands disappear and come toward me
> mutilated.

The weightiness of this marble head surely results from the concentration of meaning packed into it. It is at once a piece of marble, a "carved remain" as in Part 1; a face which brokenly mirrors the speaker's face; a head, seat of human consciousness; and a figment of the past which may bear a warning message of guilt (the epigraph, from *The Libation Bearers,* adjures the dead Agamemnon to remember his murder). The accumulated portentousness of the head makes it literally almost unbearable ("it exhausts my elbows"). Nevertheless it must be borne: "I don't know where to put it down." Having met on the borderline between dream and reality, the head and the speaker seem to be inextricably bonded ("our life became one"), yet the head is disabling and disabled, crippling to its new alter ego and itself unable to speak. Neither half of the strange new entity seems able to benefit the other half, in fact they become mutual mutilators; but the sense of kinship and mutual recognition is not thereby lessened.

Section 21 of *Mythical History* contains a somewhat similar interplay of energy between a living person and stone.

> We who set out on this pilgrimage
> looked at the broken statues
> we forgot ourselves and said that life is not so easily lost
> that death has unexplored paths
> and its own particular justice;

that while we, still upright on our feet, are dying,
become brothers in stone
united in hardness and weakness,
the ancient dead have escaped the circle and risen again
and smile in a strange silence.

The head in Section 3 has developed into a complete stone body
or bodies: statues. Statues, one of the most striking guises of
stone in Seferis, combine the durability and monumentality of
stone with the familiarity and vulnerability of the human bodies
they represent. Asked to explain the "meaning" of his statues,
Seferis replied that "the statues symbolize nothing other than
human bodies which have been hardened by insensibility . . .
bent by love, or . . . mutilated by the ravages of time."[20] Like any
writer's exegesis of his own work, this is partial. Seferis skirts
the fact that the statues inevitably connote art, recalling as they
do a product of the human spirit pitted against such destroyers of
form as insensibility or "the ravages of time." Statues of course
have a more direct and as it were larger-scale emotional impact
than such carved remains as a seal-ring or an inscription; but
basically they too are stones in the great wall of tradition, words
in the text or palimpsest of art.

ii   *The houses I had they took from me*

For Seferis as for Frost, houses are an important construct, a
significant combination of stone building blocks into a human
shelter. But if Frost's houses are often abandoned, in Seferis
they are repeatedly *lost.* "House" and "home" are usually expressed by the same Greek word *(spíti),* and the loss of houses in
Seferis's work means the loss of what *home* means. The very
impulse to build seems to get lost somewhere in the long journey
from past to present.

We find it strange that once we were able to build our
    houses, huts, and sheepfolds.
And our marriages, the cool coronals and the fingers, become
    enigmas inexplicable to our soul.
How were our children born, how did they grow strong?
                                    (*Mythical History* 10)

This inability to make houses takes place in a country where
"bodies . . . no longer know how to love," for houses mean
domesticity, regeneration, the normal cycle of human life. Some-

times, as above, their loss or destruction seems fairly recent. At other times the vision of homes destroyed is archaeological—not a matter of skills or knowledge lost within a couple of generations but of memories all but buried over the course of millennia.

> having known this fate of ours so well
> wandering around among broken stones, three or six
>   thousand years
> searching in collapsed buildings that might have been our
>   homes
> trying to remember dates and heroic deeds:
> will we be able?

> (22)

Because these "collapsed" buildings are so fragmentary, they come to signify both public and private ruin, the disintegration of both the civic and domestic realm. Either way, a construct is reduced to its component fragments. The resulting rubble is sifted in a manner that looks ahead to "The King of Asine," with its careful search on a stony acropolis and its reiterated question as to what "really exists" under "these ruined lines, edges, points, hollows, and curves."

> And the poet lingers, looking at the stones, and asks himself
> does there really exist . . .
> does there exist the movement of the face, shape of the
>   tenderness
> of those who've shrunk so strangely in our lives . . .
> or perhaps no, nothing is left but the weight
> the nostalgia for the weight of a living existence
> there where we now remain unsubstantial. . . .

The shrinkage of the present in comparison to a nostalgically recalled past is the central image in one of Seferis's most compelling poems about houses—a poem which also inevitably deals with loss. *Mythical History* could be called a voyage of exile; in this poem, "The Return of the Exile," the wanderer finds that his old home has grotesquely diminished. Seferis's admiration for Lewis Carroll can perhaps be detected in the images:

> "I'm looking for my old garden;
> the trees come to my waist
> and the hills resemble terraces
> yet as a child

> I used to play on the grass
> under great shadows
> and I would run for hours
> breathless over the slopes."
>
> . . . .
>
> "I'm looking for my old house,
> the tall windows
> darkened by ivy;
> I'm looking for the ancient column
> known to sailors.
> How can I get into this coop?
> The roof comes to my shoulders. . . ."

Most of the images are of peaceful childhood memories, yet the poem ends—strongly—on a note of dreadful and warlike violence.

> "Now I can't hear a sound.
> My last friend has sunk.
> Strange how from time to time
> they level everything down.
> Here a thousand scythe-bearing chariots go past
> and mow everything down."

The house in "Return of the Exile" begins as a personal emblem of a lost childhood paradise, but it ends as a more public omen of historical havoc. The poem is dated "spring '38."

"Piazza San Nicolo" is another poem in which a house is lost to the past, becoming shrunken, engulfed, or inaccessible. The image of the house here is primarily private, in the manner of Proust, as Nasos Vayenas points out in the most valuable discussion of this poem:

> As in Proust, so too in "Piazza San Nicolo" the return to lost time is an act of memory. But Seferis does not seem to feel that a moment, freed with the help of memory from the order of time, suffices to release him from time. The hand of time is so crushing that all memory can offer is a feeling like that of the coolness of the mountain, which may refresh him for a moment but is incapable of changing him. . . . I believe this is what Seferis means when he says that the coolness of the mountain never reaches the bell-tower. One carries "the house" around within him. One is the "house." And from the moment one has left the timeless age of childhood, the

"house" has lost its coolness, which is turned into memory; and, just as he is himself, it is locked inside the "stone church" all of whose doors are "locked by the huge hand of Saint Nicholas."[21]

But the intimate Proustian mode of "Piazza" and the personal scale of "Return" are bracketed in Seferis's oeuvre by the more monumental and public images of collapsed houses in the earlier *Mythical History* and the later *Thrush,* both poems which locate personal events or memories firmly within the larger context of history.

Thrush begins as a summation of all the lost houses in Seferis, with a line that rivals in resonance the "ancient remains and the contemporary sorrow" of "The King of Asine."

> The houses I had they took away from me. The times
> happened to be unpropitious: war, destruction, exile. . . .
>
> I don't know much about houses
> I know they have their own nature, nothing else.
> New at first, like babies
> who play in gardens with the tassels of the sun,
> they embroider colored shutters and shining doors
> over the day.
> When the architect's finished, they change,
> they frown or smile or even grow stubborn
> with those who stayed behind, with those who went away
> with others who'd come back if they could
> or others who disappeared, now that the world's become an
>   endless hotel.
>
> I don't know much about houses,
> I remember their joy and their sorrow. . . .
>
> Houses, you know, grow stubborn easily when you strip
>   them bare.

Exile means the loss of both public and private domains: of a personal dwelling, a country, and a past. Such divestment appears to be necessary in order to make possible the fresh beginning at the close of *Thrush,* when the house is restored in a transfigured way:

and you find yourself

in a large house with many windows open
running from room to room, not knowing from where to look
    out first. . . .

The houses of the past are replaced by a mysteriously exhilarating "house" of emptiness and silence, radiance and darkness (see the chapter on Light). But the vibrating silence at the end of *Thrush* is very different in quality from the tentative, wistful sifting of rubble in *Mythical History* or the nostalgic weariness of "Piazza San Nicolo" or "The Return of the Exile"—or even of the homeless cosmopolite at the beginning of *Thrush*. If stones are one's heritage and a house is the personal (or national) edifice they construct, then the loss or destruction of such a house, however painful and wasteful, also becomes a source of possible imaginative freedom. At the end of *Thrush,* with the image of the empty house with open windows, the sights and sounds—the inscriptions and burdens—of an entire culture seem to have vanished. The question is what will replace them.

   iii   *Watching the rising islands, watching the islands sink*

Beyond the human scale of carved reliefs or statues or houses, Seferis is also much concerned with the larger forms of stone: islands. *Gymnopaidia,* the pair of poems written soon after *Mythical History,* is devoted to stone in this shape. The epigraph of the poem, an excerpt from a Guide to Greece, announces that the poem's stones should be understood in the context not only of human culture but also of geological cycle.

> Santorini is geologically composed of pumice stone and china clay; in her bay, islands have appeared and disappeared. This island was once the center of a very ancient religion. The lyrical dances, with a strict and heavy rhythm, performed here were called: Gymnopaidia.

"Santorini," the first poem, begins with what sounds like a set of instructions—perhaps choreography for the "lyrical dance" of the epigraph.

> Bend if you can to the dark sea forgetting
> the sound of a flute on naked feet
> that trod your sleep in the other, the sunken life.

> Write if you can on your last shell
> the day the name the place
> and fling it into the sea so that it sinks.
>
> We found ourselves naked on the pumice stone
> watching the rising islands
> watching the red islands sink
> into their sleep, into our sleep.

The dynamic of *Mythical History,* where stones as repositories of culture allow us to carry the past along with us, is now reversed; we must fling away our own inscriptions. Nor is it ever clear whether "we" participate in the rising and sinking of islands or whether we are spectators who have somehow found a foothold outside the cycle of geological time.

The gesture of flinging the shell into the sea recalls both the epigraph of *Mythical History* 12, "Bottle in the sea," and the epigraph to *Logbook II:* "Sometimes it crosses my mind that the things I write here are nothing other than images that prisoners or sailors tattoo on their skin." The impulse to record "the day the name the place" on whatever material is available (one's own skin; "your last shell") is balanced by the impulse to disseminate these data by losing them, flinging them down, "carving a few signs on the stones / which now have touched the depths under memory," as Seferis puts it in "The Decision to Forget." The end of "Santorini" suggests just such a serendipitous finding through losing, with a sensual mood of surrender:

> Let your hands go traveling if you can
> here on time's curve. . . .
> when you can't any longer choose
> even the death you wanted as your own . . .
> let your hands go traveling if you can
> free yourself from unfaithful time
> and sink—
> sinks whoever raises the great stones.

To be lost, released from time, does not preclude some kind of survival; the "great stones" are raised. This image is less puzzling if we recall the cultural survivals of inscribed stone from *Mythical History.* In a chiasmic pattern we have seen before, submersion or oblivion is balanced by the act of recording. Seferis's poems are written in such a way that it is tempting to think of some of them as the ostrakha, inscribed shards, "carved reliefs" which the poems themselves describe. For example, the above-quoted epigraph of *Logbook II* encourages us to perceive the poems in that volume as intimate graffiti. The directive in "Santorini," "write if you can the day the name the place," is scrupulously followed in much of Seferis's work by notes as to the date and place of composition. Thus although the islands of "Santorini" are sinking "into their sleep, into our sleep," *the fact of the poem resists such oblivion.* Late in the poem the pattern is repeated. The voice nearly lapses into silence:

> in the land that was scattered, that can't resist,
> in the land that was once our land
> the islands—rust and ash—are sinking.

But after a pause, the impulse to record details even about a vanishing world galvanizes the utterance into spasms of detail, like a telegram from a battlefield:

> Altars destroyed
> and friends forgotten
> leaves of the palm tree in mud.

The epigraph to *Gymnopaidia* leaves us guessing as to whether islands that have once been submerged reappear or vanish forever; either way, the rhythm is of rising and falling. It is fitting that the poem falls into two parts, the dying note of the end of "Santorini" repeated on a rising key in "Mycenae":

> Sinks whoever raises the great stones;
> I've raised these stones as long as I was able
> I've loved these stones as long as I was able
> these stones, my fate.

Unlike the stones in *Mythical History* 22, "sinking into time" and "dragging me with them," these great stones seem to be lifted from oblivion as the speaker goes down, in a chiasmus reminiscent of *Mythical History* 3.

Can the cultural inscriptions of a tradition ("my own soil . . . my own gods, these stones") be resurrected only at the price of submerging the present? This is how a Greek critic reads the lines.

The sunken pieces of Santorini are the same as the sunken ancient world and the tombs and Cyclopean walls of Mycenae, which his memory wishes to resurrect. . . . But that man "sinks" who wishes to resurrect them—and both the national memory and the memory of the poet have "raised these stones as long as they were able."[22]

Such a reading responds to the solemnity of tone and elegiac note of the image of sinking stones, but ignores the resilience implied by the word *rhythm* and indeed by the rhythm of Seferis's language. The rhythm of the dance in the epigraph is "strict and heavy," but still for the downward motion of sinking there is a corresponding push upward. The poems attest that the raiser of the great stones has not sunk into nothingness. Memory remains in the form of language, as the injunction to write things down in "Santorini" has already apprised us. In "Mycenae," words are not written but spoken.

> Voices out of stone out of sleep
> deeper here where the world darkens,
> memory of toil rooted in the rhythm
> beaten upon the earth by feet
> forgotten.
> Bodies sunk into the foundations
> of the other time, naked.

Beyond the grave tone, the imagery has an autonomous pattern of energy. The stones naturally sink, but in the dictum of Heraclitus dear to Seferis (and to Eliot), the way up and down is one and the same. For every solemn sinking in Seferis's world there is some moment of ascension.

> A little farther
> we will see the almond trees blossoming
> the marble gleaming in the sun
> the sea breaking into waves
>
> a little farther,
> let us rise a little higher.
>
> (*Mythical History* 23)

"Mycenae" ends not with a sinking into oblivion but with a kind of transcendence (rather than actual ascension): a recess from time which breaks the rhythm of reciprocity, when the millstones stop turning. Ought we to read this aorist moment as a crack of light in the predominantly somber world of *Gymnopaidia* or as a doom-laden sign of apocalyptic cessation? In either case, the image of the millstone represents a further evolution of the link connecting stones with time. The carved remains of *Mythical History* are small enough to be carried (diachronically) *through* time. The islands in *Gymnopaidia,* larger than people but still on an earthly scale, obey geological laws of ascension and descent. It is possible to regard the millstones as cosmic in scale, obedient to a temporal scheme beyond human understanding ("not even the silence is now yours / here where the millstones have stopped turning"). What we can grasp is that when the millstones cease to turn, time stops. A rather cryptic journal entry of August 1947, when Seferis was facing major surgery, broods about millstones, mortality, metamorphosis:

> And when all has been said, the moment comes when you understand that the mechanism of transformation [?] returns from the other side and brings back what is unique—what has blossomed, as if it were a seed which follows the other seeds between the millstones.[23]

The millstones as they turn will crush the seed, recalling the image from a Greek folksong about wrestling with Death on "the marble threshing floor." When the millstones stop turning, Death itself may be suspended.

"Engomi," published in *Logbook III,* combines and summarizes, although it never wholly resolves, the themes of verticality, excavation, cycle, cessation of time, and messages from the past. These various strands are woven into a coherent texture in a poem apparently occasioned by a visit Seferis made to an archaeological site in Cyprus. The beginning of "Engomi" describes the approach to the ruins; almost at once the vision shifts from horizontality to things partly obscured beneath the surface.

> The plain was broad and level; from a distance you could see arms in motion as they dug.

Then we move closer to the actual site of the digging, where the buried life of the past is being laid bare.

And I moved on toward those at work,
women and men digging with picks in trenches.
It was an ancient city; walls, streets and houses
stood out like the petrified muscles of cyclopes,
the anatomy of spent strength under the eye
of the archaeologist, anesthetist, or surgeon.
Phantoms and fabrics, luxury and lips, buried
and the curtains of pain spread wide open
to reveal, naked and indifferent, the tomb.

Rising again from the depth of the tomb, the poem returns to the sight of the living, whose task is the revelation of the past.

And I looked up toward those at work,
the taut shoulders, the arms that struck
this dead silence with a rhythm heavy and swift
as though the wheel of fate were passing through the ruins.

Compare the "rhythm heavy and swift" with the rhythm of the dances in the epigraph of *Gymnopaidia,* the "wheel of fate" with the millstones in "Mycenae." As in the latter poem, the wheel of fate here signals (paradoxically, despite the "stretched shoulders and the arms that struck") the cessation of motion.

Suddenly I was walking and did not walk
I looked at the flying birds, and they had stopped stone dead
I looked at the sky's air, and it was full of wonder
I looked at the bodies laboring, and they were still
and among them a face climbing the light. . . .

This epiphany (closely following a passage from the Apocryphal New Testament) seems to emerge from the open grave but to transcend it.

"The face climbing the light" turns out not to be a fragment— like the marble head in *Mythical History* 3—but an entire figure.

. . . the body
emerged from the struggling arms stripped
with the unripe breasts of the Virgin,
a motionless dance.

And I lowered my eyes to look all around:
girls kneaded, but they didn't touch the dough
women spun, but the spindles didn't turn

lambs were drinking, but their tongues hung still
above green waters that seemed asleep
and the ploughman transfixed with his staff poised.
And I looked again at that body ascending;
people gathered like ants,
and they struck her with lances but didn't wound her.
Her belly now shone like the moon
and I thought the sky was the womb
that bore her and now took her back, mother and child.
Her feet were still visible, adamantine
then they vanished: an Assumption.

The transcendent vision of plenitude and tranquillity recalls the
journal passage about the blossoming seed between the millstones: the budding apparition (mother and child, belly and
womb) vanishes, taken back to the sky.

The apparition recalls the earlier poem "Spring A.D.," and a
similar female vision:[24]

But she smiled
wearing light colors . . .
and walked along lightly
opening windows
in the delighted sky
without us, the luckless ones.
And I saw her breast naked
the waist and the knee,
as the inviolate martyr
inviolate and pure
issues from the torment
to go to heaven,
beyond the inexplicable
whispering of people. . . .

In both "Engomi" and "Spring A.D.," the withdrawal of the vision signifies a return to the world of time and mortality. In
"Engomi" there is also a return to the surface of the earth with
all its terrestrial imperfections.

The world
became again as it had been, ours:
the world of time and earth.

Aromas of terebinth
began to stir on the old slopes of memory

breasts among leaves, lips moist;
and all went dry at once on the length of the plain,
in the stone's despair, in eroded power,
in that empty place with the thin grass and the thorns
where a snake slithered heedless,
where they take a long time to die.

These snakes are not the evil creatures of "Mycenae," where "the Furies began whistling / in the meager grass . . . snakes crossed with vipers / knotted over the evil generation. . . ." Rather they are symbols and victims of the earthly landscape to which, when the vision has passed, we must return.

A map of "Engomi" which might also throw light on *Gymnopaidia* and *Mythical History* would be easy to sketch.[25] Mystery and beauty lie either below the surface of the earth, among the excavated "phantoms and fabrics, luxury and lips," or else they have risen above the human sphere like the vision of the Assumption. The two kinds of otherness, that above and that below the surface, are joined by a vertical line (the way up and down). Perpendicular to this line, along the surface of the earth, runs the horizontal axis of clock time and process, where thousands of years pass, grass is thin, and "they take a long time to die."

Frost and Seferis use virtually the same image cluster to express and develop a range of kindred themes. Stone begins as a solid chunk of landscape, but its meaning hardly ends there. It can be combined with other chunks to construct tangible things like walls or houses; it can be carved or shaped to inscribe a text or form a statue. Because of the durability of anything made of stone, all these forms of it can be eloquent messengers of the past. Moreover, stone is an excellent synecdochic unit, adequate alone but suggesting extension to larger ideas. The two poets are able both to extrapolate constructs from the image and also to reduce it to its most abstract essentials. Building out from the single idea of stone enables Frost and Seferis as it were to put together walls, houses, even whole islands; yet even houses and islands are subject to decay and will eventually be reduced to their component parts or what we started with: chunks of rock.

The connotations of the image of stone tend to be collective rather than individual, for walls, houses, and art are social creations which answer to the needs of a community (even a community of only two). In Frost, although the image of the wall first offers itself as a breach between inside and outside, a boundary between the self and the world, we soon learn that the wall is also an occasion for fellowship and for form, the kind of form needed in creating works of art. In Seferis the image of stone has from the beginning a collective force, for it is by means of stone that the collective cultural heritage of the past is stored, coded, or carried on.

Beyond these broad similarities in the two poets' use of the image, there are illuminating differences. In Frost, whether two men converse over a wall ("A Time to Talk," "Mending Wall") or a solitary speaker uses language to enliven an abandoned dwelling ("The Black Cottage," "The Census-Taker," "A Cliff Dwelling"), the wall/house image tends to be an occasion for speech. Walls (and by extension human habitations) nurture the poetic process both by creating a protective envelope of space and by symbolizing constructed form, the quality of a *made* artifact with its attendant values of craft, patience, skill, and tradition. Thus for Frost the subtext of the image of stone is form, boundary, decorum: finally, the exigencies of language itself. "In making a poem," Frost says, "you have no right to think of anything but the subject matter. *After making it, no right to boast of anything but the form.*"[26] (Italics mine.)

In Seferis, stone and stone constructs are of course also the occasion for a great deal of language, but more basically they are repositories of culture. The bottle in the sea or carved reliefs of *Mythical History,* the death mask in "The King of Asine"—all these contain and recapitulate the past more succinctly than houses can. Houses, indeed, are felt by Seferis as frail and fugitive as against the powers of exile and destruction they suffer. Nevertheless, this sense of loss is balanced in the Greek poet by a greater sense of community in the projects of civilization, as we can see when we observe the frequency with which Seferis uses the pronoun *we,* as if mindful of Makriyannis's injunction about national achievement and the greater nobility of *us* than of *me.* The following quotation captures this sense at once of loss, of artifact as repository, and of communal oneness; fittingly, it was not written by Seferis himself but by his sister Ioanna Tsatsou, who is expressing the feeling of a brother and sister, a family, a generation, and a nation: "The greatest lesson of the ancient world was something we carried within ourselves. The smile of the ancient *kore,* the temple's rhythm opened a deep channel of aesthetic response. But broken stones surrounded us; they dissolved time and confronted us squarely with our plight."[27]

Such differences of emphasis between the two poets' sense of an image no doubt have to do with the respective times and places of the composition of the two oeuvres. Some of Frost's poems about houses were written before the First World War; some of Seferis's about stone, after the Second World War. And there are inevitable differences between the New and Old World poets when it comes to their experience of and response to landscape and history.[28] But it would be a distortion to claim that one poet cherishes the lost past while the other thinks only of sturdy individuality and the future. That both poets feel the need of the past is shown by their shared attention to some of the forms it takes. In their hands, chunks of the planet become a surprisingly fruitful source of imaginative endeavor. It is the power of that imaginative energy that turns inanimate rock, in both the oeuvres, into what Elizabeth Bishop called a mirror in which to dwell—a potential mirror not only of self but of cultural values, and not only of landscape but of history.

Notes

1. William James, *Principles of Psychology,* 1890, quoted by Frank Lentricchia, "Robert Frost and Modern Literary Theory," in *Frost: Centennial Essays,* compiled by the Committee on the Frost Centennial of the University of Southern Mississippi (Jackson: University Press of Mississippi, 1974), 320–21.

2. Lentricchia, 322.

3. Lentricchia, 322.

4. Frost, quoted in Reginald L. Cook, *Robert Frost: The Living Voice* (Amherst: University of Massachusetts Press, 1974), 240.

5. Ioanna Tsatsou, *My Brother George Seferis* (Athens: Hestia, 1973), 257.

6. Seferis, *Days* (Journal), Vol. 5, entry for 4 June 1946 (Athens: Ikaros, 1975).

7. Frost, quoted in Lawrance Thompson, *Robert Frost: The Years of Triumph, 1915–1938* (New York: Holt, Rinehart and Winston, 1970), 322–23.

8. Frost, "To the *Amherst Student,*" printed 25 March 1935, cited by Elaine Barry, *Robert Frost on Writing* (New Brunswick, N.J.: Rutgers University Press, 1973), 112–14. I am indebted to Richard Poirier *(Robert Frost: The Work of Knowing)* for pointing out the connection between "A Drumlin Woodchuck" and the *Letter.*

9. Richard Poirier, *Robert Frost: The Work of Knowing* (New York: Oxford University Press, 1977), 104–5.

10. Gaston Bachelard, *The Poetics of Space,* trans. Maria Jolas (Boston: Beacon Press, 1964), 36.

11. Robert Frost, quoted in Helen Bacon, "Dialogue of Poets: *Mens Animi* and the Renewal of Words," *Massachusetts Review* 19, no. 2 (Summer 1978): 323.

12. *Poetics of Space,* 91, 98.

13. Vladimir Nabokov, *Pnin* (New York: Atheneum [6th printing], 1967), 20.

14. As Poirier points out *Work of Knowing,* 85–86).

15. Seferis, "Letter to a Foreign Friend," in Seferis, *On the Greek Style: Selected Essays on Poetry and Hellenism,* translated and introduced by Rex Warner (London: Bodley Head, 1966), 170. Note: "Letter to a Foreign Friend" in this volume was translated by Edmund Keeley and Nanos Valaoritis.

16. "An Interview with Edmund Keeley," conducted by Warren Wallace (unpublished), 1979–80, 11–12.

17. Seferis, "Cavafy and Eliot—A Comparison," in *On the Greek Style,* 161.

18. Seferis, "Makriyannis," in *On the Greek Style,* 31–32.

19. "Makriyannis," 28–29.

20. Seferis to Robert Levesque, quoted in M. Argyriou, "Proposals about *Thrush,*" in *For Seferis* ed. G. P. Savidis (Athens: Ikaros, 1961), 268.

21. Nasos Vayenas, *The Poet and the Dancer* (Athens: Kedros, 1979), 258ff.

22. Markos Avgeris, "The Poetry of Seferis," in *For Seferis,* 43.

23. Seferis, *Days,* 5:106.
For the image of cosmic millstones in the Greek tradition see Giorgio de Santillana and Hertha von Dechend, *Hamlet's Mill* (Boston: David R. Godine, Publisher, 1977), especially Chapter 9, "Amlodhi the Titan and His Spinning Top," 137–48. See especially the quotation (p. 137) from Cleomedes (A.D. 150) on the northern latitudes: "The heavens there turn around in the way a millstone does." And Petronius (*Satyricon* 39, p. 138): "Thus the orb of heaven turns around like a millstone, and ever does something bad."

24. Savidis makes this connection in his section on "Engomi," in *For Seferis.*

25. For the notion of mapping Seferis's landscape in this way, I am indebted to Northrop Frye, *T. S. Eliot* (New York: Capricorn Books, 1972), 77: "A book this size has no space for full commentary on *Four Quartets,* and some 'audiovisual aids' will have to do instead. . . ."

26. Frost, quoted in Gorham Munson, *Robert Frost: A Study in Sensibility and Good Sense* (New York: George H. Doran Co., 1927), 47–48.

27. *My Brother GS,* 187.

28. See for example the essays on Robert Frost and on American poetry in W. H. Auden, *The Dyer's Hand and Other Essays* (New York: Vintage Books, 1968), 345ff.

CHAPTER II

Trees, Gardens, Sea

This chapter moves away from walls and houses to touch on a very different kind of image, or rather pair of images, whose more seductive surfaces present another set of challenges to both poet and reader. In the case of Frost, the image in question is of gardens and growing things in general, particularly trees; in that of Seferis, the sea.

At first trees and the sea might seem a more incongruous pair than walls and stones. But if we consider the terrain of New England and coastal Greece—the respective landscapes of the two poets—it is clear that trees and the sea constitute some of the most ubiquitous and hence familiar forms of nature. Where the works of men stop, woods or water begin. The attractive autonomy of woods and water, moreover, has always offered itself as an appropriate and suggestive theme for poetry. To walk among trees, plant a garden, pick a flower, gaze at or plunge into water—these are symbolic deeds in ways more dramatic than picking up a stone or pondering a wall. Whereas the latter acts are ratiocinative, the former involve participation, even immersion, in the stuff of nature.

Trees and the sea, for Frost and Seferis respectively, are not occasional decorative motifs but major subjects to which the poets return again and again. In using these images as frequently as they do, both writers are doing two things at once. Obviously each is responding to a conspicuous feature of a familiar environment as a subject and source of art. Beyond this, each poet is also participating in a tradition of poetry of place that goes as far back as the Garden of Eden for trees and the *Odyssey* for salt water. (It is not farfetched to mention such prototypes; in many poems Frost and Seferis themselves refer to such models. "Carpe Diem," "Nothing Gold Can Stay," "Upon a Foreign

Verse," and "The Companions in Hades" are only a few examples.)

But a venerable and still-flourishing tradition poses problems for those who would carry it on and still retain some originality. This chapter is therefore organized according to the major ways in which Frost and Seferis bring their technical and imaginative resources to bear on the problem of originality within a tradition. Neither poet violently breaks with the past, but each has distinctive ways, not only of responding to nature, but even of looking at it.

First, both poems avoid monotony by varying the stance and focus of their poems about trees and the sea. Even as they scrutinize and cherish nature, both often station themselves so as strikingly to acknowledge the limitations of human vision. The resulting poems stress the perpetual curiosity of human spectators in the face of natural mysteries, however familiar such mysteries may be. To read Frost on gardens or Seferis on the sea is to be constantly reminded how partial our knowledge of the world is. Even when planting a garden or sailing over the ocean—two archetypal images of human cultivation and exploration of the wilderness—we remain ignorant of what goes on beneath the surface. Yet the same pair of images can also occasion moods of clarity and perspicacity, as when Frost counters the mysteriousness of nature by setting up parallels between "inner and outer weather," or when Seferis, gazing at the sunken wreck of the "Thrush," envisions the bright bodies of divers still cleaving the dark water.

Some of the most notable (and original) moments in both poets' visions of nature occur when the central image is transcended rather than actually contemplated. As if growing impatient with his own perennial scrutiny of trees, Frost in several remarkable poems uses trees as celestial vehicles, modes of transport between earth and heaven. The section on Frost in this chapter concludes by discussing "Birches," "Wild Grapes," and "After Apple-Picking," poems in which trees are dynamic agents of experience as well as classic objects of poetic revery.

Like Frost, Seferis has recurrent longings to "get away from earth awhile." But whereas Frost can turn a tree into a ladder to heaven, Seferis cannot use the sea as a passageway to the Happy Isles; a major theme of his *Mythical History* is indeed the impossibility of such an enterprise. Searching for some other mode of transcendence, Seferis is sometimes tempted actually to reject

the sea—to get away from his beloved Aegean just as Frost gets
away from his beloved earth. Hence a culminating moment of
Seferis's marine poetry is this dismissal at the end of *Thrush:*
"the sea will drain dry . . . from north to south."

Such a statement might seem to announce the poet's wish to
free himself from all the mythological and psychological baggage
associated with the image of the sea—*to do without the sea* in
some "other life." Yet the very words Seferis chooses to express
this wish inextricably involve him in a tangle of tradition, for the
draining of the sea is an image borrowed from a line in Aeschylus's *Agamemnon*—a line Seferis used repeatedly. I conclude my
discussion of Seferis's sea imagery by tracing his various adapta-
tions of the Aeschylean line "There is the sea—and who will
drain it dry?"—a line which in its defiant proclamation of the
sea's inexhaustibility seems to pose a prophetic challenge to all
poets after Aeschylus. By a similar paradox, it is just when Frost
most wishes to rise above the earth that he clings most tena-
ciously to such literary and mythological antecedents as the
story of the Bacchae or of Leif the Lucky in "Wild Grapes," or
the Tree of Knowledge in "After Apple-Picking."

What, then, relates trees and the sea as major images in the
two poetic oeuvres? In each case, the poet takes a characteristic
and important feature of the landscape he knows and loves;
circles it, observing and pondering, from many angles; and eventually gets (or wishes to get) beyond it altogether. In observing
this process, part of the interest, as I have said, lies in the way
traditional poetic themes impose the need for freshness of perception. But literary history apart, Frost and Seferis are grap-
pling with whatever symbolic quality it is that has made these
images so central a poetic *topos*. To isolate that quality, it is
helpful to contrast the character of trees/sea with that of the
image discussed in Chapter I, stone.

Since stone is not conspicuously, vitally attractive in the way
living plants or moving water are, its use as a major poetic image
requires a kind of abstraction, whereas flowers or waves are
immediately eloquent—but of what? Stone, we have seen, is
chiefly perceived by our poets as raw material for human purposes, a kind of tablet on which an entire cultural heritage can be
inscribed. By contrast, trees or the sea are relatively free of the
marks of civilization; we touch but cannot change them. Their
subtext for both poets would seem to be not—as stone's is—
human culture as recorded by people in time, but time itself—

time as cycle and metamorphosis, decay and rebirth. A natural rhythm beyond the scope of our individual lives is regularly recapitulated in the growth of plants or fall of leaves, or in the mysteries that take place beneath the strangely renewable earth and the familiar, inscrutable surface of the sea.

It was noted in the Preface that both Frost and Seferis at some point described themselves as obstinate or single-minded or limited. This somewhat obsessed quality of concentration may have been what enabled them to discern likeness amidst multiplicity. There is no such thing as a typical Frost tree poem or Seferis sea poem; each poet respects the protean nature of his cherished image. And yet time and again, the many guises of the image prove to be variations of the same underlying theme. The message coded in the sprouting of seeds or the murk of waters is above all *time*—time in its cyclical, mythical aspect rather than the linear, historical dimension which might be traced by an archaeologist or an epigrapher.

It is the aura of myth that keeps a blooming garden, bare tree, or sea surface tantalizingly fresh and strange to the poet, however familiar they may be to the gardener or the fisherman. These everyday things become, in Frost's and Seferis's work, corresponding emblems of the unknowable, because always changing, things of this world. The third and final chapter, on stars and light, will take us to these poets' pictures of what is unknowable beyond our planet.

1. Frost: Growing Things and the Cycle of Seasons

The most cursory glance at the Table of Contents of Frost's *Collected Poems* reveals a profusion of growing things and related activities—"Birches," "Wild Grapes," "Rose Pogonias," "Putting in the Seed," "Flower-Gathering," and "A Leaf Treader" are only a few items in what can seem a rapt almanac of natural objects and events. Indeed, so many of Frost's shorter poems, in particular, respond to the rural calendar and landscape that the result might well be a monotonous, if picturesque, catalogue of beauties. How is it that these poems manage to avoid monotony?

Frost can scrutinize a flower or scan a forest; he takes nature in close up and at a distance. Reginald Cook has noted that Frost's poems can be divided into those with vertical and those with horizontal gazes;[1] in fact, the subject of a Frost nature poem may be a sight that greets the viewer as he looks up or down, near or far. Equally important is the way the voice in these poems varies, moving from anecdotal or wry or indulgent or deadpan to rapt, perplexed, abstracted, terrified. This range of tone reflects the varying status—real or imagined, humdrum or emblematic—of some of the natural sights we come upon in Frost.[2] Finally, the role of imagination in Frost's nature poems is protean. Some poems celebrate a perceived scene; others go halfway toward transforming what is perceived and then withdraw. In a poem like Tennyson's "Flower in the Crannied Wall," a firm decorum separates the flower from the speaker who plucks it, observes it, addresses it, and moralizes upon it. In Frost such decorum is undependable; it tends to waver like the "pane of glass" in "After Apple-Picking":

> It melted, and I let it fall and break.

Yet even after the ice/pane breaks, the speaker "cannot rub the strangeness" from his sight. In Frost's poems, the boundary between perceiver and perceived, or between nature and the imagination, constantly shifts in this manner. It can be hard to tell whether the strangeness inheres in the seer or the sight.

In examining even a fairly modest sample of Frost's nature poems, I have found varying degrees of firmness in the boundary between self and world—variations that can also be seen as different degrees of participation in the theme of mutability or in the pathetic fallacy, those strands of poetic tradition that are never far away from poems about blooming gardens or falling leaves, as Frost would have been the first to agree. I assume no intentional divisions on the part of the poet. The divisions are marked here for the sake of clear articulation, and even so they tend to run together. They are (i) the imagination's push to fill in the incompleteness of a given moment; (ii) curiosity, ecstatic or somber, as to what goes on beneath the surface; (iii) partial identification of the observer with the natural process, which can become (iv) a progressive blurring of the borderline that separates us from nature, "inner" from "outer weather," and (v) the actual (if temporary) physical merging of man and nature in an action of ascent which—more than the other imaginative responses—tends to be enriched by allegorical and mythical resonances.

i   *Filling in the moment*

In "Carpe Diem," a poem which illustrates with unusual clarity the poet's claim that "many of my poems have literary criticism in them—*in* them,"[3] Frost discusses the mutability theme and concludes with an almost Proustian resistance to the pressure of the present.

> "Be happy, happy, happy,
> And seize the day of pleasure."
> The age-long theme is Age's.
> 'Twas Age imposed on poems
> Their gather-roses burden
> To warn against the danger
> That overtaken lovers
> From being overflooded
> With happiness should have it
> And yet not know they have it.
> But bid life seize the present?
> It lives less in the present
> Than in the future always
> And less in both together
> Than in the past. The present
> Is too much for the senses,
> Too crowded, too confusing—
> Too present to imagine.

This poem's dissent against the traditional *carpe diem* or "gather-roses burden" takes a subtler, less programmatic form in two of Frost's most exquisite brief lyrics, "Spring Pools" and "In Hardwood Groves." Both poems bear out the point that it is impossible to perceive the present in isolation, to seize on a single moment, however beautiful. Both poems take the occasion of an observed point in time to complete, in thought, the seasonal cycle. Thus both poems manage to encompass, as well as the unique stillness of a particular instant, the inevitability and imminence of change. Both capture something of the pendulum swing of what Wallace Stevens, in "The Poems of Our Climate," called "the never-resting mind."

The very syntax of "Spring Pools" tells us from the start that Frost is not merely naming or admiring the pools. He begins by anticipating their disappearance.

These pools that, though in forests, still reflect
The total sky almost without defect,
And like the flowers beside them, chill and shiver,
Will like the flowers beside them soon be gone,
And yet not out by any brook or river,
But up by roots to bring dark foliage on.

The trees that have it in their pent-up buds
To darken nature and be summer woods—
Let them think twice before they use their powers
To blot out and drink up and sweep away
These flowery waters and these watery flowers
From snow that melted only yesterday.

The suavity and compactness of this performance lend it an air of simplicity. Yet the poem's statement is complex. Like "Carpe Diem," it finds the present "too present to imagine," and as if against its will is hurried on at once. No sooner is the pools' presence stated ("*these* pools") than their transience is suggested, first by "still" and then, more fully, by "will soon be gone." The pools will vanish "like the flowers beside them," but this is no ordinary lament at the evanescence of spring; rather the pools will be pulled "up by the roots" (notice how the cliché springs to aptness and life) to nourish the foliage of next summer. The second stanza is a subdued request for what the speaker hardly expects to be granted—a slowing down of time.[4]

The elliptical manner of "Spring Pools" is appropriate to the unbroken process of the natural cycle it implicitly (and elliptically) describes—implicitly because the poem's decorous economy requires that it omit mention of much of the passage of time it *shows* us.[5] Nature's thrift miraculously encloses the leaves of summer in the tight buds of late winter/early spring. The never-resting mind, contemplating a scene of early spring, blots up the waters and puts leaves on the bare branches—envisions the whole process of burgeoning. Such is the thrift of the imagery that three of the four seasons of the year are adumbrated in this brief poem whose ostensible subject is *one* season. So effortlessly does the syntax assimilate seasonal transition that Reuben Brower finds it undecorous to declare that such change is in fact the poem's subject. "The awkwardness of using terms like cycle and eternal return of 'Spring Pools' is only another sign that the chainlike, unbroken process is in the movement of impressions and 'things': snow-into-pools-into-flowers-into-trees."[6]

Yet of course "Spring Pools" *is* about cycle, since it both depicts a single point in a year and spans the whole seasonal cycle. The tension between moment and cycle is felt as movement in a poem which at first seems more like a still life, a Monet-like impression of "flowery waters and watery flowers." That motion is chiefly an upward pull, a sucking skyward as the melted snow, having sunk into the ground, is tugged up "by the roots" to water the embryo leaves. Appropriately for a poem whose gaze and imaginative process both travel upward, "Spring Pools" ignores fall. The temporal cycle takes us from late winter or early spring to summer, season of "dark foliage." The motion toward summer is too full of knowledge to be exuberant, even if fall is not mentioned. I would not, with Brower, call the movement one of "darkness and terror," but there is solemnity in the poem's inability to ignore, even for an instant, the imminence of change.

"In Hardwood Groves" expresses a similarly inexorable awareness of cycle. The direction here is as emphatically downward as that of "Spring Pools" is ascendant. Nature's imperative gesture, obeyed by the leaves, points down:

> The same leaves over and over again!
> They fall from giving shade above
> To make one texture of faded brown
> And fit the earth like a leather glove.
>
> Before the leaves can mount again
> To fill the trees with another shade,
> They must go down past things coming up.
> They must go down into the dark decayed.
>
> They *must* be pierced by flowers and put
> Beneath the feet of dancing flowers.
> However it is in some other world
> I know that this is the way in ours.

The view presented here has a daunting completeness, like a painting of a blooming garden which shows earthworms, leaf-mold, and bones beneath the surface. But rather than either grimness or gaiety, the chief sense is of *completeness,* a cycle filled out from a given part. The poem's final two lines extend the pattern of falling-in-order-to-rise beyond a particular deciduous grove in autumn to everything in our mortal world. By advanc-

ing within a single line the possibility of other worlds where
gravity, decay, and mutability may work differently, may not
exist at all, and then returning to our world, "In Hardwood
Groves" emphasizes its terrestriality.

Both these poems extrapolate the imperative of cycle from a
sign of one season: melting snow, a falling leaf. Our sense of the
brevity of New England seasons and then by extension of any
earthly spans is sharpened by the poems' insistence on what
comes next. Both express temporal imminence in part by spatial
aggressiveness, the sense that things in nature must get out of
the way of other things (this will recur in "Pea Brush"). But of
course what really must get out of the way of the oncoming
moment is time itself. In the light of these extensions and com-
pletions so deftly executed by the "never-resting mind," the request in Frost's early "A Prayer in Spring" seems especially
poignant:

> Oh, give us pleasure in the flowers today;
> And give us not to think so far away
> As the uncertain harvest; keep us here
> All simply in the springing of the year.

Such a request is denied in poems like "Carpe Diem," "Spring
Pools," and "In Hardwood Groves." But the germ of denial is
contained within the very words of the petition, for only the
mind's tendency to push beyond the present makes it necessary
to pray for the limitation of awareness to a "simple" pleasure.

ii   Under the earth (The strong are saying nothing)

Completion of the present moment such as we have seen involves a visualizing imagination which can supply leaves to bare
branches and see the leafmold beneath spring flowers. But the
seasonal metamorphoses that take place underground are usually difficult to visualize and even, in Frost, to imagine. It is as if
a bedroom door were shut upon the secrets of generation and
regeneration. In the absence of knowledge or a clear image,
there are speculation and curiosity about subterranean process;
there is also a certain prohibition of speech. "The Strong Are
Saying Nothing" stoically denies the propriety of speech about
hidden things; it also protests too much.

> Wind goes from farm to farm in wave on wave,
> But carries no cry of what is hoped to be.
> There may be little or much beyond the grave,
> But the strong are saying nothing until they see.

The poem calls attention to its own status as an act of speech by the provocative metaphor "beyond the grave." The use of such a metaphor for "underground" is surely hardly the same as "saying nothing," for the phrase gives the annual crop the intensely awaited significance of an afterlife even while it also refuses to visualize the transformation which is mysteriously taking place. A similar refusal to imagine a hidden process (a refusal which amounts to just such an imagining) occurs in "Goodbye and Keep Cold":

> I wish I could promise to lie in the night
> And think of an orchard's arboreal plight
> When slowly (and nobody comes with a light)
> Its heart sinks lower under the sod.
> But something has to be left to God.

"Beyond the grave," "left to God"—this is the language of mystery or revelation, religious faith in the invisible. But humanity, being fallible, is not really satisfied with what cannot be seen. The strong may *say* nothing "until they see" but the poem shows that they imagine. Similarly, since much of "Goodbye and Keep Cold" is a litany of possible sources of harm to the orchard, the owner *does* lie awake and think about his trees, even if he knows that thought is useless and that the trees must be "left to God."

The act of planting is rather grimly referred to in "The Strong Are Saying Nothing" as "stringing a chain of seed in an open crease." The image is sexual without losing its sense of isolation: "Men work alone, their lots plowed far apart." A happier focus on the act of planting is "Putting in the Seed," perhaps one of the most evocative garden poems ever written. Since the speaker is down on his knees in the dirt, the poem brings us close to earth and also close to worship. "Putting in the Seed," as well as a description of planting seeds, is several kinds of hymn at once: a celebration of the springing of new life and also a call to the beloved to join in such a celebration and in the work that occasions it. "You come to fetch me," the poem's opening, is the same kind of resonant call—embracing the beloved, the reader, and the world—as that in Frost's theme poem, "The Pasture" ("I shan't be gone long.—You come too.").

> You come to fetch me from my work tonight
> When supper's on the table, and we'll see
> If I can leave off burying the white
> Soft petals fallen from the apple tree
> (Soft petals, yes, but not so barren quite,
> Mingled with these, smooth bean and wrinkled pea;)
> And go along with you ere you lose sight
> Of what you came for and become like me,
> Slave to a springtime passion for the earth.
> How love burns through the Putting in the Seed
> On through the watching for that early birth
> When, just as the soil tarnishes with weed,
> The sturdy seedling with arched body comes
> Shouldering its way and shedding the earth crumbs.

In this paean to human and vegetative springing, potential awareness of the cycle of life is encapsulated by the image of planting peas and beans as "burying." The legumes are "buried" in order to turn into something else; but so too are the flower petals, which will be transformed to earth and whose decay will feed new life. Celebrating the joy of a particular occasion, "Putting in the Seed" thus finds room to suggest the metamorphoses inherent in the natural cycle. The "wrinkled" bean will turn into a "sturdy seedling with arched body," while the buried petals will invisibly turn into "earth crumbs." (There is a similar richly sensuous textural contrast in "The Strong Are Saying Nothing"; "To the fresh and black of the squares of early mold/The leafless bloom of a plum is fresh and white.") The speaker's "springtime passion for the earth"—a passion that we feel keeps him on his knees not only for hours but for weeks, until that "early birth"— is a fascination with hidden process. Because the speaker has himself done the planting, the growth of the seed synecdochically extends itself here not only to human sexuality but to another kind of human creativity: the making of art, the growth of poetry.[7]

A passage from Frost's prose piece "The Figure a Poem Makes" recapitulates the image developed in "Putting in the Seed." Again we have the miracle of invisible metamorphosis followed by emerging organic development, with the creator

both spectator and participant. Frost is describing the act of
writing poetry, but the passage might also be about gardening:
"For me the initial delight is in the surprise of remembering
something I didn't know I knew. I am in a place, in a situation, as
if I had materialized from cloud or risen out of the ground. There
is a glad recognition of the long lost and the rest follows. Step by
step the wonder of unexpected supply keeps growing."[8] Perhaps
the chief difference between a seedling and a poem is that the
latter is more surprising; the plant is awaited, passionately expected, from the moment the seed is put in. But the progressive
curve from delight to direction, as Frost never tired of pointing
out, is the same whether we think of lovemaking, conception,
gestation, birth, and nurture, or the equally rapt, hard-to-leave-
off labor of planting, followed by growth. The movement is from
hiddenness to manifestation.

"Pea Brush," which immediately precedes "Putting in the
Seed" in *Mountain Interval,* also deals with human participation
in the natural cycle and human concern for what is above and
below the surface. The surface in this case is not the concealing
earth but a layer of birch boughs "piled everywhere, / All fresh
and sound from the recent ax." "Pea Brush" shows the violence
inherent in the dialectic of up-and-down, over-and-under which
is almost as common in Frost's work as it is in nature. The birch
stumps are still "bleeding their life away"; yet there is an up-
thrusting of life in the poem.

> Birch boughs enough piled everywhere!—
>   All fresh and sound from the recent ax.
> Time someone came with cart and pair
>   And got them off the wild flowers' backs.
>
> They might be good for garden things
>   To curl a little finger round,
> The same as you seize cat's-cradle strings,
>   And lift themselves up off the ground.
>
> Small good to anything growing wild,
>   They were crooking many a trillium
> That had budded before the boughs were piled
>   And since it was coming up had to come.

Human cultivation here first upsets and then restores the appropriate layering of over/under. Curiosity as to subterranean

growth has here become the inevitability of the upward push of growth. The poem is a riot of moisture, warmth, reaching tendrils—as sensuous in its way as "Putting in the Seed" is exuberantly sexual. Planting, growth, death, birth, the way one generation makes room willy-nilly for another—all this is scaled to a human size in the context of gardening, a context whose central emblem is the mysterious layer between life and death—earth.

iii   *Halfway into Nature*

Not all the people in Frost's nature poems are farmers. Instead of planting they may gather leaves or wander in the woods—rural activities which posit no specific relation between man and nature and which leave room for vagueness as to where one ends and the other begins. "Gathering Leaves" keeps such vagueness at bay by comparing the leaves to a crop, so that the leaf-gatherer is a kind of farmer: "a crop is a crop, / And who's to say where / The harvest shall stop?" Where there is no incorporation of the leaves into a fruitful cycle, the autumnal mood can be much murkier. The best example of a peculiarly Frostian kind of confusion vis-à-vis nature is perhaps "A Leaf-Treader."

The difference between "A Leaf Treader" and other poems of natural observation such as "Spring Pools" or "In Hardwood Groves" is that here the speaker participates somewhat in the downward dynamic he sees around him in nature. In participating, he becomes himself affected by the downward mood of that rhythm.

> I have been treading on leaves all day until I am autumn
>   tired.
> God knows all the color and forms of leaves I have trodden
>   on and mired.
> Perhaps I have put forth too much strength and been too
>   fierce from fear.
> I have safely trodden underfoot the leaves of another year.

The voice is full of trouble, as if a recent act of violence still in the air had to be justified. "Fear" and "safely" crystallize the tone of exhaustion and uneasiness.

> All summer long they were overhead, more lifted up than I.
> To come to their final place in earth they had to pass me by.

> All summer long I thought I heard them threatening under
> their breath.
> And when they came it seemed with a will to carry me with
> them to death.

This second stanza is a variation of the chiastic motion familiar
from "In Hardwood Groves" ("They must go down past things
coming up"). The difference is that here a human being is uneas-
ily aware of being located in the middle of the chiasmus. He
takes the leaves personally; a certain pique can be heard in "all
summer long they were overhead, more lifted up than I," and in
the following line a fear of proximity, as if the leaves' mortality
were contagious. Stanza two divides neatly into two more or less
factual statements about the leaves' summer height and autumn
falling, and the affective human response (envy; apprehension)
to each of these natural facts.

> They spoke to the fugitive in my heart as if it were leaf to
> leaf.
> They tapped at my eyelids and touched my lips with an
> invitation to grief.
> But it was no reason I had to go because they had to go.
> Now up my knee to keep on top of another year of snow.

If he has responded to the leaves, the third stanza seems to
show, they respond to him as well. Loverlike, they approach the
vulnerable openings in his body—lips, eyelids—with a Keatsian
"invitation to grief." This invitation the poem's last two lines
staunchly refuse. But the bluster of those lines does not screen
out the sense of desolation, the fear of falling which must be
actively resisted by "keeping on top of" things.

"A Leaf Treader" is remarkable for the conflict which pervades the voice almost to the point of stifling it. The speaker's
mild participation in autumnal process seems to be both cause
and result of his greater fear of fall. He sees the connection
("Perhaps I have put forth too much strength . . . from fear"), but
fear of what? If it is fear of the cycle which first lifts the leaves
overhead and then consigns them to earth, he can only be feed-
ing his own fear by accelerating the process, treading the leaves
down. The nature of this fear is sketched in the leaves' speaking
"to the fugitive in my heart as if it were leaf to leaf": the speaker
is halfway a tree himself. Yet this identification with nature

means being "trodden on and mired." No wonder he has to
reassure himself finally that "It was no reason I had to go because they had to go"—a brave denial which probably does not
convince the speaker for a moment. It hardly needs to be said
that Frost's poems repeatedly *do* find a "reason" to connect
autumn and death (and not only Frost's; think of Shakespeare's
Sonnet 73). The end of Frost's early "Reluctance" reads like a
gloss on "A Leaf Treader":

> Ah, when to the heart of man
>   Was it ever less than treason
> To go with the drift of things,
>   To yield with a grace to reason,
> And bow and accept the end
>   Of a love or a season?

A sympathetic confusion is the subject (and not merely the
atmosphere) of "A Boundless Moment," a poem which calls into
question the difference between observing and participating in
nature. (One meaning of the poem's title is surely that of a lack
of clear distinction, of limits laid down, both in the mind and in
nature.)

> He halted in the wind, and—what was that
> Far in the maples, pale, but not a ghost?
> He stood there bringing March against his thought,
> And yet too ready to believe the most.
>
> "Oh, that's the Paradise-in-bloom," I said;
> And truly it was fair enough for flowers
> Had we but in us to assume in March
> Such white luxuriance of May for ours.
>
> We stood a moment so in a strange world,
> Myself as one his own pretense deceives;
> And then I said the truth (and we moved on).
> A young beech clinging to its last year's leaves.

Perceptions of what is being seen waver in this poem; so do
critical perceptions of its tone.[9] Knowing that it is two months
too early for a flower to be out, the speaker nevertheless purposefully blurs boundaries, "as one his own pretense de-
ceives"—but (as the title of the poem and its ninth line both
remind us) *only for a moment.* After that moment, the poem

turns back to the unfictive world of what the seasons allow (there is a similar turning in "Stopping by Woods on a Snowy Evening," similar strictures in "There Are Roughly Zones").

According to Richard Poirier, "A Boundless Moment" describes "without disillusionment, indeed with wit and pleasure, how nature and man participate in that creation of illusion which is essential to the sequestering power of poetry . . . This is a poem about 'pretending' whenever nature gives you any sort of license . . . for doing so. And it is out of such moments of illusion or extremity that images emerge which belong to and are perpetuated by poetry."[10] What Poirier terms the participation of nature and man is just that blurring of boundaries I have been trying to describe. It is symptomatic of the blur that the speakers here do not engage in the natural scene to the extent of picking a flower, planting a bean, or even treading down a leaf. Yet neither do they merely gaze; one of them in particular participates immediately in the scene, effecting an illusion of change from which, after a moment, he withdraws.[11]

Lingering at the division between the world perceived and the world imagined, "A Boundless Moment" shares with more stable poems such as "Spring Pools" and "Putting in the Seed" the tendency to cram more time into a single vista than nature, strictly speaking, allows. When Frost is working at his full poetic capacity (as often in brief poems such as these), he loads his rift with ore in more ways than one, squeezing every drop of significance from what might have seemed a wrung-out cliché ("up by the roots") and extracting more experience of cycle from a "boundless moment" than the usual traffic of time would bear. Such an imaginative voracity, reaching out for and often triumphantly keeping more than time "really" affords us, is gloated over in "I Could Give All to Time" because it has won out, has successfully smuggled its contraband of *temps retrouvé:*

> I could give all to Time except—except
> What I myself have held. But why declare
> The things forbidden that while the Customs slept
> I have crossed to Safety with? For I am There,
> And what I would not part with I have kept.

iv   *Inner and outer weather*

Sometimes the blurring of boundaries in Frost gets out of control. A more or less tentative identification with nature gives way to a merging (fearful or pleasurable) with the landscape, particularly with trees. (The sequence "The Hill Wife" and the dramatic narrative "The Fear" are more psychological studies than landscape poems; but in the context of Frost's nature poems it is relevant that fears in these poems often take the form of the fantasy that trees are turning into, or menacing like, people.)

"An Encounter," "The Oft-Repeated Dream," "Tree at My Window," and "The Sound of Trees" are variations on the theme of person meets tree—a peculiarly Frostian brand of encounter, and one for which a necessary condition is usually loneliness. In most cases, these poems about human-arboreal confusion are not strictly outdoor pieces; the person is likely to be on the inside, looking at and listening to the tree, which is on the outside looking in. Listening is at least as important as looking in the exchanges that ensue. For trees not only mirror human appearance in odd ways; they also serve as sounding boards, expressing what human language in isolation cannot or will not say. Frost's imagination was strongly aural.[12] He justly complained in an early letter that the Imagist movement concentrated on visual images to the exclusion of sound, and later wrote "I cultivate . . . the hearing imagination rather than the seeing imagination though I should not want to be without the latter." I shall concentrate on "Tree at my Window" and especially "The Sound of Trees" because these latter two poems are *hearings,* rather than readings, of nature in which the indoor listener struggles with the sense of boundary between himself and an outdoor instrument.

The prevailing tone of "Tree at My Window" is a sort of bemusement, a slightly skeptical scrutiny.

> Tree at my window, window tree,
> My sash is lowered when night comes on;
> But let there never be curtain drawn
> Between you and me.
>
> Vague dream-head lifted out of the ground,
> And thing next most diffuse to cloud,
> Not all your light tongues talking aloud
> Could be profound.
>
> But, tree, I have seen you taken and tossed,
> And if you have seen me when I slept,
> You have seen me when I was taken and swept
> And all but lost.

> That day she put our heads together,
> Fate had her imagination about her,
> Your head so much concerned with outer,
> Mine with inner, weather.

The poem establishes a mirrorlike symmetry with grace and delicacy, down to the *abba* rhyme scheme. Yet the impulse toward reciprocity is constantly, if gently, thwarted, notably in the beautiful second stanza. "Light tongues" is more than a conceit for rustling leaves; it is something the tree and the man share, since the speaker is a poet. (Similarly, the "vague dream-head" is also shared by man and tree, since we are shown the man asleep in stanza three.) The tree's plurality of tongues cannot "be profound." Is this the same superficiality as that implied in the last stanza, where the tree cannot penetrate interiors? In spite of the companionable mode of the poem, a certain competitive edge is detectable in its waverings of emphasis from the similarity between man and tree to their differences. The speaker's equanimity in facing this arboreal emanation of himself openly ("let there never be curtain drawn") seems to depend on his (the man's) having the last word. Having used language to assert his parallels with the tree, he ends by using it to reassert his own humanness. Whereas in "An Encounter" the lonely wanderer in the woods improvises a dialogue between a telegraph pole and himself, pretending it has questioned him, the tree in "Tree at my Window" is never assigned any kind of speech; its "light tongues" are silent in the poem, and it is hard to imagine it rejoining "Man at your window. . . ." As long as the tree does not seem to speak, there can be no real confusion of identities; yet the poem can also be read as dissatisfied with the inner/outer division, wanting to surmount human loneliness in the face of the inanimate. (Such is certainly the theme of one of Frost's most suggestive poems about speech and silence in nature, "The Most of It," whose "he" could easily be the speaker of "Tree at My Window" in a more truculent mood:

> He thought he kept the universe alone;
> For all the voice in answer he could wake
> Was but the mocking echo of his own
> From some tree-hidden cliff across the lake.
> Some morning from the boulder-broken beach
> He would cry out on life, that what it wants

Is not its own love back in copy speech,
But counter-love, original response.)

In "The Sound of Trees," obviously, noise and speech are
again important; indeed, the trees dance too, attractive as a
grove of pied pipers. The poem itself is infectiously and disturb-
ingly musical, with its pulls and syncopations, its irregular
rhyme pattern which conveys the ebb and flow of the trees'
motions. (Is the speaker conducted, like a musician, by their
myriad batons?) "The Sound of Trees" begins by wondering
rather petulantly why we "wish to bear" the trees' noise. Instead
of answering his own question, the speaker proceeds to describe, interpret, and ponder the trees' sounds and movements
in such a way as to establish beyond any doubt how closely akin
trees and listener are. This mirroring is attended by ironies. The
trees "talk of going" but never go, and it seems likely that the
speaker is doing exactly the same thing, even to the point of
forgetting that unlike the trees he has legs and can walk away.[13]

They are that that talks of going
But never gets away;
And that talks no less for knowing,
As it grows wiser and older,
That now it means to stay.
My feet tug at the floor
And my head sways to my shoulder
Sometimes when I watch trees sway,
From the window or the door.
I shall set forth for somewhere,
I shall make the reckless choice
Some day when they are in voice
And tossing so as to scare
The white clouds over them on.
I shall have less to say,
But I shall be gone.

Even if the speaker really were to set forth, the poem leaves us
in doubt as to whether he would be dancing to the trees' tune or
fleeing them, "scared on" like a cloud. Such a doubt is not
merely a reader's quibble or an irrelevant attempt to fix "plot"
beyond the boundaries of the poem's scope. The doubt is a
response to an ambiguity that shapes and pervades "The Sound
of Trees" from its first line ("I wonder about the trees") and

which is never resolved. Indoors and outdoors, person and trees, cause and effect, wish and fear, have been inextricably blended. What seems to emerge from the mingling is that the trees are both an emanation of the listening self (speaker) in the poem and its dramatic other. Such doubleness is akin to what Poirier calls man's and nature's participation to create an illusion, and to what Radcliffe Squires describes as a turning away from people in Frost's poetry in order "to converse with nature itself. . . . Nature . . . often takes up the role deserted by human beings in the poetry of Frost."[14] But in taking up this role nature invariably acquires (if it does not already have) human characteristics. (As Squires says elsewhere, man and nature "have an agreement: they mirror each other.") It is when the mirrored and the mirror begin to melt into each other that human affinities with nature are most strangely and vividly felt and expressed in Frost's poetry; not that he is portraying a looking-glass world of dream transformations, but that he is so sensitive to the illusions we create when we look at nature or that (perhaps) nature perpetrates on us.

v   *To get away from earth awhile*

A few of Frost's poems about the contemplation of nature substitute a ladder for a window. The direction of confusion becomes vertical, not horizontal; no longer inner/outer but up or down, on the ground or off it. In "Birches" a remembered boy swings on birches and returns to earth; in "Wild Grapes" a little girl is swept off the ground by a birch tree and returned to earth; in "After Apple-Picking" the picker, whose ladder remains in the tree pointing upward, has already returned to earth. The upward trajectory is followed by a return; abdication of earthliness, as we might expect in Frost, is temporary. Nevertheless the subject has a certain sublimity which expresses itself in these poems, all three of which have a more overtly literary quality than is commonly found in Frost's nature poems. All three poems read both like anecdotes and like allegory. They are anecdotal in being (far more than a disembodied lyric like "Spring Pools") tales or reminiscences from childhood or a working day. It is into this informal narrative texture that the vertical urge toward heaven is artfully inserted (artfully by the poet; but also, if the narratives are true, by life or nature imitating art). As Squires says, the symbol is "a guileless one—a ladder, a tree, some perpendicular

. . . geometric in clarity and simplicity, yet organic always within the poem itself."[15] But the very introduction into the poems of this "guileless" symbol creates resonances beyond anecdote— hints of allegory, archetype, and poetic tradition. The Edenic association of apple trees and apple picking and the classical references in "Wild Grapes" make themselves felt not far below the surface of the words, or even on the surface.

Discussing the power of images over the imagination in *The Poetics of Space,* Gaston Bachelard refers to the doubleness of an image, its strangeness and familiarity (what I have called the blend of allegory and anecdote):

> Great images have both a history and prehistory; they are always a blend of memory and legend, with the result that we never experience an image directly. Indeed every image has an unfathomable oneiric depth to which the personal past adds special color. Consequently it is not until late in life that we really revere an image, when we discover that its roots plunge well beyond the history that is fixed in our memories. In the realm of absolute imagination, we remain young late in life. But we must lose our earthly Paradise in order actually to live in it, to experience it in the reality of its images, in the absolute sublimation that transcends all passion.[16]

Bachelard is describing the familiar Romantic project of re-capturing youthful intensity of experience both through memory and through imagination. If memory is the source of anecdote and imagination, the source of what Bachelard calls the "un-fathomable oneiric depth" of an image, or archetype, then "Birches" swings freely (if slyly) between the two. Because of the dialectical bent of Frost's mind, the anecdotal and archetypal sides of the birch-swinging image do not so much combine in this poem as they undermine each other—a process formally ex-pressed in the increasingly rapid transitions between up and down, swinging out and returning, as the poem unfolds. I say "undermine," a word with associations of irony, on purpose. Irony signifies instability of stance, tone, attitude; and it is difficult to assign the various tones and digressions in "Birches" to stable categories. Like "Mending Wall," "Birches" must owe some of its enormous popularity to being less simple than it at first appears; to being, finally and excitingly, inscrutable but ca-pable of very varying readings under its anecdotally simple sur-face.

The opening of the poem sounds like a factual observation veering toward chatty reminiscence.

> When I see birches bend to left and right
> Across the lines of straighter darker trees,
> I like to think some boy's been swinging them.

This boy, "too far from town to learn baseball," swings away in the central portion of the poem with a vividness that makes him its focus, the image most readers of "Birches" presumably remember and cherish. By contrast, the image of ice-storms which extends from the fifth to the twenty-second line of "Birches" seems to belong to the world of trope and ornament. Its "girls on hands and knees that throw their hair / Before them over their heads to dry in the sun" have the kind of reality, sturdy but remote, that Homeric similes often offer; and like a Homeric simile the image of the ice-storms offers itself as a digression, the strong caesura in line 5 clearly preparing for a parenthetical lowering of voice: "As ice-storms do. Often you must have seen them. . . ."

Such impressions are of course matters of tone and poetic decorum rather than fact. Perhaps fact hardly matters; certainly it is relegated to second place when "Birches" resumes (line 21):

> But I was going to say when Truth broke in
> With all her matter-of-fact about the ice-storm
> I should prefer to have some boy bend them. . . .

What does matter is Frost's ability to keep us suspended between anecdote and something else, whether we call it fiction, allegory, archetype, or vision. Poirier says of this suspension that Frost's "visionary life is linked ineluctably to physical sensations and realities generally considered 'natural.' So subtle are his driftings from one kind of experience to another that it is possible in reading 'Birches' . . . to forget that the trees are bent because of ice-storms and not because boys have been swinging in them. The latter is only the poet's preference."[17] A hint of the visionary quality of the birch-swinging boy is given when the speaker refers to the ice-storm digression as "Truth . . . with all her matter-of-fact," thus presumably relegating the boy to fiction. Already, too, the boy's journey has become associated with the swoops and dips of poetic imagination, whereas ice-storms bend the trees down "to stay," and the girls in the long simile, unlike the boy, are firmly planted on earth.

Once we are even partly aware of the deliberate shifts in tone, direction, and perspective in "Birches," it is easier to abandon expectations of a straightforward narrative line and notice instead various ways the poem pulls us first to one side and then another. In the opening lines, for example—lines which are almost impossible to visualize or to hear because they are so familiar—the birches bend, a grove of graceful white lines, across the lines of "straighter darker trees." Is the poem an exercise in reading across (or between) such sober "lines"? Furthermore, we learn as early as line 4 that "swinging doesn't bend them down to stay / As ice-storms do" (nature overmastering art?) and can therefore expect that after the trees have dipped down to earth and released the young birch-swinger, there will be a movement back upward, a kind of resurgence. The pattern of there-and-back-again will not be neatly resolved but will continue to oscillate. And such a second taking off from earth does indeed happen, on a smaller scale and at a quickened pace, in the final section of the poem, the lines beginning "So was I once myself a swinger of birches."[18]

With this shift of tense from past (or more properly imperfect) to present, and of person from third to first, the poem begins its cycle afresh. Along with tense and person, it has undergone a change of scale and situation. Instead of looking at things from some distance, as in the poem's (also first-person) opening, the speaker has lost his perspective and plunged into the midst of a "pathless wood." This *selva oscura,* like the boy, is figurative but takes on its own reality; Frost has merely said that life seems *like* a wood. The tall white birches naturally represent relief, transcendence, youth regained. Yet the rhythms of thought still return to earth as insistently as they venture away from it. "I'd like to get away from earth awhile"—but this impulse to reach out with pure yearning turns out at once to be subject to the same inexorable gravity that in "In Hardwood Groves" governs the ways of earth: "However it is in some other world, / I know that this is the way in ours." The indecisive rhythms beginning with "I'd like to get away" accumulate and accelerate as the poem approaches a close, oscillating in a flurry of indecisiveness that seems to continue beyond the actual words of the last line.

> I'd like to get away from earth awhile
> And then come back to it and begin over.

> May no fate willfully misunderstand me
> And half grant what I wish and snatch me away
> Not to return. Earth's the right place for love:
> I don't know where it's likely to go better.
> I'd like to go by climbing a birch tree,
> And climb black branches up a snow-white trunk
> *Toward* heaven, till the tree could bear no more,
> But dipped its top and set me down again.
> That would be good both going and coming back.
> One could do worse than be a swinger of birches.

Two of Frost's statements about dialectic make more sense in light of "Birches," and it in the light of them—both its ascendant motion and its nostalgia for earth.

> The most exciting movement in nature is not progress, advance, but expansion and contraction, the opening and shutting of the eye, the hand, the heart, the mind. We throw our arms wide with a gesture of religion to the universe; we close them around a person. We explore and adventure for a while and then we draw in to consolidate our gains. The breathless swing is between subject matter and form.[19]

> Narrative is a fearfully safe place to spend your time. Get up there high enough and the differences that make controversy become only the two legs of a body the weight of which is on one in one period, on the other in the next. Democracy monarchy; puritanism paganism; form content; conservatism radicalism; systole diastole; rustic urbane; literary colloquial; work play. I should think too much of myself to let any teacher fool me into taking sides on any of these oppositions. Maybe I'm wrong [note the slight oscillation even here!].[20]

Perhaps no teacher could "fool" Frost, but the poet also wrote that

> Nature within her inmost self divides
> To trouble men with having to take sides.[21]

"Wild Grapes," which was apparently conceived as a kind of companion-piece of "Birches," resembles the earlier poem in describing an excursion upward from earth via a tree.[22] The affinity between the two poems goes deeper than subject matter; both blend homely reminiscence (or what offers itself as such) with very different material. "Wild Grapes" is apparently based on an incident in the life of Frost's friend and editor Susan Hayes

Ward; it is more anecdotal than "Birches" in being a more or less true account of an episode rather than a mere "preference." But the core of childhood memory is overlaid with additions, afterthoughts, and interpretations in much the manner described by Bachelard. "It is not until late in life that we really revere an image, when we discover that its roots plunge well beyond the history that is fixed in our memories" applies to the narrator of "Wild Grapes," who is explicitly middle-aged, well-read in classics, and interested in the "roots" of images—so much so indeed that the central incident of the poem can easily be imagined as being narrated to a Jungian psychologist. The reference to Eurydice early in the poem and the description of the birch/dryad prepare us for the mythical nature of the roots which "plunge well beyond . . . history." Behind the figure of the boy in "Birches" are Wordsworthian resonances, solitary excursions, intimations of childhood and freedom. Behind the girl's experience in "Wild Grapes" is a classical world of Dionysiac revelry, as Helen Bacon has brilliantly shown. I will not discuss her thesis in any detail here; but the archetype behind the anecdote of "Wild Grapes" ought to be apparent as soon as we read the description of the tree.

> One day my brother led me to a glade
> Where a white birch he knew of stood alone,
> Wearing a thin head-dress of pointed leaves,
> And heavy on her heavy hair behind,
> Against her neck, an ornament of grapes.
> Grapes, I knew grapes from having seen them last year.
> One bunch of them, and there began to be
> Bunches all round me growing in white birches,
> The way they grew round Leif the Lucky's German. . . .[23]

A critic like Squires who is irritated by the self-consciously literary tone of a passage like this misses what it is doing. The connection between the wild grapes growing on the birch and Leif the Lucky's German, like the connection with Eurydice ("The day I swung suspended with the grapes, / And was come after like Eurydice / And brought down safely from the upper regions"), has been made by the grown woman. Like the imagined boy in "Birches," such images are retrospective *preferences,* embroideries of the mind on the raw episode ("Wild Grapes") or on unadorned nature (the ice-storms in "Birches"). The incident of being swept off her feet by the tree was originally inarticulate, according to the narrator: "Grim silence on my part as I sank lower." But the adult speaker/poet rescues the silent, frightened child from oblivion by using the image in all its "oneiric depth."

"Wild Grapes" has a doubleness of motion similar to that of "Birches"—a there-and-back-again arc. But there is a more emphatic identity between the woman who is speaking and the child who is remembered than in "So I was once myself a swinger of birches/And so I dream of going back to be." The path from child to woman does not veer nostalgically back to childhood; its doubleness is an achieved thing, which the woman is enjoying even as she writes. Having been brought back from the beyond like Eurydice,

> the life I live now's an extra life
> I can waste as I please on whom I please.
> So if you see me celebrate two birthdays,
> And give myself out as two different ages,
> One of them five years younger than I look. . . .

This sense of having acquired an extra life is the narrator's interpretation of the doubleness that pervades "Wild Grapes." She both is and is not the same person as she was before her ascent into the birch tree. Her own term for the change, "translation," means both a carrying across and a rendering into another idiom; both meanings are alive in "Wild Grapes."

Despite the similar trajectories in "Birches" and "Wild Grapes," the poems contrast with each other in ways that suggest alternate attitudes toward the worlds of nature and imagination. The boy in "Birches" has taught himself to swing the trees because he is "too far from town to learn baseball" and his "only play was what he found himself." *Faute de mieux,* the boy illustrates Frost's saying that "no forms are more engrossing, gratifying, comforting, staying, than those lesser ones we throw off like vortex rings of smoke, all our individual enterprise and needing nobody's cooperation: a basket, a letter, a garden, a room, an idea, a picture, a poem. For those we haven't to get a team together before we can play."[24] Without a team, the boy's reliance is on craft; on form.

> He learned all there was
> To learn about not launching out too soon
> And so not carrying the tree away

Clear to the ground. He always kept his poise
To the top branches, climbing carefully
With the same plans you use to fill a cup
Up to the brim, and even beyond the brim.

"Learned," "poise," "pains," "carefully"—this is the vocabulary of a severely self-administered discipline, at once aggressive and austere. The adult's nostalgic dream of "going back to be" a swinger of birches is less a longing for innocence and simplicity than a desire for a controllable, *learnable* environment.

The little girl in "Wild Grapes," on the other hand, is caught up beyond her own control, against her wishes, all but without her own knowledge of what is happening. "I said I had the tree. It wasn't true. / The opposite was true. The tree had me." The poem stresses knowing; far from having invented and perfected a technique, she "knows" nothing before her ascent and is proud of still knowing little after it. Of course this is ironic; if what one learns from growing up is to become cold-hearted, to let go, then to be an ignoramus becomes a virtue.

So I was translated
To loud cries from my brother of "Let go!
Don't you know anything, you girl? Let go!"

After she has returned to earth (with the brother's help):

My brother said: "Don't you weigh anything?
Try to weigh something next time, so you won't
Be run off with by birch trees into space."
It wasn't my not weighing anything
So much as my not knowing anything—
My brother had been nearer right before.
I had not taken the first step in knowledge;
I had not learned to let go with the hands,
As still I have not learned to with the heart,
And have no wish to with the heart—nor need,
That I can see.

Earlier in the poem we have seen that the girl's knowledge, such as it is, is unlearned, instinctive:

But I, with something of the baby grip
Acquired ancestrally in just such trees
When wilder mothers than our wildest now

> Hung babies out on branches by the hands. . . .
> I held on uncomplainingly for life.

Her achievement is not to *unlearn* that instinct to hold on.

The boy in "Birches" and the girl in "Wild Grapes" represent two kinds of mingling with nature: hers artless and clinging, his crafted and cautious, both intent and solitary.

The warm-hearted girl who holds on so tight is abstracted into Love in "Bond and Free." Should we read the figure of Thought in that poem as an image of the boy in "Birches"?

> Love has earth to which she clings
> With hills and circling arms about—
> Wall within wall to shut fear out.
> But Thought has need of no such things,
> For Thought has a pair of dauntless wings.
>
> On snow and sand and turf I see
> Where Love has left a printed trace
> With straining in the world's embrace.
> And such is Love and glad to be.
> But Thought has shaken his ankles free.

In fact "Wild Grapes" and "Birches" escape such classification by the generous ballast of anecdote they retain. Moreover, "straining in the world's embrace"—some kind of union with nature—is a marriage achieved by both the boy and the girl. Frost knew too much about men and women and the imagination to assign experience according to sex (even though the girl in "Wild Grapes" conforms to some sexual stereotypes, she is also "a little boyish girl"). To strain in an embrace is an ambiguous image, connoting both desire and a desire to escape—in the poems we have just seen, a desire to escape the world's gravity, to ascend. To defy gravity is not easy; we see this in the birch-swinger's studied poise, in the almost painful image of the girl's "small wrists stretching till they showed the banjo strings." The poems return to earth; but even aloft, the children have never lost their human values of craft and kindness. To leave nature for a little renews love for it. To Yeats's "Once out of nature I shall never take / My bodily form from any natural thing," Frost would retort that "Earth's the right place for love"; moreover, our shape is human and "we love the things we love for what they are."[25]

"After Apple-Picking" is a very different version of a journey out and back. The speaker is an adult, not a child, and his climbing into the tree is connected with the world of work, not play. Rather than a nostalgic dream or a fond memory, the poem seems to be a humdrum depiction of tiredness, a description after the fact. Yet "After Apple-Picking" is anything but a matter-of-fact poem; it is far dreamier, in its own way, than the other two. The central incident of the poem, the apple-picking, is over with, according to the title—or is it really in progress? or about to begin? Time is scrambled in a way unusual in Frost. "I am done with apple-picking now," says the speaker, yet, a little later,

> My instep arch not only keeps the ache,
> It keeps the pressure of a ladder-round.
> I feel the ladder sway as the boughs bend.
> And I keep hearing from the cellar bin
> The rumbling sound
> Of load on load of apples coming in.

His weariness ("I am overtired / Of the great harvest I myself desired") results as much from hallucinatory memories and sensations of work as from the work itself—yet of course the weariness is the cause of such memories and sensations. Pleasure and pain, sleep and waking, even rising and falling are confused in this poem, which begins with a heaven-pointing ladder, moves down to barrels on the ground, and finally burrows beneath the surface to the hibernating woodchuck. "The fact is the sweetest dream that labor knows," Frost had written in "Mowing"; but the end of "After Apple-Picking" works retroactively to make the whole experience of labor into a dream.

As with the facts and fictions of "Birches," once we have been alerted to the wavering categories in "After Apple-Picking," it becomes hard to be sure of the simplest "facts" about the poem. Where are we? What time is it? The sinuous line of the verse traces its way through contradictions.

> Essence of winter sleep is on the night,
> The scent of apples; I am drowsing off.
> I cannot rub the strangeness from my sight
> I got from looking through a pane of glass
> I skimmed this morning from the drinking trough
> And held against the world of hoary grass.
> It melted, and I let it fall and break.

But I was well
Upon my way to sleep before it fell,
And I could tell
What form my dreaming was about to take.
Magnified apples appear and disappear,
Stem end and blossom end,
And every fleck of russet showing clear.

This phantasmagoria constitutes the central portion of "After Apple-Picking." It removes the poem from the dependable seasonal or quotidian round of harvest and cycle, work and sleep, at the same time that the poem remains rooted in earth. Poirier comments that "the laborer, who may also be the poet, becomes vaguely aware that what had before seemed solid and unmalleable is also part of a collective 'dream' and partakes of myth."[26] Yet in Frost the dream retains a kind of solidity, the allegory's underpinning of anecdote remains firmly in place, like the ladder whose feet are on the ground but whose head is in the clouds.[27] The ladder's double nature, earthly and heavenly, is like a metaphor's doubleness, like poetry. Frost said in "Education by Poetry,"

> We still ask boys in college to think . . . but we seldom tell them what thinking means; we seldom tell them it is just putting this and that together; it is just saying one thing in terms of another. To tell them that is to set their feet on the first rung of a ladder the top of which sticks through the sky.[28]

The ladder mediates between earth and heaven, but—closer to the speaker—the "pane of glass," a reflector of dubious and evanescent transparency, shapes his view on earth. As a window on the world, it wavers as Frostian boundaries so often do, melting and breaking; yet the "strangeness" it has given the world remains in the speaker's sight. The resulting confusion between what Poirier terms solid and malleable on the one hand and dreamy and mythlike on the other epitomizes the doubleness of "After Apple-Picking," the way the poem is pulled both toward archetype and anecdote. The poem's earthiness lies in its frank account of weariness, its desire to burrow into the ground like the woodchuck; its *other*worldliness lies in the hazy visionary quality which lingers from the labor, pervades the world seen through the "pane of glass," and "will trouble/This sleep of mine, whatever sleep it is." Nowhere in Frost does the boundary between the self and the world waver more beautifully—a delicate balance one feels is reproduced in the care with which the apples must be handled or in the ladder balanced against the tree.

If we compare "After Apple-Picking" with a lyric like "Spring Pools," the activity of the never-resting mind in poems like the latter, busily filling out cycles and drawing analogies between human and plant life, seems to have been transformed into a physical ache, a response of the whole body. Bodies figure in "After Apple-Picking," "Wild Grapes," and "Birches" more directly than in most of Frost's nature pieces, as if the body had decided to follow the questing mind and found it could not sustain the journey. The figure we have been following throughout this section—that of imaginative response to nature—can be envisioned as consisting of increasingly bolder forays into nature, increasingly active interpretations of the meaning of reflection. Not all the people in Frost's nature poems actually climb the tree toward heaven; but all begin by seeing some kind of reflection of themselves in the natural world and to one degree or another all reach out toward what they see.

2. Seferis: The Sea

As Frost's titles often show fascination with nature and the seasons, so those of Seferis bespeak the Greek poet's preoccupation with the sea and voyaging. For Seferis, much in life and literature can be expressed through the figure of a sea journey. The epigraph to *Logbook I,* for example—"we remain in this position awaiting orders"—indicates both political and aesthetic uncertainty. But rich and flexible though the sea as symbol is, as poetic subject it is not without difficulties. Its very multitudinousness can lead to monotony, a kind of becalmed imagination embarrassed by too many riches.

For Seferis, as for most of his countrymen, the sea is of an importance that can scarcely be exaggerated. It represents at once the familiar and the beautiful; nostalgia for the lost, magical world of childhood; adventure and romance; history and tradition; and a linkage with the body of Greek myths. Its protean quality would seem to make the sea a poetic symbol par excellence, evocative yet amorphous, needing a distinctive imagination to shape it into significance. Without such an imaginative treatment, the danger is that the sea will signify everything in general and nothing in particular.

The boundless, hard-to-pin-down character of a sea which is nevertheless intensely loved is well shown in an essay by G.-A. Mangakis on Greek landscape. Mangakis calls the sea

> . . . an uninterrupted, ever-changing element with its radiant beauty and incessant motion, the endless open sea ever travelling with the wind . . . limitless, determined by a power unseen but strongly felt, which derives from boundlessness. . . . Thus, the first image of Greece is illuminated in a child's soul, as something so real it overflows all sensation and floods the heart to the brim, but at the same time as something intangible, sibylline, something passionately yearned for throughout life . . . yet never grasped in its definite shape, its true form.— This is the first experience: *the sea.*[29]

I quote this passage because it illustrates so well the splendors and miseries of the sea as a poetic subject. Like the experience it tries to describe, the language is charged with feeling yet oddly lacking in individuality, whether because the feeling for the sea the essayist is describing is so universal among his Greek readers that no definition is needed, or because the nature of the sea is to clude sharp evocation. A similar rhapsodic quality sometimes marks the passages in Seferis's journal which concern the sea, though the poet is less rhetorical than Mangakis:

> Inexplicable sorcery of the sea. How it changes me all at once: astonishment, deep amazement down to my bones. I can't understand. To go closer, to cross this line of separation for another world. . . . How is it possible to be the same man who was swimming in the water and who now is reading the newspaper? Here is something which is absolutely inconceivable to me.[30]

Amidst the yearning, however, a central idea is discernible: emphasis on the metamorphic power of the sea, its particular properties of cleansing and renewal, is more important in the passage than a raptly intangible boundlessness.

Moreover, the passage is in prose. Seferis rarely lost his sense of the difference between journalistic (if sincere) rhapsodizing about the sorcery of the sea and the sea-change which had to be wrought by the sorcery of poetry. He seems to have been wary of writing directly, *in his poetry,* about the wonders of the sea; and as a result his poems about the sea avoid monotony and shapelessness to a remarkable extent. Seferis accomplishes this feat by different means. First, many of the poems, especially earlier ones, treat times and places whence the sea is inaccessible or barely visible, an expanse glimpsed out of the corner of the eye. Another version of the sea perceives it as present but unsatisfactory: polluted or puzzling, becalmed, endless. A third approach penetrates the sea's surface and heads for the depths. Finally (and this method also touches almost every other use of the sea in his work) Seferis avails himself of classical references to the sea, above all the *Odyssey* and Aeschylus's *Agamemnon.* The use of myth bestows richness of perspective on an element whose nature is to appear flat and timeless. To write about statues, stones, inscriptions (Chapter I) is to ponder some of the most obvious remnants of the Greek past. To write about the sea means that the poet risks floating out of time (note Mangakis's use of words like "limitless" and "boundless" to evoke the unfettered quality, both temporarlly and spatially, of voyaging). By referring to the companions of Odysseus or to the Argonauts, Seferis makes the Aegean into a continuum.

i   *The mermaid at the prow*

In Seferis's first volume of poems, *Turning Point,* the sea is at its most fugitive. One indication that the young poet is still finding his voice and subject is the paucity, in this volume, of the sense of place, whether the place is Greece or anywhere else. The poems exist in a brittle, tenuous, and sparsely imagined world. When the sea does appear in *Turning Point* it has a Laforguesque air of urbanity; it is not the Aegean but a French Symbolist sea.

> And life's cold as a fish
> —Is that how you live?—Yes, how else?
> So many are the drowned
> down on the sea's bed.
>
> Trees are like corals
> their color gone,
> carts are like ships
> sunken and lonely . . .[31]

("Fog")

As Nasos Vayenas points out, the chief function of this submarine vignette is to cast a despairing light onto the life up above. "Fog" moves away from the depths; its last stanza shows us firelight, red fingernails, someone coughing (a juxtaposition that recalls several such in *The Waste Land,* which Seferis had not yet read). The following poem in *Turning Point,* "The Mood of a Day," in contrast to "Fog" moves *toward* the sea. As the epigraph from *Arthur Gordon Pym* suggests, both the cityscape and the ship in "The Mood of a Day" have a nightmarish air; the ship is full of dead people. Yet the movement from the third to the final stanza—from city to sea—is one of overwhelming relief, as of motion after long stalling, open air after claustrophobia.

Part of the relief is perhaps the reader's at hearing a true Seferic tone:

He worries: if they knock at the door who will open it? If he
    opens a book whom will he look at? If he opens his soul
    who will look? Chain.
Where is love that with one stroke cuts time in two and stuns
    it?
Words only and gestures. A monotonous monologue in front
    of a mirror under a wrinkle.
Like a drop of ink on a handkerchief, the boredom spreads.

Everyone in the ship is dead, but the ship keeps going the
    way it was heading when it put out from the harbor
how the captain's nails grew . . . and the boatswain, who had
    three mistresses in every port, unshaven . . .
The ship swells slowly, the rigging fills with pride, and the
    day is turning mild.
Three dolphins flash black, glistening; the mermaid smiles,
    and a forgotten sailor waves astride the yardarm.

The ship which moves purposefully out of the harbor whether its crew are dead or not is an image, compounded of hope and despair, of a tradition both moribund and hardy. The same paradox makes nails grow on a corpse. The question at this point in Seferis's work is where the ship is going—but it does seem to be going somewhere. The smiling mermaid and waving sailor seem to be responding to something, sending out some signal of recognition, unlike the narcissistic mirror-monologue in the preceding stanza.

It is characteristic of the stylistic veerings in *Turning Point*

that "The Mood of a Day" is followed by "Rocket," a poem
which begins "It isn't the sea" and ends

>   I can't live
>   only with peacocks,
>   nor travel always
>   in the mermaid's eyes.

"Rocket" expresses impatience with the exotic trappings of symbolism, in the light of which (an elusive light which is neither the
sea nor the world) the mermaid is doubly unsatisfactory. Like a
peacock she is exotic, ornate; like the "monotonous monologue
in front of a mirror" in "The Mood of a Day" she represents a
self-communing gaze which narcissistically reflects itself alone.
After *Turning Point,* Seferis did indeed avoid traveling "in the
mermaid's eyes." The hall of mirrors, peacock, and pentacle of
the first volume do not reappear, and the mermaid becomes
rather a representative of the sea than a mode of consciousness.

The poems Seferis wrote in London after the publication of
Turning Point are stylistically simpler and more uniform than
before. Both these qualities are related to the persona of Stratis
Thalassinos (Stratis the Mariner). Through the eyes of the nostalgic sailor, a poem like "Hampstead" expresses homesickness
for the Mediterranean. But the work is cautious. Just as Seferis
wears the mask of the seafarer, "Hampstead" approaches the sea
gingerly, transforming the wished-for expanse of blue into a theatrical scrim. In fact Stratis just wants a *symbol* of the sea.[32]

>   Now I long for a little quiet
>   all I want is a hut on a hill
>   or near a seashore
>   all I want in front of my window
>   is a sheet immersed in bluing
>   spread there like the sea. . . .

With the sequence "Mr. Stratis Thalassinos Describes a Man,"
Seferis moves a little closer to the water. The accessibility or
forbidding quality of the sea is presented in terms of the psychological development of "a man," and vice versa: with the advent
of puberty, the young man moves instinctively toward the sea.
The following passage combines archetypal imagery with a kind
of sea-yarn. It also reinforces the sense we have already gotten
from the sparse references to the sea so far in Seferis that the sea

is difficult of access, both attractive and forbidding but hard to reach.

> In the summer of my sixteenth year a strange voice sang in
>   my ears;
> it was, I remember, at the sea's edge, among the red nets and
>   a boat abandoned on the sand, a skeleton
> I tried to get closer to that voice by laying my ear to the sand
> the voice disappeared
> but there was a shooting star
> as though I were seeing a shooting star for the first time
> and on my lips the salt taste of waves.
> From that night the roots of the trees no longer came to me.
> The next day a journey opened in my mind and closed again,
>   like a picture book;
> I thought of going down to the shore every evening
> first to learn about the shore and then to go to sea;
> the third day I fell in love with a girl on a hill. . . .
>
> ("Adolescent")

(Compare this passage to the later "Stratis Thalassinos among the Agapanthi," which links sea-voyaging and sexuality:

> The first thing God made is love
> then comes blood
> and the thirst for blood
> roused by
> the body's sperm as by salt.
> The first thing God made is the long journey. . . .)

In "Mr. Stratis Thalassinos Describes a Man," the linking of sex and the sea begins by being negative. After the failure of love on a hill, "I left and went back to sea," but the sea grows mellower. With the opening of "Young Man," Seferis's work advances simultaneously along several different fronts. The simple, colloquial language spans a synchronicity that can accommodate Aghia Sophia, a mermaid, "Captain" Odysseus, and an easy narrative mode:

> I sailed for a year with Captain Odysseus
> I was fine
> in fair weather I made myself comfortable in the prow beside
>   the mermaid
> I sang of her red lips as I gazed at the flying-fish,

in storms I took refuge in a corner of the hold with the ship's
    dog who kept me warm.
One morning at the end of the year I saw minarets
the mate told me:
"That's Saint Sophia, tonight I'll take you to the women."

Like the logo he chose for his books, a two-tailed mermaid,
the mermaid figurehead on the prow in "Young Man" links the
various stages of Seferis's vision. Half-human, half-monstrous,
and a fairytale creation associated with art and magic, she is
surely the same apparition who smiled from the deck at the end
of the "Mood of a Day." Barly glimpsed as long as the poems
barely dare approach the sea, she is cuddly and companionable
in "Young Man" for the hero, who is no longer an onlooker but a
voyager himself. Disappearing in "The Mood of a Day," rejected
in "Rocket," welcoming in "Young Man," the mermaid mirrors
the poet's feeling for the sea. (To turn back for a minute to
Mangakis's essay: "Thus Greece becomes danger . . . . it appears, this danger, with the blue body of the sea, clothed in
golden scales, and like the lovely mermaids of the fairy tale,
summons you to a fatal, alluring adventure. . . ."[33])
    The Stratis Thalassinos poems fall midway between *Turning
Point* and the mature, characteristic voice Seferis found in
Mythical History. Also in this transitional group are "Syngrou
Avenue 1930" and "Foreign Verse," two poems which have in
common the appearance of a mermaid at their close. "Syngrou
Avenue" uses marine metaphors to describe the Acropolis and
its surroundings; though less artificial than that in "Fog," the
effect is labored when the Acropolis is called "the petrified ship
traveling with broken rigging toward the depths." (The Acropolis "travels" for the same reason that in "In the Manner of G.S."
Greece itself travels, so basic is the trope of a voyage in Seferis.)
But the marine mode is more appropriate, naturally, when Phale-
ron and the sea are glimpsed at the end:

> Break Ariadne's thread and look!
> The blue body of the mermaid.

Again, the mermaid/sea is precariously located at the tail end (so
to speak) of the poem, just appearing or vanishing. She may
seem like a habitual means to poetic closure by now; but a
variation on the image distinguishes a much greater poem than
"Syngrou," "Reflections on a Foreign Line of Verse."

Dated Christmas 1931, "Foreign Verse" was written at around the same time as the Stratis Thalassinos series I have discussed. Rather than using a persona, the poem focuses on a single intensely imagined presence who is to pervade the rest of Seferis's work in a more muted way—the figure of Odysseus. Since the native habitat of Odysseus is marine, the sea functions structurally in "Foreign Verse" as a thing experienced rather than a hastily glimpsed streak of blue. The reference to Odysseus is not straightforward; Seferis takes his first line from the sonnet "Heureux qui comme Ulysse" by Joachim du Bellay, who was himself looking back longingly at the Odysseus archetype.[34] But far from being hobbled by complexities of literary reference, the poem is unencumberedly eloquent in a way new for Seferis.

"Foreign Verse" is partly about language and tradition.[35] But, like the language and tradition which were Seferis's heritage, it never gets far from, and incessantly returns to, the sea, since even emotion is expressed in terms of a voyage: "Fortunate if on setting out he's felt the rigging of a love strong in his body, spreading there like veins where the blood throbs." And Odysseus has been battered and shaped by the sea. We have progressed a long way from hanging up a sheet "immersed in bluing" before the window.

And again and again the shade of Odysseus appears before
    me, his eyes red from the waves' salt,
from his ripe longing to see once more the smoke ascending
    from his warm hearth and the dog grown old waiting by
    the door.

A large man, whispering through his whitened beard words in
    our language spoken as it was three thousand years ago.
He extends a palm calloused by the ropes and the tiller, his
    skin weathered by the dry north wind, by heat and snow.

Odysseus is clearly the most important representative of the sea in this poem; it is as if he carries it with him wherever he goes. Yet the other emblem of the sea—the mermaid—appears in "Foreign Verse" as well, in the same place we found her in "Mood of a Day" or "Syngrou"—at the end, vanishing from sight.

He speaks . . . I still see his hands that knew how to judge
    the carving of the mermaid at the prow
presenting me the waveless blue sea in the heart of winter.

Like almost every other object in the poem, the mermaid becomes a measure of Odysseus's wisdom and experience. As a
carved figure whose craftsmanship is judged by his skilled
hands, she signifies art which is subject to scrutiny by those who
are learned in its tradition. The mermaid is plastic art, of course,
like the "carved reliefs of a humble art" we meet with in the first
part of *Mythical History*. But since so much of "Foreign Verse"
is about language, the verbal heritage passed on by Odysseus-
like figures ("certain old sailors of my childhood who . . . used to
recite, with tears in their eyes, the song of Erotocritos"), the
mermaid can also be seen as the art that can be made of the sea:
its timeless lyric aspect, whereas Odysseus is the grizzled epic
narrator. Some kind of tradition in the etymological sense of
handing down is going on at the end of the poem. Odysseus's
wise hands (which we have already been told are callused) are
shown "presenting me" [the speaker] with that sea of which the
mermaid is an emblem. Such a transaction shows how much
bigger Odysseus is than the mermaid who in other poems
(though not here) has been equated with that waveless blue sea.
Odysseus can judge the mermaid; she cannot judge him. She
embodies the sea, but he travels on it. He, in fact, is human; she
is not, though both here have a kind of immortality.

Seferis's early visions of the sea are tantalizingly fraught with
significance but hard to grasp, like a dream which ends before its
point is reached. In "Foreign Verse" for the first time the alluring
but inscrutable mermaid is juxtaposed with the symbol par excellence in Western literature of hard daily experience of salt
water.

ii   *The sea that embittered us*

Mythical History, a 24-part sequence written in 1933–34, presents a vision of the sea almost directly opposed to that
epitomized by the attractive but fugitive mermaid. In *Mythical
History* the sea is often present; the problem becomes how to
escape it, or at least how to impose various kinds of limitation on
its expanse. Without such markers the voyage might be endless.
I want to consider especially sections 4, 8, 10, and 12.

In section 4 *(Argonauts):*

> We went past many capes many islands the sea
> leading to another sea, gulls and seals.

> Sometimes unfortunate women wept
> lamenting their lost children
> and others raging sought Alexander the Great
> and glories buried in the heart of Asia.
> We moored on shores full of night-scents
> with birds singing, waters that left on the hands
> the memory of great happiness.
> But the voyages did not end.
> Their souls became one with the oars and the oarlocks
> with the solemn face of the prow
> with the rudder's wake
> with the water that shattered their image.
> The companions died one by one,
> with lowered eyes. Their oars
> mark the place where they sleep on the shore.
>
> No one remembers them. Justice.

The note is monotony and weariness that end in oblivion.
Loveliness is located now on land, where scents and sounds
recall happiness. Water seems to be inimical to memory: "the
water . . . shattered their image. . . . No one remembers them."
The same sea that shaped Odysseus in "Foreign Verse" has
weathered these Argonauts into indistinguishability. In section 8
they or people very like them do the talking (Seferis constantly
switches persons in *Mythical History*), questioning the purpose
of their continuing voyage in lines that effortlessly encompass
broader meanings about quests and goals. One of the most representative sections of the sequence, the section is worth quoting
in full.

> What are they after, our souls, traveling
> on the decks of decayed ships
> crowded in with sallow women and crying babies
> unable to forget themselves either with the flying fish
> or with the stars that the masts point out at their tips?
> Grated by gramophone records
> committed to non-existent pilgrimages unwillingly,
> murmuring broken thoughts from foreign languages.
>
> What are they after, our souls, traveling
> on rotten brine-soaked timbers
> from harbor to harbor?
>
> Shifting broken stones, breathing in

the pine's coolness with greater difficulty each day
swimming in the waters of this sea
and of that sea,
without the sense of touch
without men
in a country that is no longer ours
nor yours.

We knew that the islands were beautiful
somewhere round about here where we are groping—
a little lower or a little higher,
the slightest distance.

As if in search of something tangible, the poem moves from
the decayed ship to the more palpable brine-soaked timbers and
finally into the water. Surely the sea is neither nonexistent nor
foreign. Yet the sensation of being in the water is also disappoint-
ing; the senses seem to fail, the power to distinguish gets lost,
and finally the islands (which are revealed at the end to be one
goal of the journey) cannot be located. The boundlessness and
freedom from limitation which look so attractive from shore
when the mermaid smiles prove to be a frightening expanse of
anonymity.

Section 10 takes place back on land—a dry, shut-in land.

Our country is closed in, all mountains
that day and night have the low sky as their roof
We have no rivers, we have no wells, we have no springs,
only a few cisterns—and these empty—that echo, and that
we worship.

Such a country might well make one long for the sea again. The
world of *Mythical History* takes shape as one where voyages are
wearisome shuttlings between the harsh alternatives ("two black
Symplegades," they are called here) of boundless sea or arid
land where dryness and sterility have invaded the people as well
as the soil. Between these alternatives a dialectic rhythm prevails. If the poems are located on land, as 10 is, there is a longing
for the sea's openness ("we go down / to the harbors on Sunday
to breathe"). Section 5 also shows the tug of the sea:

Dawn finds us beside the tired lamp
drawing on paper, awkwardly, with effort,
ships mermaids or sea-shells;

at dusk we go down to the river
because it shows us the way to the sea;
and we spend the nights in cellars that smell of tar.

Yet that magically alluring sea, once you have set out on it, spells exhaustion, confusion, endless voyaging. Approaching either pole—either of the clashing rocks—Seferis's imagination recoils. The effect is gloomily paradoxical, as in section 16 where the sea can be neither escaped nor reached by the runner Orestes; but this gloomy paradox is the device that keeps *Mythical History* afloat and moving.

Section 12's two stanzas are about land and sea respectively and are bracketed by a one-line epigraph, "Bottle in the Sea," and a final closing line.

Bottle in the Sea

Three rocks, a few burnt pines, a solitary chapel
and farther above
the same landscape repeated starts again:
three rocks in the shape of a gate-way, rusted,
a few burnt pines, black and yellow,
and a square hut buried in whitewash;
and still farther above, many times over,
the same landscape recurs level after level
to the horizon, to the twilight sky.

Here we moored the ship to splice the broken oars,
to drink water and to sleep.
The sea that embittered us is deep and unexplored
and unfolds a boundless calm.
Here among the pebbles we found a coin
and threw dice for it.
The youngest won it and disappeared.

We set out again with our broken oars.

Rusted, burnt, dried, buried—the land is depicted in repeated images of desiccation. The sea, while more mysterious, is not very positively seen either; it has "embittered" us. Yet since it is unexplored it still, unlike the land, has secrets and can draw the voyagers on. The poem is in fact a brief rest before they reembark. Like salty quotation marks, the epigraph and last line enclose the utterance within a marine world; indeed, the epigraph

turns the poem into a message which the last line hints may be all
that remains of a shipwreck. (It is fair to add that Mrs. Tsatsou
says the last line became a Seferis family slogan for persever-
ance under difficult circumstances.)[36]

Occurring at the dead center of a 24-part sequence, section 12
epitomizes the dialectic between sea and land, inwardness and
outwardness, venture and retreat (and one could multiply categories like wet and dry) which shapes the entire sequence, taking
on the task of narrative. Frost was quoted earlier as having said,
"Narrative is a fearfully safe place to spend your time. Having
ideas that are neither pro nor con is the happy thing."[37] Frost
goes on to envision a series of dialectical oppositions above
which the thinker can remain suspended. Both opposition and
suspension characterize the motion of *Mythical History*. The
sea's alternations of attractiveness and repulsion propel a continued movement but also a kind of removal, a complex disen-
chantment.[38]

Discussing the pessimism of *Mythical History* in historical and
mythological terms, a Greek critic writes about the prototypical
voyages to which the poem constantly refers.

> Both [the voyage of the Argonauts and that of Odysseus] had
> tragedy for their climate. Thus mention of them constitutes a
> continual reminder of the role of the voyage as an element in
> our history and of the tragedy of that history. For the age when
> Seferis is writing, however, the voyage is no longer a cam-
> paign or a triumphant war; it is a shipwreck . . . it is endless
> vicissitudes, it is loss, or it is simply myth, an unfulfilled long-
> ing, for no one has the strength—or has the strength remain-
> ing—to undertake such a venture. None of those on board
> wished for this adventure; they are victims of fate and play-
> things of history. They have neither set out, like Argonauts, on
> an expedition, nor are they, like the companions of Odysseus,
> on their way home from a war which they sought out.[39]

The "endless vicissitudes" Karapanayiotis mentions translate
structurally   into   the   ambivalent   pattern   of   longing/
disappointment which accompanies and shapes the image of the
sea in *Mythical History*—a pattern which is perceptible whether
or not we link the poem to any particular mythology or history.

Another way of describing the uneasy dialectic which pervades *Mythical History* is as a succession of approaches to and
retreats from edges (shores). To call such edges historical or

ethical (i.e., to interpret them as decisions or victories, references to particular moments) is possible; but what is basic to the
poem is the pattern of advance and retreat. The unsatisfactory
nature of the sea in *Mythical History* is illuminated, I think, by
Bachelard's account in *The Poetics of Space* of an equivalent
dialectic.

> Outside and inside form a dialectic of division, the obvious
> geometry of which blinds us as soon as we bring it into play in
> metaphorical domains. It has the sharpness of the dialectics of
> *yes* and *no,* which decides everything. Unless one is careful, it
> is made into a basis of images that govern all thoughts of
> positive and negative. . . . Being is alternately condensation
> that disperses with a burst, and dispersion that flows back
> toward a center. Outside and inside are both intimate—they
> are always ready to be reversed, to exchange their hostility. If
> there exists a border-line surface between such an inside and
> outside, this surface is painful on both sides . . .
>
> In this drama of intimate geometry, where should one live?[40]

Or in Seferis's terms, "What are they after, our souls, traveling . . . ?"

iii *Free yourself from unfaithful time and sink*

Neither the fugitive mermaid nor the frustrating expanse image of the sea gets beneath the surface of the water. Occasionally, though, Seferis ventures below the beautiful blue surface.
The imaginative effort to penetrate the depths constitutes a third
perspective of the sea.

The Cistern (1932) deserves mention but it is a special case.
Personally I find the poem nearly impossible to read or discuss
because overluxuriant language chokes the meaning like an un-
pruned vine. Beneath the richness of the poem's linguistic surface, which Seferis labored over for years, consistency of
thought is hard to find. So far as one can tell, the cistern contains
fresh water. This, and the fact that it is underground, make the
cistern's nature as different as possible from the exposed
breadth of the sea. The hiddenness of the water means that its
symbol, its message, is a secret one—and this hiddenness sorts
well with the style of the poem. Also the cistern seems not to
change, since it is beyond the reach of the other elements:

> Here in the earth a cistern has taken root
> den of secret water that gathers there.
> Its roof, resounding steps. The stars
> don't blend with its heart. Each day
> grows, opens, shuts, doesn't touch it.
> . . . .
> But here in the earth a cistern has taken root
> warm, secret den that hoards
> the groan of each body in the air
> the battle with night, with day
> the world grows, passes, does not touch it.
>
> Time goes by, suns and moons,
> but the water has hardened like a mirror. . . .

Finally the cistern is said to "teach silence/in the flaming city." The image of patient, timeless subterranean waters quenching the flames of the upper world leaves one with contradictory senses of doom and consolation.[41] Such contradictions as organic ("taken root") yet unchanging; secret yet teaching; warm quenching—perhaps these are what the poem has to teach us about the depths.

Certainly *The Cistern* associates water and verticality. In *Gymnopaidia* Seferis further explores this association, this time in the clear, spare, yet hermetic style of *Mythical History* (*Gymnopaidia* was written in 1935). Like *Mythical History*, *Gymnopaidia* moves not by narrative but by a dialectic of opposition, though on a much smaller scale, since *Gymnopaidia* consists of only two poems. Where the longer sequence, with its stoppings and startings, pauses and renewals, departures and arrivals, is generally horizontal in movement, the direction of *Gymnopaidia* is not over the sea but into it. Islands rise, bodies sink; a shell is flung into the sea so that it sinks; "whoever raises the great stones" sinks. Seferis has taken the image of sinking from the description of Santorini in the Guide to Greece quoted in the epigraph of *Gymnopaidia*, endowing a neutral geological fact with poetic richness.

The sinking that fills *Gymnopaidia* is presumably a sinking into the sea. But this sea is quite a different sea from that in *Mythical History*. Instead of oblivion and mystery it offers an escape from time: "Free yourself from unfaithful time and sink." An escape from time may be an escape into death, but not any usual kind of death, since what sinks in this poem seems destined to rise again. The sea is mystically envisioned in *Gymnopaidia* above all as *otherness*—an alternative to the world above the surface, an alternative which, however enigmatic when seen from our standpoint, can nevertheless (with a little courage) be entered and experienced. It would be a falsification for any account of *Gymnopaidia* to clarify what is obscure in the poem, which may be Seferis's most hermetic. No easy revelation awaits us; in the first line of "Santorini" we are told to "Bend if you can to the dark sea," and after many perusals the poems remain dark. But the darkness belongs to the depths, not the surface.

These depths of *Gymnopaidia,* with their paradoxical life/death/escape from time, recall Emily Vermeule's evocation of the ambivalent attitude of early Greeks to the sea.

> Because the Greeks were interested in unseen possibilities, the horizon between what they knew and what they imagined was easily represented for them by the water surface, which provoked a kind of double vision. Painters and poets were both attracted by the two realms which were mutually invisible . . . The sea makes a double viewpoint easy, as in the famous simile of the dead suitors in the Odyssey (xxii.384 ff.) . . . the shape of the sea gives the fisherman's viewpoint; the feelings of being at home in the dark and vulnerable to the sun belong to the fish, as though man's world and the sea's world were in mirror image, sometimes inimical, sometimes sympathetically linked, like men and gods.[42]

But such a mirror can only be envisioned if one is curious about what goes on beneath the surface. Some of the opacity of *Gymnopaidia* results from the opacity of the medium. Seferis refuses to make clear what is obscure by nature, and the poetic result is a prophetic blend of authority and vagueness.

> Voices out of stone out of sleep
> deeper here where the world darkens,
> memory of toil rooted in the rhythm
> beaten upon the earth by feet
> forgotten.
> Bodies sunk into the foundations
> of the other time, naked. Eyes
> fixed, fixed on a point

that you can't make out, as much as you want to:
the soul
struggling to become your own soul. . . .[43]

In *Thrush* (1947) the plumbing of depths is a more luminous
process. The very name of the poem points to at least some
clarity as to what lies beneath the surface of the sea; "Thrush"
was a small craft that had been sunk off Poros, the island where
Seferis was staying at the time he wrote the poem. The poem is
in three sections of which the third is the longest, in some ways
the most obscure, and the most powerful; it is also the section
closest to the sea. The first part of this section is entitled *"The
wreck 'Thrush'";* the poet is trying to discern what is barely
visible under the water.

              I heard the voice
as I was gazing at the sea trying to make out
a ship they'd sunk there years ago;
it was called "Thrush," a small wreck; the masts,
broken, swayed at odd angles deep underwater, like tentacles,
or the memory of dreams, marking the hull:
vague mouth of some huge dead sea-monster
extinguished in the water. Calm spread all around.

This wreckage, this vague monster, is given a voice in the passage that follows, if we take the necessary step of equating the
submarine darkness with the darkness of Erebus, the ghost-filled
underworld whence the voices come.

     And gradually, in turn, other voices followed,
     whispers thin and thirsty
     emerging from the other side of the sun, the dark side;
     you might say they longed for a drop of blood to drink;
     familiar voices, but I couldn't distinguish one from the
     other.

Without the lines devoted to the wrecked ship, these "other
voices" would seem to be coming from a Homeric world of
blood-sipping ghosts such as also appears in *Mythical History 24*
and "Stratis Thalassinos among the Agapanthi." But the sight of
the fairly recent wreckage mediates the classical vision by
filtering it through the depths of a sea that is at once contemporary and timeless. The wreck is familiar; the poet knows its

provenance and name. Yet like the "bodies sunk into the foundations / of the other time, naked" in "Mycenae," the fact that the wreck is sunken signifies the *otherness,* "sometimes inimical, sometimes sympathetically linked, like men and gods," mentioned by Vermeule.

In "The King of Asine" Seferis gives the act of searching for "ancient remains" a significance that transcends archaeology. Similarly, the act of peering at sunken wreckage here is a richly emblematic one. Peering beneath the surface of water to make out indistinct shapes is a symbol of understanding the past, the unconscious, and their artistic blend in poetry. It is probably with the above passage from "Thrush" in mind that Mrs. Tsatsou writes about her brother:

> . . . I have his soul before me, outwardly liquid and translucent, and in its depths, a black monster is swimming! The suffering of the race. Sometimes we see its shadow, sometimes its wings, sometimes, beneath the trembling of the water, whirlpools, hollows, humps, sometimes other signs.

> How he struggled to kill his emotional nature. He ironized events, above all himself. But did he indeed kill it? He covered it with stones and seaweed.[44]

The other underwater passage in *Thrush* is concerned with movement toward the depths rather than scrutiny of them from a distance. The repetition of "still" emphasizes the continued presentness of the downward thrust.

> And the boys who dived from the bow-sprits
> go like spindles twisting still,
> naked bodies plunging into black light
> with a coin between the teeth, swimming still,
> while the sun with golden needles sews
> sails and wet wood and colors of the sea;
> still they're going down obliquely,
> the white lekythoi,
> toward the pebbles on the sea floor.

This passages transforms boys into vases—a metamorphosis of life into art which we can actually witness rather than guessing at it (as in the sinkings in *Gymnopaidia*). Such a metamorphosis is surely the key to escaping from "unfaithful time." Metamor-

phosis, sea-change, is the characteristic gift of Proteus, the Old
Man of the Sea who is the master of transformations in *Odyssey*
4 and who recurs in Seferis's work. For example, in "On Stage,"
the second of Seferis's *Three Secret Poems* (1966), the image of
diving and of pebbles on the sea floor we have seen in *Thrush*
recurs with the addition of Proteus.

> Yet the sea was sweet
> where I plunged in and swam as a child,
> and later, as a young man,
> while searching for shapes in the pebbles,
> trying to discover rhythms,
> the Old Sea-god said to me:
> "I am the place you belong to;
> I may be nobody,
> but I can become whatever you want."

The "boys who dived from the bow-sprits" embody the poet
who seeks knowledge of the depths, looks for patterns in pebbles; they also represent that transformation of life into art
which is finally the only way of escaping from time. The sea-
change of life into art, the present into the aorist, cannot be
accomplished if the voyager is content to remain on the surface.
One answer to the question posed in *Mythical History 8* ("What
are they after, our souls?") and a solution to that aporia may be:
the depths.

   iv   *And who shall drain it dry?*

Edmund Keeley has written that Seferis uses "myth and symbol to shape the formless present."[45] For *present* we may substitute *sea* without the observation's losing its truth. The sea may
be glimpsed, traveled over, plunged into—but who or what *is* it?
In order to give the sea a shape Seferis often personifies it; we
have already seen the mermaid and the figure of Odysseus as the
latter appears in "Foreign Verse." Insofar as Odysseus is the
prototype of a voyager, he is also present in the Stratis Thalassinos poems, in *Mythical History,* and in *Thrush*—that is, all
Seferis's major work. Whether we call the effect synchronic or
anachronistic, figures with classical names and attributes fit into
Seferis's world with remarkable ease. We do not protest when
we find the Argonauts and Alexander the Great or the Symplegades and Sunday or Adonis and a cannon cohabiting the

same poem. Elpenor's cigarette in Part II of *Thrush* hardly gives us pause. The poetic sleight of hand that makes these juxtapositions so acceptable is not in question, but it is explained by two critics in ways that are diametrically opposed.

"Seferis's secret," writes Keeley,

> is that he always offers an appropriate setting—a poetically realistic setting—before he allows any ghosts to appear on his stage; before he attempts to carry the reader to the level of myth, the level of timeless universalities, he wins his sympathy and belief by convincingly representing the present reality sustaining his myth—a contemporary, Greek reality always.[46]

According to Walter Kaiser, on the other hand, Seferis moves from mythic generality to contemporary particularity—at least for the non-Greek reader:

> Whereas normally in poetry of such classicism we perceive the particular and move on from there to the universal, in this case the process is curiously reversed. Most probably, it is the general applicability of Seferis' message which reaches us first, as these poems become almost instantaneously *our* poems and we relate them to our own experience of the world. To see how they are also *his* poems, to comprehend, that is, how they grow out of the personal and specific experiences of an individual Greek—this is what poses a greater difficulty for a foreigner. What is universal in his poetry we can test on our very pulse; what is personal and local we can, at best, only experience vicariously.[47]

It should be borne in mind that Keeley is writing about Seferis's middle period and Kaiser chiefly about *Three Secret Poems;* also that some of the difficulties of grasping the "personal and local" are owing to the language gap to which Kaiser frequently (and rightly) refers in his introduction to his translations of Seferis. In saying that Seferis's poems "grow out of the personal and specific experiences of an individual Greek," Kaiser is essentially repeating Keeley's point about "present reality."

Nevertheless, there is an interesting opposition in these two fine critics' perceptions of how the poetry works. For one, Seferis uses "present reality" to win sympathy and belief for the "timeless universality" which, it is implied, is the poet's real interest. For the other, it is the "general applicability" of Seferis's "universal" message which—regardless of the poet's intention—first becomes available to the reader and which then earns that reader's sympathy for the "personal and local."

I propose another way of looking at the problem. Instead of regarding personal and local detail as a sort of sugar coating for the pill of universality and myth, or vice versa, we might imagine Seferis as perceiving no distinction between these categories. The same quality of mind that gave the poet a synchronic view of Greek tradition, in the prose passage quoted below, made it possible for him to write the poetry quoted after that. In both, various eras huddle side by side in a happy disregard for chronology and history.

Writing about Cavafy's "basic characteristic, his unity," Seferis moves on to the larger and related unity of Greek culture (and not merely literary culture) as a whole:

> . . . we might attempt to place him and to feel him within the framework of the Greek tradition, the whole tradition, indivisible as it is. For this tradition is not, as some see it, an affair of isolated promontories, some great names, some illuminating texts; instead it is like what others of us see and feel in the little mosaics of a humble Byzantine church—the Ionian philosophers, the popular verses of the period of the Comneni, the epigrams of the Anthology, Greek folk song, Aeschylus, Palamas, Solomos, Sikelianos, Calvos, Cavafy, the Parthenon, Homer, *all living in a moment of time,* in this Europe of today and looking at our devastated homes. With this point of view Cavafy will not seem to us alien. . . .[48] (Italics mine.)

In the light of such a passage as this, it seems beside the point to read "Stratis Thalassinos among the Agapanthi" as a battleground of past and present, universal and particular. Seferis needs past voices, names, and images in order to say what he is saying in the present.

> The first thing God made is love
> then comes blood
> and the thirst for blood
> roused by
> the body's sperm as by salt.
> The first thing God made is the long journey;
> that house there is waiting

with its blue smoke
with its aged dog
waiting for the homecoming so that it can die.
But the dead must guide me;
it is the agapanthi that keep them from speaking,
like the depths of the sea or the water in a glass.
And the companions stay on in the palaces of Circe:
my dear Elpenor! My poor, foolish Elpenor!
Or don't you see them
—"Oh help us!"—
on the blackened ridge of Psara?

This poem was written in South Africa in 1942; Seferis was
serving with the Greek government in exile. The sense of exile
from home and the need of guidance recall the *Odyssey;* the war
for freedom recalls Solomos's famous elegy of 1825, "The Destruction of Psara."[49] To non-Greek readers the second reference
in particular may be obscure; but I see no way of separating the
universal from the local in what Seferis is saying about war.

The references to incidents and a character from the *Odyssey,*
and the use of Solomos's actual words, accomplish two things.
First, Seferis avoids the kind of nonspecific, ultimately bland
expression of feeling we saw in Mangakis's essay. Secondly, the
presence of other voices gives an appropriate timelessness to the
timeless theme of war. In exile, feeling cut off from Hellenism,
Seferis reaches back to the Greek tradition—a reaching which is
the real subject of "Stratis Thalassinos among the Agapanthi" as
well as much of his other work.[50]

It's painful and difficult, the living are not enough for me
first because they do not speak, and then
because I have to ask the dead
in order to go on farther.

Talking to the dead is Seferis's most striking use of myth in
poetry, his strongest means of showing that Elpenor and the
Independence Fighters of 1821 exist "in a moment of time." His
use of quotation from ancient sources is far more interesting as a
shaping device than the mere use of ancient names for timeless
figures; it is also one of the most interesting ways Seferis approaches the sea. Proteus is Proteus, the same in Seferis as in
the *Odyssey;* but a more distinctive proof of the mul-

titudinousness (in fact the protean quality) of the sea can be found in the changes Seferis rings on line 958 of the *Agamemnon,* "There is the sea—and who will drain it dry?"

"The dead must guide me," says the mariner in "Stratis Thalassinos among the Agapanthi"; "the living are not enough for me . . . I have to ask the dead / in order to go on farther." The quotation from Solomos at the end of that poem is an example of such guidance in a difficult moment. What kind of guidance does Aeschylus's line and its context provide? It appears—with variations—twice in "Notes for a Week," once in *Mythical History,* and at the close of *Thrush.* Comparing these different uses of the line ought to show some of the ways Seferis uses myth and dead voices to shape and dramatize the sea.

Even in its Aeschylean context, the line has a Delphic quality. Its enigmatic character is of course appropriate in that the line is spoken by that rhetorical riddler Clytemnestra as she welcomes Agamemnon home and tempts him to walk on the purple carpet. I use the Fagles translation.

> Ag.   . . . And now,
>   Since you have brought me down with your insistence,
>   Just this once I enter my father's house,
>   trampling royal crimson as I go.
>
> Clyt.   *There is the sea*
>   *and who will drain it dry?* Precious as silver,
>   inexhaustible, ever-new, it breeds the more we reap it—
>   tides on tides of crimson dye our robes blood-red.
>   Our lives are based on wealth, my king,
>   the gods have seen to that.
>   Destitution, our house has never heard the word.[51]

The image is deeply ironic and full of double-edged truth. It extends into the past and future as the purple fabric ripples beneath Agamemnon's feet. Clytemnestra boasts of the sea as proudly as if she owned it; indeed, she goes on to say that the Atreid house, reaping continual wealth from the red dye of the sea, *does* as good as own it. The speech beginning "There is the sea" is thus both outrageously arrogant and outrageously reasonable.

The sea is both the reservoir of their riches and the incarnation of their never-ending strife, a harvest and a grisly reaping both. Thus the sea reflects the tapestries and Clytemnestra's victim, the deadliness beneath the surface grandeur of the fabrics and the man. The sinuous red line they form is in the vein of Agamemnon—they fuse his slaughters and his bloodline, his will and his hereditary guilt. And at every step he takes upon them he exceeds his limits and retraces his descent: an Olympian outrage to be punished by the forces of the Earth. For as he tramples on the gods he re-enacts his trampling on the innocents of Troy and on his daughter—just as his forebear trampled on the banquet of his children—and so the king reactivates the curse. As if caught in a slow-motion camera, all his murderous acts dissolve into a single act, deliberate and majestic and profane, that accelerates toward the murder that awaits him.

An entire history of violence marches toward its violent but valid retribution.[52]

Fagles's and Stanford's vivid and poetic reading of the image unfolds like a brilliantly successful synecdoche from the sea to an entire history which we realize retrospectively is encapsulated in the line which begins the speech. The richness of association is more than poetic in its evocations; it is moral, historical, religious if we are aware of the family story Clytemnestra has in mind (and she knows that Agamemnon *is* aware of it, as Aeschylus knew his listeners were).

If then we read Seferis's variations on the line as references to the whole of Clytemnestra's speech and thus to the whole moral problem of the house of Atreus, it is clear that he could hardly have chosen a more humanly and complexly charged image of the sea. And if the reference escapes the reader? Seferis wrote of a comparable Aeschylean adaptation in *Thrush,* "I don't think that I'm unjustified in considering these things [Aeschylus; tragedy; ancient Greek; Greek culture] as the common possession of us all; if they are not, so much the worse for us."[53] Unfortunately things *are* the worse for us; most of us now need notes to explain the line's provenance, let alone its larger context and suggestiveness.

If we are unaware of the Aeschylean reference, much of the effectiveness of the line is inevitably lost. But Seferis has preserved some of the dramatic quality of the original context of Clytemnestra's (largely rhetorical) question by emphasizing the line's interrogative tone in most of its recurrences. Whatever we take the sea to mean, it is often an open question in Seferis

whether it can or will be or has been drained dry or not—and
beyond this uncertainty, whether or not it ought to be. The answer to that question of course depends on how we interpret the
sea. Recall in Aeschylus its double burden of riches and guilt,
self-renewal and pollution. The sea is a synecdoche for both
wealth and blood; beyond that, for a royal house and its violent
past. If we know nothing of the house of Atreus or Clytemnestra's speech, the line as Seferis uses it still pulsates with ambivalence; it is a question to which there is no easy answer. Feeling
that, we feel (I here agree with Kaiser; see p. 139) the "general
applicability" of the line before we sense its specific import. But
it is questionable how specific the import ever becomes in the
quotations that follow; the question of the sea is nearly always
bigger than its context.

In "Notes for a Week," some of the poems written in London
in the early thirties, both "Monday" and "Wednesday" refer to
the line.

> the river doesn't roll, it has forgotten the sea
> and yet there is the sea and who will drain it dry? . . .
> I look at the river
> sudden light puffs of wind pass under the impotent sun
> nothing else, the river waits;
> pity those who wait.
>
> ("Monday")

> Brothers, we've shared our bread and our pain.
> No one hungers any longer, no one suffers
> and all of us have the same stature. Look at us!
> We look at you. We too. We too. We too.
> There is nothing beyond.
> —But the sea:
> I don't know why they've drained it dry.
>
> ("Wednesday")

In both these poems, written far from home and imbued with the
same nostalgia as "Hampstead," the sea is desired but out of
reach and out of sight. It is not quite certain that the sea exists at
all; it has been forgotten by the river, it has perhaps been drained
dry. The sea-less world is also a world without heroism, a world
where the sun is "impotent" (as of course English sun is in
comparison to Greek), where no one is greater than anyone else
and there is no other life, no escape from unfaithful time: "noth-

ing beyond." The violence that in Aeschylus makes the sea run red is absent from these pale poems, but so is its splendor and ability to renew itself.

In *Mythical History 20,* subtitled *Andromeda* in the Greek edition, the speaker is closer to the sea and senses it as a real thing: threat? escape? Both the first and second lines of this passage can be read as either fearful or yearning:

> These stones sinking into time, how far will they
>   drag me with them?
> The sea, the sea, who will be able to drain it dry?
> I see the hands beckon each dawn to the vulture and
>   the hawk
> bound as I am to the rock that suffering has made mine,
> I see the trees breathing the black serenity of the dead
> and then the smiles, so static, of the statues.

A kind of transcendent sublimity as splendid in its way as Clytemnestra's arrogance raises the tone of these lines above the usual human hopes and apprehensions. Andromeda, or a nameless consciousness, is able to perceive on a geological scale the processes of nature such as stones moving, trees breathing, the sea being (or not being) slowly depleted. What becomes of the sea is of vital but not personal importance to this consciousness, rather as in the opening of *Prometheus Bound.*

In the close of *Thrush,* for the only time, the sea *does* drain dry.

>   and you find yourself
> in a large house with many windows open
> running from room to room, not knowing from where
>   to look out first,
> because the pine-trees will vanish, and the mirrored
>   mountains, and the chirping of birds
> the sea will drain dry, shattered glass, from north
>   and south
> your eyes will empty of daylight
> the way the cicadas suddenly, all together,
>   fall silent.

Emptiness and cessation are presented with a lighthearted, almost rapturous rhythm and tone; Seferis himself called this section the *allegro* of *Thrush.*[54] Silence, darkness, emptiness do not preclude an apocalyptic radiance; the silence seems to herald a new beginning, as does the cessation in "Engomi," another transcendent moment (see Chapter I). But "Engomi" returns at its close to a world of sparse grass where "they take a long time to die"; here death is simply the stoppage of the poem on a note of paradoxical exultation.

Seferis has made extraordinarily varied, though consistently mysterious, uses of Aeschylus's line. The earlier work, emphasizing the life-giving quality of the sea, uses its possible draining as a source of apprehension, a sign of alienation consonant with the alienation of being in London. *Mythical History* moves closer to the world of Greek myth and Greek landscape, with its sinking stones, vulture, and statues; but with the dialectic familiar from our earlier discussion of this sequence, the sea is not necessarily more precious as it is more closely approached. Here it is inscrutable, perhaps dangerous, perhaps life-saving.

The actual draining of the sea at the end of *Thrush* sends us back to Aeschylus. What would such an exhaustion of resources mean in Clytemnestra's terms? Her sea is "inexhaustible, ever-new"; "Our lives are based on" the wealth it produces and do not understand deprivation. For that inexhaustible sea to dry up is unheard of, terrifying, and ultimately cleansing, even if it means death. Seferis is suggesting the end of a rich tradition with its wealth, for the poet, of history and legend; a final freeing, both exhilarating and dreadful, from the bond of the past. Instead of peering underwater in order to decipher the past, the poet can now run from room to room of unfulfilled potential. It is hard to know what kind of resource will replace Clytemnestra's rich and bloody sea; *Thrush* ends at this point, and so does the great majority of Seferis's best work. In *Logbook III* (1955) he turned to Cypriot legend and myth, and in *Three Secret Poems* language and continuity sometimes seem tenuous, the work of a tired man. Yet it is in "On Stage," the second of these three poems, that Seferis comes closest to confronting Clytemnestra in all her sinister splendor—that Clytemnestra who remains in the background in all the changes run on her great line. In some kind of theatrical performance, a female figure appears on stage, unnamed but "Leaving the sheets to grow cold / and the avenging baths." Has Agamemnon already been murdered; is this *The Libation Bearers?* All we are shown is the figure's courage in the face of nameless attackers.

> They drew the knives from the sheaths,
> looked for a place to stab you.
> Only then did you cry out:
> "Let anyone come and sleep with me
>   who wants to:
> am I not the sea?"

Arrogant, unanswerable, finally mysterious, this question is perhaps Seferis's final version of *Agamemnon* 958 and his final vision of the sea, as if the cleansed quality of the end of *Thrush* had to give way to the familiar elemental and mythological forces of tradition. In the following section, to which I referred on page 138, Seferis is questioning his own vision, the use he has made of myth and symbol. "The sea: how did it become so, the sea?" To which the only answer is that given by Proteus: "I may be nobody, / but I can become whatever you want." In other words, *know thyself.*

Proteus is a reminder that the most constant thing about this changeable element is its truthfulness. As Emily Vermeule points out, sea-prophets like Proteus may be hard to catch, but, once caught, they never lie.[55] Vermeule also observes (what we have already seen in the line about the sea draining) that the sea is "double-faced and changeable, sometimes the way to paradise and sometimes the jaws of death, but never predictable." Life-giving and death-giving, the sea is the emblem of dialectic, and any symbol of it must be contradictory or incomplete. Yet in its formlessness it must be symbolized; it cries out for poetic treatment and challenges the poet's control over his own tradition. What Seferis says of the sea in his Makriyannis essay is true as well of his own struggle for equilibrium, his attempt to maintain a synchronic sense of Greek tradition and his place in it: "this element that, although always tormented, never stops striving towards a balance, towards a 'measure.'" Writing about the sea was a harsh test for Seferis: could he both be original and tell the truth? In his different ways of viewing the sea and especially his heed of "the dead" for guidance, Seferis managed to hold his own against the formlessness of the element as timeless as Homer, Aeschylus, Solomos.

I said at the end of Chapter I that the power of the imagination turns inanimate rock into "a mirror in which to dwell." Trees and the sea, of course, are mirrorlike in much more obvious ways. They reflect not only the constantly changing faces of nature but also ourselves—reflect, finally, the sense of life or death, hope or despair, we bring to a contemplation of natural metamorphosis. In Frost and Seferis gardens are blossom or decay; the sea is renewal or disappearance.

As if occasionally weary of the protean character of some of their preferred emblems, Frost and Seferis sometimes conjure them out of existence. In "After Apple-Picking" the world is perhaps no more than a dreamlike apparition; in Seferis's variations on the Aeschylean line about the sea, the sea itself vanishes. A powerful ambivalence about the beloved landscapes with which they are so familiar underlies such exorcisms; it is an ambivalence that will reappear more strongly when the poets turn from earthly landscapes toward the inaccessibilities of stars and light and their human mirrorings.

Notes

1. Reginald Cook, *The Dimensions of Robert Frost* (New York: Barnes and Noble, 1958), 105.
2. Richard Poirier, *Robert Frost: The Work of Knowing* (New York: Oxford University Press, 1977), 18.

[of "Spring Pools"]: [Frost] is speaking not of some pools in particular, but of pools in his mind, pools of such unusual visionary sharpness as to be immediately present to him, "*these* pools."

3. Robert Frost, "On Extravagance," quoted in *Work of Knowing,* xi.
4. *Work of Knowing,* 199.
5. Compare the elliptical technique of "Spring Pools" with A. E. Housman's poem "Loveliest of Trees."
6. Reuben Brower, *The Poetry of Robert Frost: Constellations of Intention* (New York: Oxford University Press, 1963), 37.
7. *Work of Knowing,* 220:

Frost wants to show how an ordinary man discovers in the round of housekeeping and planting, which he shares with his wife, the larger patterns of time that include different forms of gestation and birth. The "seed" grows in every sense: it is a seedling in the field which unlike the weeds comes arching out of the earth thanks to the human agent who planted it; it is an "arched body" emerging from the womb because of another human planting; and it is the language of poetry which begins in the opening line with "a selection of language really used by men" and develops, as Wordsworth might further describe it, toward a "personification."

8. Frost, "The Figure a Poem Makes," in *Collected Poems* (Holt, Rinehart & Winston, 1967), vi.
9. Nina Baym and Poirier, for example, have very different reactions to the passage. See Baym's essay in Lewis P. Simpson, comp., *Profile of Robert Frost* (Columbus, Ohio: Charles E. Merrill Publishing Co., 1971), 86–87.
10. *Work of Knowing,* 214.
11. See note 9. The delicacy of the gesture the poem executes may be gauged by the way it hoodwinks readers (as its speaker does his companion). Baym calls the move-

ment of "A Boundless Moment" "that of a mind away from a comforting illusion toward a harsh truth." Yet that same mind has wished to foster the illusion before withdrawing it; and how "harsh" is the fact that March is not May? I think the poem is at least as much about the tricky pleasure of creating and maintaining a precarious illusion as it is about the pain of giving that illusion up.

12. See Theodore Roethke's anecdote in "What Do I Like?" Harvey Gross, ed., *The Structure of Verses* (reprint, New York: Ecco Press, 1979), 250:

I remember the first time I heard RF read. . . . a line, I think it was from Shakespeare, came into his head. He recited it. "Listen to that," he said. "Just like a *hiss,* just like a *hiss.*" It is what Eliot has called the "auditory imagination."

See also Frost's letter to his daughter Lesley in Arnold Grade, ed., *Family Letters of Robert and Elinor Frost* (Albany: State University of New York Press, 1972), 162:

An Imagist is simply one who insists on clearer sharper less muddled half realized images (chiefly eye images) than the common run of small poets. That's certainly good as far as it goes. Strange with all their modernity and psychology they didn't have more to say about ear images . . .

The passage quoted in the text is from Lawrance Thompson, ed., *Letters of Robert Frost* (New York: Holt, Rinehart & Winston, 1964), p. 130.

13. See *Work of Knowing,* 81–82, on equivocations in "The Sound of Trees."

14. Radcliffe Squires, *The Major Themes of Robert Frost* (Ann Arbor: University of Michigan Press, 1961), 50.

15. *Major Themes,* 3.

16. Gaston Bachelard, *The Poetics of Space,* trans. Maria Jolas (Boston: Beacon Press, 1969), 33.

17. *Work of Knowing,* 275.

18. Like many crucial transitions within Frost's longer poems, this one is not signaled by any line-break.

19. Robert Frost, "The Poetry of Amy Lowell," first pub. in *The Christian Science Monitor* 16 May 1945, reprinted in Elaine Barry, *Robert Frost on Writing* (New Brunswick, N.J.: Rutgers University Press, 1973), 136.

20. Lawrance Thompson, *Robert Frost: The Years of Triumph 1915–1938* (New York: Holt, Rinehart & Winston, 1970), 290.

21. Quoted in F. D. Reeve, *Robert Frost in Russia* (Boston: Atlantic–Little, Brown, 1963), 43.

22. For an account of the genesis of "Wild Grapes" and a superb reading of the poem see Helen Bacon, "For Girls: from 'Birches' to 'Wild Grapes,' " *Yale Review* LXVII No. 1 (Autumn 1977): 13–29.

23. On "Leif the Lucky's German," see Bacon, "For Girls," 27–28:

. . . the allusion to Leif the Lucky's German links the miracle of the Mediterranean Dionysus to the Norsemen's discovery of grapes in America. According to the *Greenland Saga,* Leif Ericson took with him when he left Greenland to explore the New World a German named Tyrker. . . . At one of their landing-places . . . Tyrker, who had gone exploring with half the ship's company, was missing when they returned to camp in the evening. Leif in great distress organized a search party, which soon came upon Tyrker so full of joy and excitement that for a long time he could only babble in German and roll his eyes. But at last he spoke in the language of the Norsemen. "I did not go much further than you and yet I have something of novelty to relate. I have found vines and grapes."

24. Frost, "Letter to the *Amherst Student,*" in *RF on Writing,* 113.

25. "Hyla Brook."

26. *Work of Knowing,* 293–94.

27. *Work of Knowing,* 293–94.

28. Frost, "Education by Poetry," *Selected Prose of Robert Frost,* ed. Hyde Cox and Edward Connery Lathem (New York: Collier, 1968) 41.

29. Georgios-Alexandros Mangakis, "My Greece," trans. Rachel Hadas, *The Charioteer,* No. 19 (1977): 66–67 (first appearance in *Eighteen Articles,* Athens, 1972).

30. Seferis, *Days,* journal entries for 12 May and 14 August 1946 (my translation).

31. On the influence of Verlaine and Laforgue on the early Seferis, see Naso Vayenas, *The Poet and the Dancer* (Athens: Kedros, 1979), 118–20. Vayenas derives "Fog" from Laforgue's "Complainte de l'automne monotone" and quotes:

Nuits sous-marines!
Pourpres forêts,
Torrents de frais,
Bancs en gésines.

To be sure [writes Vayenas] the meaning of the images in the two poets is not the same. For Laforgue the submarine world is the symbol of nirvana, of a vegetable, unorganized life, relieved of every human anxiety. Seferis remains on the first level of the comparison, suggesting the essential futility and inertia of human existence. (Translation mine.)

32. See also Vayenas, *Poet and Dancer,* on the possible derivation of "Hampstead" from Sikelianos's poem, pp. 197–200.

33. "My Greece," 66–67.

34. See W. B. Stanford, *The Ulysses Theme.*

35. See my paper "Upon a Foreign Verse: Translation and Tradition," *Translation Review,* no. 11 (1983): 31–36.

36. For the graffito-like aspect of Seferis's work, see Chapter I. The Tsatsou reference is from *My Brother George Seferis* (Athens: Hestia, 1973).

37. Robert Frost, quoted in Lawrance Thompson, *Robert Frost: The Years of Triumph,* 290.

38. See John Vernon, *The Garden and the Map,* 145:

It is insufficient to talk simply about spatial cross-references . . . The point of repeated images, of cross-references, is that the image accumulates new meaning with each new appearance, since it is arrived at in the act of reading, in time; it therefore possesses not only its first appearance but a whole intermediary part of the poem or novel, as the part that constitutes its presence.

39. L. B. Karapanayiotis, "Mythistorema '61," in G. P. Savidis, ed., *For Seferis* (Athens: Ikaros, 1961), 225.

40. *Poetics of Space,* 211, 217.

41. On the confused and contradictory images in *The Cistern,* see also *Poet and Dancer,* 129–32.

42. Emily Vermeule, *Aspects of Death in Early Greek Art and Poetry* (Berkeley: University of California Press, 1979), 180.

43. Compare this passage with the opening of Section 4 of *Mythical History,* itself in turn a quotation from Plato's *Alcibiades,* p. 133B.

And if the soul
is to know itself
it must look
into a soul:
the stranger and the enemy, we've seen him in the
mirror.

44. *My Brother GS,* 190, 269.

45. Edmund Keeley, "T. S. Eliot and the Poetry of Seferis," *Comparative Literature* 8 (Summer 1965): 225.

46. Edmund Keeley, "Seferis' Elpenor: A Man of No Fortune," *Kenyon Review* 28 (June 1966): 378–79.

47. Walter Kaiser, trans. *Three Secret Poems by George Seferis,* Cambridge, Mass.: Harvard University Press, 1969), ix–x.

48. Seferis, "Cavafy and Eliot—a Comparison," in Rex Warner, editor and translator, *Seferis on the Greek Style* (London: Bodley Head, 1966), 161.

49. "On the blackened ridge of Psara":

This line is from Solomos's "The Destruction of Psara" (1825). The island of Psara was razed and its people massacred during the Greek War of Independence (1821–1829). The complete poem is among the more famous in modern Greece. . . .

Keeley and Sherrard, "Notes" to *George Seferis: Collected Poems (1924–1955)* (Princeton, N.J.: Princeton University Press, 1971), 265.

50. See my unpublished paper, "Talking to the Dead: Seferis and Tradition" (delivered at the MLA, Houston, Texas, 12/28/80).

51. Aeschylus, *The Oresteia,* trans. Robert Fagles (New York: Bantam Edition, 1977), 145.

52. Robert Fagles and W. B. Stanford, "A Reading of the Oresteia: The Serpent and the Eagle," *The Oresteia,* 27.

53. Seferis, "Letter on *Thrush,*" *English-Greek Review.*

54. Seferis, quoted in *Poet and Dancer,* 278–79.

55. Vermeule, *Aspects of Death,* 190–91.

CHAPTER III

Stars and Light

This chapter is about the third and final image-cluster: Frost's poems about stars, Seferis's about sunlight and light in general. As we consider the several groups of poems, it becomes possible to see that each of them has or creates its own generic needs. Images of stone evoke a voice which, as it ponders the past, is generally meditative and abstracted (or abstracting). Since subjects which belong to the past—to history—have stories attached to them, such a voice can often be a narrative one (especially, for example, in Frost's poems about houses). By contrast, trees and the sea usually occasion lyric moments whose intensity is timeless; they celebrate a fixed point in nature rather than a sequence of events, though what is fixed is also transient. Especially in Seferis, in addition, the sea can provide a backdrop for a questlike series of actions; thus *Mythical History*'s framework is apparently narrative. By and large, however, the sea-tree cluster is lyrical, the stone-wall-house group either narrative or meditative.

Now that we have reached the poems about stars and light, it becomes apparent that many of them are written in a style different from any we have seen before. Two poetic voices which were never lavish become markedly sparser. For Frost and Seferis to turn their gazes skyward means that each leaves behind the familiarities, not only of earth, but also of such generic frameworks as lyric or narrative. Thus we feel a double sense of isolation: both from terrestrial minutiae and from the stabilities of the poetic tradition. Under the stars, human history shrinks to a speck. The earth-scaled mutabilities of flowers and water are eclipsed by the cosmic mutabilities—or is it immutability?—perceived by the two poets as they ponder the skies.

Change or changelessness: such is the yawning choice presented in Frost's star and Seferis's light poems. These are works which characteristically move between two extremes. In both poets, the bareness of this often late work allows us to discern the outlines of a great dialectic, an either/or whose poles govern the gestures of the poem. Rather than lyrical or narrative, such gestures are, in their own way, dramatic.

Dramatic, that is, in thought and substance rather than explicitly in form. The counterpoint of voice on voice, at which Frost was particularly skilled, which is the method of drama, is absent from these poems. But their compression of tragic dilemmas and paradoxes into tight, almost lyrical dimensions gives an effect of foreshortening which *is* dramatic. Poems like Frost's "Any Size We Please," "Skeptic," or "An Unstamped Letter in Our Rural Letter Box," or Seferis's "Our Sun" or "Agianapa II" all combine a human foreground with a limitless dimension in a limited, but not a lyric, space: the effect, unique and intense, is dramatic in its energy if not in its lineaments.

Frost's "The Bear," which images his vision of the cosmic dialectic of possibilities, is Beckett-like in its portrayal of mankind as a caged animal whose movements are restricted to an arc between "two metaphysical extremes." The dramatic element, and the key to much of Frost's star poetry, is an alternation between two choices. These choices are first sensed as spatial. Unable to rely on the sense of sight for something as remote as stars, Frost tends to oscillate in his sky poems between a somewhat abstract idea of the universe's immensity and a more viscerally felt cosmic claustrophobia.

Like the restlessness of the caged bear, such a pendulum swing entails extremes of mood between the hope for some general harmony and meaning in the universe and the fear or suspicion of present disorder and future nothingness. The alternation can be seen, too, as between skepticism and a sense of mystery. At almost all times Frost admits a vast world beyond comprehension; what swings back and forth is his response to such a world. The following passage from Santayana, an important philosopher for Frost, conveys something of the sense of alternation the star poems cumulatively give, as if one were looking now out of one end of a telescope, now the other:

. . . I am not myself a believer in the ordinary sense, yet my *feeling* on this subject is like that of believers, and not at all like that of my fellow materialists. The reason is that I disagree utterly with that modern philosophy which regards *experience* as fundamental. Experience is a mere whiff or rumble, produced by enormously complex and ill-deciphered causes of experience; and in the other direction, experience is a mere peep-hole through which glimpses come down to us of eternal things.[1]

For Seferis, the experience of light, of sun, is overwhelming in its intensity; thus the cosmic dialectic first of all is simply the result of visual impact. The alternation between sense and disorder, meaning and mystery, is for Seferis something like the way too bright light, dazzling the eyes, produces an afterimage of darkness. The alternation of dark and light becomes an *agon*, a kind of wrestling match in which each partner ought to win. In this pulsating pattern of black and white, mythological resonances abound; but the myths, even where they are thickest, as in *Thrush*, never quite mesh into a narrative texture. Rather, Seferis maintains a note of abstraction. *Three Secret Poems*, the last poetic work published in his lifetime, compresses the brightness and its dark antagonist into the small, intensely personal framework of "the blank page, difficult mirror"—the world of the poet's own mind and oeuvre.

Readers of poetry commonly cavil at changes in a favorite poet's matter or manner, missing the mastery of modes which the poet may have transcended. Frost's star poems are not among his best known; and in *Three Secret Poems* Seferis leaves behind the nexus of mythical references which has come to be a signature, preferring a purgative directness. It is precisely when they have left the beauties of earth and the familiarities of tradition behind, and have begun to look beyond their usual terrain, that these poets, paradoxically, come into their own. Frost on stars, Seferis on light, are at their most vulnerable and their most courageous. Vulnerable because they are no longer guarded by the carapace of familiar tradition and locale; courageous because, facing final things, they never pretend to have arrived at final certainties.

This courage and this vulnerability make the later Frost and Seferis poems perhaps the most true of all. Two distinctive but moderate poetic voices are—unobtrusively—wrenched by the strain of addressing themselves to the cosmos. The effect of such stresses for both poets is similar: they maintain an embattled equilibrium, but at the cost of a good deal of terrestrial coziness.

The voices do not rise to shrill heights of rhetoric; neither do they drop to incoherent or nihilistic growls. But both poets are tempted by the silence of the infinite spaces. Instead of cracking with the strain, the voices are pulled toward dialectical halves: the cosmic poems become conversations between the two halves of a voice, or between a voice and an Other. They are dialogues that have not yet concluded when Frost's and Seferis's voices fall silent.

1. Frost on Stars

I guess I don't take life very seriously. It's hard to get into this world and hard to get out of it. And what's in between doesn't make much sense. If that sounds pessimistic, let it stand. There's been too much vaporous optimism voiced about life and age. Maybe this will provide a little balance.[2]

There's a good deal of God in everything you do. It's like climbing a ladder, and the ladder rests on nothing; and you climb higher and higher, and you feel there must be God on top. It can't be unsupported up there.[3]

I contain opposites. I can hold a lot. I can get up a phrase to handle almost everything that happens.[4]

These three quotations are all excerpted from interviews Frost gave during the last three years of his life. Their shifting tones of serenity and trouble, strength and puzzlement, balance and paradox swirl about a single core of concern: last things. Frost's late poetry shares the preoccupation with eschatology shown in these statements, and shares too their shifting emphases from pessimism to faith.

Frost is not best known and loved as a poet of eschatological concerns. Last things demand a new focus; they also require a renunciation of old subjects. "Come In" offers a foretaste of the celestial scrutiny of the later poems and also of the renunciations that accompany it:

> Far in the pillared dark
> Thrush music went—

Almost like a call to come in
To the dark and lament.

But no, I was out for stars:
I would not come in.
I meant not even if asked,
And I hadn't been.

"Come In" turns away from any possible proffering of human companionship and also away from birds and trees (Frost's earlier preserves par excellence, territory the poet had made his own) toward the stars which become visible as daylight dies—though only to one willing to stay out of doors and look up. The staunchness of the speaker here presages the spareness of many of Frost's late poems, where the poet is "out for stars" to the exclusion of much else.

Sometimes throughout his career, but increasingly often in and after *Steeple Bush* (1947), Frost was out for stars. Like the passages quoted on the previous page, many of the poems he wrote during the last dozen years of his life are cosmic meditations, eschatological musings whose precise tone can be hard to catch. Some poems have forsaken, even if they have not forgotten, the beauties of earth. They tend to see life, with all its thrush music, weather, seasons, trees, houses, and people, *sub specie aeternitatis,* or at least as near to eternity as one curious old mind can get.

Have Frost's astronomical and extraterrestrial poems given offense because they are too abstract (insufficiently lyrical, detailed, musical) or because they are not abstract enough (in the sense that Frost never seems to arrive at a final religious or scientific conclusion about how to regard the world)?[5] What has seemed hardest for some critics to forgive is that the very poems which seem speculative rather than poetical nevertheless arrive nowhere.

It is true that Frost's star poems shy away from finalities. Rather, these poems, with their pendulum-like swings back and forth between moods and possibilities, provide an unusually clear view of the dialectical path of a mind's track—a view unimpeded by the terrestrial underbrush and seasonal change that adorn and vary the earlier work. As a reflection of some, if not all, kinds of human ratiocination, the back-and-forth of Frostian

speculation has a compelling history. Coleridge had been thinking along the same lines in *Biographia Literaria:*

> Most of my readers will have observed a small water-insect on
> the surface of rivulets . . . and will have noticed, how the little
> animal wins its way up against the stream, by alternate pulses
> of active or passive motion, now resisting the current, and
> now yielding to it in order to gain strength and a momentary
> fulcrum for a further propulsion. This is no unapt emblem of
> the mind's self-experience in the act of thinking.[6]

Like the water-bug, Frost's cosmic poems alternate between
active and passive motion, now yielding to the current and now
resisting it. Far from answering ultimate questions, "Frost's
poems are directly about struggle; the terms of the struggle are
defined with satisfying honesty and exactness, even to the epis-
temological difficulties that man encounters in getting to know
the world."[7] "Mind is the uniquely human characteristic, and
man defines himself therefore as man by asserting it against the
push of matter."[8]

In the passage quoted on page 155 above, note how rapidly the
terms *pessimism, optimism,* and *balance* follow upon one
another. Since each of these terms seems to carry with it an
entire way of looking at the world, the effect of such rapid shifting is bewildering, as if the earth were to spin faster under our
feet. The giddiness induced by trying to follow the rhythms of
Frost's thought is a frequent sensation for readers of the late
poems. As the cosmological speculations move between dialectical poles, the resulting arcs can be wearying to follow. Wearying but not monotonous; for although the principle of motion is
constant in these poems, the terms of the dialectic vary. In
Frost's poems about the stars or more generally about what
exists beyond our planet, I discern three major versions of the
dialectic. First, there is repeated emphasis on the reciprocal
senses of the nearness or farness, immensity or smallness, of the
cosmos—emphasis expressed in a rhythm of alternation both
within single poems and from one poem to another. Another
theme in the star poems is the limited nature of our ability to see
far, despite the persistence of our attempts to do so, and the
resulting rhythmical tugging at the leash of our limitations. In a
third group of poems, the remoteness of stars is perceived in
terms of speech as well as of visibility. That is, not only must we

on earth struggle even to catch a glimpse of the stars; being ourselves creatures of language, we want to do more than see them, we want to speak to them *and be answered.* "Say something to us we can learn / By heart and when alone repeat. / Say something!" pleads "Take Something Like a Star."

A word on the "meaning" of stars in Frost. It is obvious that stars, like Frost's other major images, are symbolic and synecdochic; they suggest a whole range of meanings beyond themselves. Whether we wish to call the technique symbolism or emblemism, synecdoche or allegory, is less important than the outwardly radiating suggestiveness all-pervasive in these poems. The openness of Frost's images is deliberate; it is accompanied by a refusal to be pinned down and, especially in late poems and interviews, a disinclination for formal closure. Perhaps it seemed to Frost that death was close enough already without the addition of artificial deaths in the form of structured endings. His interviewer Roger Kahn has a revealing anecdote in this regard.

> Some summing up seemed in order, and, for want of a better term, I intended to say that this visit had brought me into the presence of greatness. "I feel as though . . ." I began.
>
> "Now, none of that," Frost said anticipating. "We've had a fine talk together, haven't we? And we've talked to some purpose. Come now, and I'll walk with you down the hill."
>
> He got up from his chair and started down the steep path, pausing to look at the sunset as he went.[9]

The sunset, of course, provides its own kind of closure. But like Frost in this anecdote, the star poems do not seek stasis; they wind down rather than executing the formal flourishes of a conclusion.

i   *The universe may or may not be very immense*

Frost had laid out the path of the mind's track as early as his 1925 review of Amy Lowell's work, when he wrote

> The most exciting movement in nature is not progress, advance, but expansion and contraction. . . . We explore and adventure for a while and then we draw in to consolidate our gains.[10]

This theoretical scheme is filled in, in a sympathetically fleshy
and concrete way, by "The Bear," a poem which depicts mankind as a caged and pacing bear, locked up in the universe. The
compulsive back-and-forth pacing is the action of ratiocination,
but the back-and-forth movement exists also in the swing of our
sympathies as we read the poem, or in the contrast between the
unfettered ramblings of the free bear at the beginning and the
caged animal's constraint. This undeservedly obscure poem is
crucial for all Frost's star pieces, and I quote it complete.

> The bear puts both arms around the tree above her
> And draws it down as if it were a lover
> And its choke cherries lips to kiss good-by,
> Then lets it snap back upright in the sky.
> Her next step rocks a boulder on a wall
> (She's making her cross-country in the fall).
> Her great weight creaks the barbed-wire in its staples
> As she flings over and off down through the maples,
> Leaving on one wire tooth a lock of hair.
> Such is the uncaged progress of the bear.
> The world has room to make a bear feel free;
> The universe seems cramped to you and me.
> Man acts more like the poor bear in a cage
> That all day fights a nervous inward rage,
> His mood rejecting all his mind suggests.
> He paces back and forth and never rests
> The toe-nail click and shuffle of his feet,
> The telescope at one end of his beat,
> And at the other end the microscope,
> Two instruments of nearly equal hope,
> And in conjunction giving quite a spread.
> Or if he rests from scientific tread,
> 'Tis only to sit back and sway his head
> Through ninety odd degrees of arc, it seems,
> Between two metaphysical extremes.
> He sits back on his fundamental butt
> With lifted snout and eyes (if any) shut,
> (He almost looks religious but he's not),
> And back and forth he sways from cheek to cheek,
> At one extreme agreeing with one Greek,
> At the other agreeing with another Greek
> Which may be thought, but only so to speak.
> A baggy figure, equally pathetic
> When sedentary and when peripatetic.

This restless oscillation is both comic and grim. The baggy bear
is a bit of a Chaplinesque clown, but is also, in its awareness of
restrictions, an emblem of the existential hero or anti-hero in all
of us, pacing and swaying only within the walls of our cage.

The figure of the pacer in the universal cage is never as clearly
set forth in Frost's astronomical poems as it is in "The Bear";
but this poem is a paradigm of the dialectic that governs nearly
all the star poems. When man is absorbed in concentration at
either the telescopic or microscopic end of his beat, the bars of
the cage fade for a while from his consciousness and the bear is
in abeyance. (Behind the bear I hear Hamlet's "O God, I could
be bounded in a nutshell, and count myself a king of infinite
space, were it not that I have bad dreams.") But sooner or later
we again become aware of our place in the enormous scheme of
things. Marice Brown observes that a characteristic technique of
Frost's poetry is "that of approaching a subject from its furthest
points rather than from the center. The diminutive, then, becomes a foil for the 'yonder.' Somewhere between outer space
and the microscope stands the poet [or bear], towering like a
giant over an ant and, at the same time, diminished by stars."[11]
Avoidance of the center is understandable if we visualize the
center as a still point between the poles—a still point during or
on which the caged animal takes stock of its condition and helplessly recommences its pacing. The image of impotent energy,
fruitless ratiocination, is discernible even in some of Frost's telescopic pieces.

In "Too Anxious for Rivers," for example, even as the
pendulum swings far outward, celebrating infinity, we are pulled
back to the limits of what we know by a refusal to see or specu-
late too far. The landscape perceived by the eye is transformed
first into a *paysage moralisé* reminiscent of Auden ("The truth is
the river flows into the canyon / Of Ceasing to Question What
Doesn't Concern Us") and then into a series of mythical solu-
tions to the problem of the universe, charming tall tales that
relegate human curiosity to the status of childish inquisitiveness.

> The world as we know is an elephant's howdah;
> The elephant stands on the back of a turtle;
> The turtle in turn on a rock in the ocean.
> And how much longer a story has science
> Before she must put out the light on the children
> And tell them the rest of the story is dreaming?

Like "Wild Grapes" or "Birches," "Too Anxious for Rivers" comes to a halt with a gesture toward human feeling, "the essay of love"; but the pendulum will inevitably swing away from this earthly experiment back toward space, attracted by the magnet of our incorrigibly speculative appetites. Between the dreaming children and the conjectures of Lucretius paces the bear.

The bear's dilemma is more pungently conveyed in the shorter lines and restrictive form of the sonnet "Why Wait for Science," where such boundaries as rhyme scheme and syllable count emphasize the limits of our world. But a more noteworthy use of the sonnet to explore our metaphysical extremes is "Any Size We Please," a poem which, like "The Bear," benefits from being read in the light of Frost's remarks (page 158) about expansion and contraction. "We throw our arms wide with a gesture of religion to the universe; we close them around a person."[12] But there is no person here, at least no other person; the poem limns an isolation which recalls Frost's early image of form in the *Amherst Student* letter, that "The background is hugeness and confusion shading away from where we stand into black and utter chaos; and against the background any small man-made figure of order and concentration."[13] "Any Size We Please" animates this small figure:

> No one was looking at his lonely case,
> So like a half-mad outpost sentinel,
> Indulging an absurd dramatic spell,
> Albeit not without some shame of face,
> He stretched his arms out to the dark of space
> And held them absolutely parallel
> In infinite appeal. Then saying, 'Hell'
> He drew them in for warmth of self-embrace.
> He thought if he could have his space all curved
> Wrapped in around itself and self-befriended,
> His science needn't get him so unnerved.
> He had been too all out, too much extended.
> He slapped his breast to verify his purse
> And hugged himself for all his universe.

The successive gestures here are true to Frost's earlier description, only more reflexive, for the figure hugs himself. In the last line, *for* is ambiguous: he hugged himself both *on behalf of* and also *instead of* or *in place of* his universe; that is, the isolated figure has to provide its own warmth of embrace if the universe (as preoccupied with self as he?) will not embrace him.

One should remember at this point that a hug is a characteristically ursine gesture. This small figure is another version of the caged bear caught between centripetal and centrifugal impulses. Far from seeming cramped, however, the universal cage is now too vast for comfort. The self-hugging is a strategy of consolation, but consolation can only occur when the restless swing of dialectic is stilled (however briefly) by the confidence that we know certain things about the nature of the cosmos. "On Looking Up by Chance at the Constellations" is another example of human avoidance of getting "unnerved" by science, this time in temporal rather than spatial terms. "Any Size We Please" focuses on a single figure against infinite space; "On Looking Up" dwarfs the present moment by measuring it against celestial time.

It is undoubtedly because of its concern with time that "On Looking Up" uses a line that is, for Frost, notably long and leisured, a roughly five-stress line with a generous sprinkling of extra syllables allowed between stresses. The slightly padded, ponderous, and lulling effect ("You'll wait a long, long time for anything much / To happen in heaven beyond the floats of cloud") soothes us into acquiescing to the poem's comfortable denial of apocalypse ("But nothing ever happens, no harm is done . . ."). We are still nodding to the steady beat when the poem slyly surprises us:

> We may as well go patiently on with our life,
> And look elsewhere than to stars and moon and sun
> For the shocks and changes we need to keep us sane.
> It is true the longest drouth will end in rain,
> The longest peace in China will end in strife.
> Still it wouldn't reward the watcher to stay awake
> In hopes of seeing the calm of heaven break
> On his particular time and personal sight.
> That calm seems certainly safe to last tonight.

The poem reassures us ironically, by asserting the limitedness of human experience in time. In "Any Size We Please" space must be "curved" to accommodate human needs; here it seems that time must be varied to provide us with needed interest. Unadapted by or to human needs, space in both poems seems unfathomably foreign, vast, and unyielding, in contrast to the small if exigent scale of what people know and want. The poems are meditations on the note sounded in a letter Frost wrote Untermeyer in 1925: "I might sustain the theme indefinitely that you nor I nor nobody knows as much as he doesn't know. And that isn't all: There is nothing anybody knows, however absolutely, that isn't more or less vitiated as a fact by what he doesn't know."[14] But if ignorance vitiates what is known, it can also be a comforting condition. A state of semi-knowledge, or doubt, is more characteristic of the human condition than either the telescopic or the microscopic extreme, and Frost beautifully captures the uneasy teetering of doubt and belief in "Skeptic."

> Far star that tickles for me my sensitive plate
> And fries a couple of ebon atoms white,
> I don't believe I believe a thing you state.
> I put no faith in the seeming facts of light.
>
> I don't believe I believe you're the last in space,
> I don't believe you're anywhere near the last,
> I don't believe what makes you red in the face
> Is after explosion going away so fast.

Frost's negations are put to unsettling use in this cagey speculation about eschatology, or rather speculation about speculation about eschatology. "I don't believe I believe" is a good example of the way Frost extracts a maximum of significance from an idiom. "Believe" implies a creed, but the common phrase "I don't believe" has a distinct idiomatic pressure of its own (much as "I don't like her" is not the logical opposite of "I like her" but rather implies a positive dislike).

The lonely figure in "Any Size We Please" wants his space "curved" to a human shape and scale, and we believe in his wish. But "Skeptic" is tinged by an irony that makes its speaker's wishes unstable, double-edged. For example, "I don't believe I believe you're the last in space" may mean either that the universe is far larger than we have been told or far smaller. Generally the first two stanzas express discomfort with scientific doctrine and/or the evidence of the senses ("the seeming facts of light"). But the final and most successful stanza shifts to a less abstractly formulated dialectic.

> The universe may or may not be very immense.
> As a matter of fact there are times when I am apt
> To feel it close in tight against my sense
> Like a caul in which I was born and still am wrapped.

These extraordinary lines manage to embody thought in physical terms. Their connection with what has come before is tenuous in that the first two stanzas do not approach this level of poetic intensity; but there is a connection. The poem is preoccupied with the alternative ways in which we may apprehend the world. The caged animal, the earthbound being born *and still wrapped* in a caul, represent one extreme of how it feels to be human.

One critic has written of Frost's cosmology, "Moving with the wary caution of the sceptic, utilizing only the observable, Frost manages to construct a universe at once tenable to our modern eyes and satisfying to our thirst for justice and meaning."[15] Such a statement pays tribute to the unpretentious and shrewd quality of the meditative poems; but it does not adequately acknowledge the contradictory nature of "the observable" when what is observed is so enormous. Frost's mind was never less monolithic, never more apt to sway back and forth, than when he contemplated immensity. The wary caution of the skeptic implies, for Frost's work, many mental toings and froings, not at all a fixed view of any cosmic order whole or partial. The late Frost's refusal ever to *express* anything singly was a symptom of a profounder habit of *perceiving* things doubly, as witness the following anecdote.

> In 1957, when the United Nations was given a huge rock of solid iron ore by Sweden, and it was decided to build the rock into the UN building, as a symbol of nature's strength and man's unity, Frost was invited to "write a poem celebrating the ideal of the interdependence of the nations." Frost rejected the prescribed theme of the invitation, noting ironically that iron could indeed be used to strengthen the UN building, but it could also be used for weapons of war, which was historically the way with nature and men. After rejecting the UN invitation, Frost wrote a couplet which expressed his own convictions:
>
>> Nature within her inmost self divides,
>> To trouble men with having to take sides.

Later, in 1959, Frost commented upon his couplet: "I was thinking when I wrote of that lump of iron in the United Nations building, that stands for unity. *But, even as you look at it, it seems to split.* You think of tools that can be made of it, and you think of weapons. . . ."[16] (Italics mine.)

ii *The limits of looking*

The dialectical swing which tends to govern the motion of
Frost's star poems is most clearly discernible when the speaker
(stargazer, sentinel, peaceful shepherd, skeptic, chance looker-
up at the constellations) has an unhindered view of the sky, be
that view telescopic or microscopic. Some of Frost's most tren-
chant poems about the universe, however, never quite arrive at
the point of contemplating a cosmic dialectic. "Utilizing the observable," as Rechnitz calls it, may mean that precious little gets
to be observed. The same kind of refusal to declare absolutes
that charges "Any Size We Please" or "Skeptic" with wry tension is at work somewhat differently in poems like "Neither Far
Out nor In Deep" and "Afterflakes," which lay down the limits of
vision.

"Neither Far Out nor In Deep" is not specifically about stars;
it is one of Frost's relatively few poems about the ocean. Most of
all, though, it is emphatically a poem about contemplating immensity and about the limits of such contemplation. "The people
along the sand" who "look at the sea all day" do not seem to
have reached the point of alternating senses of the universe's
smallness and vastness which is captured in "Skeptic"; they are
notably unskeptical, and the poem's irony is separate from their
simple gaze.

> They cannot look out far.
> They cannot look in deep.
> But when was that ever a bar
> To any watch they keep?

Randall Jarrell's comment on this poem is also his critical
summary of those poems he considers among Frost's strongest:

> . . . so far from being obvious, optimistic, orthodox, many of
> these poems are extraordinarily subtle and strange, poems
> which express an attitude that, at its most extreme, makes
> pessimism seem a hopeful evasion; they begin with a flat and
> terrible reproduction of the evil in the world and end by say-
> ing: It's so; and there's nothing you can do about it; and if
> there were, would *you* ever do it? The limits which existence
> approaches and falls back from have seldom been stated with
> such bare composure.[17]

In "Neither Far Out nor In Deep" there is indeed a striking collocation of what Jarrell calls "the limits which existence approaches" and the actual limits of physical perception. The two kinds of limits tend to become identified with one another in late Frost. Poems about seeing the stars (or the sea) are also about perceiving universal truths; both kinds of perception are drastically limited, but the poems are free of distraction and clearly declare their own blind spots.

Whereas the omniscient speaker of "Neither Far Out" uses the third person to note the befuddlement of "the people along the sand," a first-person poem like "Afterflakes" necessarily locates the limits of looking closer to home. The speaker is caught in his own limited perspective.

> In the thick of a teeming snowfall
> I saw my shadow on snow.
> I turned and looked back up at the sky,
> Where we still look to ask the why
> Of everything below.
>
> If I shed such a darkness,
> If the reason was in me,
> That shadow of mine should show in form
> Against the shapeless shadow of storm,
> How swarthy I must be.
>
> I turned and looked back upward.
> The whole sky was blue;
> And the thick flakes floating at a pause
> Were but frost knots on an airy gauze,
> With the sun shining through.

The sky-watcher here looks up as far and deep as he can to discover a reason for darkness—a reason that turns out to be "in him." Through the prism of self, his sense of the world reverses itself between the first and third stanzas. The action of the poem is a floundering search for a center of awareness from which to launch the processes of perception. Is the world heliocentric or anthropocentric? Where are we to look for the explanation of what we perceive; and how far (or deep) can we perceive at all?

As early as Frost's first book, an inconspicuous poem, "Stars," executes a somewhat similar gesture, asking whether otherness is to be invested with human significance, whether we are to look skyward for comprehension and compassion. So it would seem; the stars "congregate . . . as if with keenness for our fate." Yet finally the stars are seen as neutral, "with neither love nor hate, / Those stars like some snow-white/Minerva's snow-white marble eyes / Without the gift of sight."

Samuel Coale has described the abrupt turn in "Stars"—from a sympathetic to a neutral heaven—as an example of Frost's preference for what Coale calls "emblemism" over symbolism in his poetics.

> Perhaps the best example of Frost's theory of emblemism can be seen in the early "Stars." The stars in the poem "congregate" above "our tumultuous snow" as if they were symbols of some more permanent meaning, as if they symbolized a "keenness for our fate." Frost, however, rejects such personification of natural objects, rejects the "symbolism" he describes, and prefers to take the stars *as they are* with neither "love nor hate." They are significant by virtue of their permanence as natural objects, by their very existence and distance from us, but they cannot be symbolically defined or personified; they remain not allegoric or symbolic but in Frost's terms emblematic of man's encounter with the very presence of existence itself. . . .[18]

But the crucial distinction here is not that between two terms which approach the synonymous, emblem and symbol—it is between two frames of mind. One imaginative attitude endows the stars with intelligence and hence significance for us; the opposing impulse drains them of animation and hence of significance. Partly because "Stars" is an early poem, there is in it no clearly felt "I" in contrast to the stars' otherness, and as a result the tension of the poem is dissipated, the location of its center of awareness blurred to a vague "we." Nevertheless, "Stars" is important and characteristic. For whether we read it as an early example of Frost's rebellion against symbolism or as a presage of his lifelong sense of the impediments to perception, "Stars" clearly defeats some of the very expectations it sets up, conjuring up the stars' concern with us, hedging such a possibility with a Frostian "as if," and finally scotching it.

"Stars" touches on a double or reciprocal limit of vision: our limited power to see or read the stars' interest, and the stars' blindness and coldness vis-à-vis us. Some of the later star pieces reiterate this double jeopardy:

> Have I not walked without an upward look
> Of caution under stars that very well
> Might not have missed me when they shot and fell?
> It was a risk I had to take—and took.
>
> ("Bravado")

But more often the limits of human vision are in the foreground.

> We've looked and looked, but after all where are we?
> Do we know any better where we are,
> And how it stands between the night tonight
> And a man with a smoky lantern chimney?
> How different from the way it ever stood?
>
> ("The Star-Splitter")

> From following walls I never lift my eye
> Except at night to places in the sky
> Where showers of charted meteors let fly.
>
> ("A Star in a Stone-Boat")

Sometimes the vastness and strangeness of what meets the upward gaze is received with almost sensuous abandonment. Contrast the deliciousness of being lost in what follows with a poem about terrestrial lostness such as "Desert Places."

> The clouds, the source of rain, one stormy night
> Offered an opening to the source of dew;
> Which I accepted with impatient sight,
> Looking for my old skymarks in the blue.
>
> But stars were scarce in that part of the sky,
> And no two were of the same constellation—
> No one was bright enough to identify;
> So 'twas with not ungrateful consternation,
>
> Seeing myself well lost once more, I sighed,
> "Where, where in Heaven am I? But don't tell me!
> Oh, opening clouds, by opening on me wide,
> Let's let my heavenly lostness overwhelm me."
>
> ("Lost in Heaven")

Rather than the opposition of two metaphysical extremes characteristic of our caged and pacing bear, these passages measure various degrees of heavenly and earthly lostness—a lostness which can be companionable, even pleasurable to wallow in, but the sense of which (like a Wordsworthian epiphany) is not always equally available to us. One might redefine Frost's dialectic of outflung arms and tight embrace by observing that sometimes the embrace is of another person, sometimes of the self, and sometimes of a vastness which can only be apprehended by risking immersion in the reaches of the cosmos.

In the late work the Brad McLaughlins, those who insistently study the heavens to "satisfy a life-long curiosity / About our place among the infinities," become more frequent, and poems are often spoken from the consciousness of such a curiosity instead of by bemused neighbors. Nevertheless, the conclusions these star-gazers reach are seldom final; rather, they gauge the extent of their heavenly lostness.

iii *Say something*

A recurrent strand in this study has been Frost's sensitivity to sound—a theme to which it is useful to return whenever we run the risk of overemphasizing the visual in his work. Cosmic intimations, of course, can be expressed in all sorts of human terms. "The Bear," "Skeptic," and "Any Size We Please" use the physiology of gesture, open or closed arms, pacing, the sensation of tightness given by a caul, to convey the stuffy tightness or expansive bagginess of the universe as it may happen to be felt at a given time. But what of the language and voice ways, the sound of sense so important to the younger Frost—are these concerns that the late poems have abandoned? Does the compelling quality of the poetry falter in the absence of such conversational modes as govern, for example, most of the work in *North of Boston?*

It seems likely that the relative neglect of much of Frost's late work results from the undramatic texture of that work. Poems about the cosmos tend to be lonely; there is rarely more than one speaker heard, so that the interplay of voice on voice so masterfully portrayed in "Home Burial" or "The Death of the Hired Man" is lacking. Readers who respond easily to voice-dramas like "The Witch of Coös" or "A Servant to Servants" must approach "The Bear" and its ilk with a different kind of aural imagination, for these later poems do not limn their dialectic by means of dialogue. The single voice which is all that is usually heard is not mimetic of a farmer's or wife's or witch's rhythms and vocabulary; rather, it is a neutral voice which is mod-

ulated—like Coleridge's water-bug—by the processes of
thought. (In "Etherealizing" Frost seems to be conscious of the
danger of aridity which pure thought poses for poetry.)

The mode of the star poems tends to be thinking aloud or
talking to oneself. There is usually no one else to talk to except
(a big except) the cosmos, or God, a word Frost seldom uses.
Not that this otherness is only present in poems about stars; it
plays a continuing role in Frost's awareness, as witness the couplet "There was never nought. / There was always thought," or,
in "A Considerable Speck,"

> I have a mind myself and recognize
> Mind when I meet with it in any guise.
> No one can know how glad I am to find
> On any sheet the least display of mind.

Assuming the presence of an indistinct otherness, this solitary
voice has the choice of addressing itself or the other—a choice
which blurs into a single process when the other is so vague (is
"Skeptic," for example, spoken to the "far star" or to the self?).
Perhaps the criterion for distinguishing between a soliloquy and
an utterance to some other is the result: does that other answer?
The question, once we have recognized it, resounds throughout
a great deal of Frost's work. "The Most of It" never quite answers the question of whether or not response is forthcoming,
but it does provide an unmatched expression of the lonely longing for not an echo but an answer. The sylvan scenery has fallen
away from the later poems, but not the impulse.

> He thought he kept the universe alone;
> For all the voice in answer he could wake
> Was but the mocking answer of his own
> From some tree-hidden cliff across the lake.
> Some morning from the boulder-broken beach
> He would cry out on life, that what it wants
> Is not its own love back in copy speech,
> But counter-love, original response.[19]

Speech; response. If this is not to be had from the cosmos, then
the speaker provides it himself in "copy speech" (compare "and
hugged himself for all his universe" in "Any Size We Please"), by
naming whatever of otherness is available for naming. In "The
Most of It" the "embodiment" is finally named by the poet (if not

the speaker) as a "great buck," but we are left in doubt as to whether the buck is the desired emanation from the universe which "he" has been seeking or merely a form of copy speech. The apparition of the buck may be an illusion—not that it does not in fact appear, but that its appearance may not have anything to do with human need. How to regard the phenomenon remains a mystery and a suspension in "The Most of It," which ends abruptly "—and that was all." The suspension of any solution of the mystery of appearances, the nature of otherness, is echoed in Frost's Delphic statement about "facts"—a statement about which Poirier goes so far as to say that "there is no use pretending that statements such as this make any immediate sense" (284):

> But people say to me: The facts themselves aren't enough. You've got to do something to them, haven't you? They can't be poetical unless the poet handles them. To that I have a very simple answer. It's this: Anything you do to the facts falsifies them, but anything the facts do to you—yes, even against your will; yes, resist them with all your strength—transforms them into poetry.[20]

Certainly the statement is playful and obscure, but hardly Heraclitean in its difficulty. Suppose the "facts" are, for example, stars—that is, things which plainly exist but which are nearly impossible to reach, grasp, define, or extort replies from. It may become a little clearer why Frost recommends (in poetic, not practical terms) wise passivity and patience over the anxious attempt to "do" something to stars, to "handle" them. Judging by "The Most of It," any reply from a star would be hard to recognize, hard to prove genuine, and hard to interpret, as if our very will for an original response had falsified whatever response came.

In "For Once, Then, Something," "All Revelation," "An Unstamped Letter in Our Rural Letter Box," and "Take Something Like a Star," a kind of dialogue is sought—and very tentatively won—between a human being and celestial otherness. Facts in these poems are "resisted" with a good deal of energy on both sides. People resist the inscrutability of stars, their reluctance to communicate or reply; and stars, or otherness, seem to resist human attempts to extract love, "original response" from them. The resulting atmosphere is far from cozily sentimental; star poems do not have happy endings. But neither is it wholly bleak;

rather the climate is one of a stimulating strenuousness, a refusal to give up easily.

The question of just what, or how much, can be salvaged from otherness by dint of persistence and imagination, is the subject of "For Once, Then, Something," a poem which itself quite successfully fends off attempts at paraphrase and easy summations. "What was that whiteness? / Truth? A pebble of quartz? For once, then, something." The poem has no intention of answering its own question definitively.

The image of looking at the sky as it is reflected in water recalls "Neither Far Out nor In Deep"; and "For Once, Then, Something," although lighter in tone, does share something of the other poem's pessimism about the human chances of ever really discerning something, or perhaps anything. The familiar Frostian dialectic gives with one hand and takes away with the other so adroitly that the end of the poem is perfectly poised between perception and deception, those twinned possibilities whose interplay has rippled and shimmered throughout the poem in a charming but ultimately frustrating version of the caged bear's swaying back and forth. At one extreme what is reflected is "me myself in the summer heaven godlike," at the other a chip of pure essence—or a rock. Comparing "For Once, Then" to "On the Heart's Beginning to Cloud the Mind," Poirier notes that " 'For Once' . . . is also a poem about trying to have a vision, trying to see 'something' which is probably only that— 'some thing' and not a metaphor for anything."[21] Probably. But to disrupt the delicate balance of Frostian perhapses is to violate the decorum of the poem.

"All Revelation" begins with what might be a reference, from another angle, to the peering figure of "For Once"; we need only locate ourselves within the well—or, as has been suggested, within the birth canal:

> A head thrusts in as for the view,
> But where it is it thrusts in from
> Or what it is it thrusts into
> By that Cyb'laean avenue,
> And what can of its coming come,
>
> And whither it will be withdrawn,
> And what take hence or leave behind,
> These things the mind has pondered on

> A moment and still asking gone.
> Strange apparition of the mind!

Perhaps even more than "The Most of It" or "For Once, Then, Something," "All Revelation" captures Frost's curiosity, his preoccupation with reaching out toward the unknown, on a scale both universal and personal (the "counter-love, original response" of "The Most of It" is here "Eyes seeking the response of eyes"). Whereas in "For Once, Then," uncertainty is located in the never precisely defined nature of the glimpsed otherness, here the nature and provenance of the seeking head are just as mysterious as the universe which is being explored. A single line such as "What can of its coming come" presents a richly polysemic spectrum of possible meanings.

In a stimulating essay, Frank Lentricchia emphasizes the "perilous balance" achieved in "All Revelation," a poem in which, as he says, Frost can somehow move in and out of the constituting mind. Doubleness of vision is thoroughgoing in this poem, extending to the double force of the final line, "All revelation has been ours." "It is we who reveal the world—as we desire to see it revealed—and by so doing we reveal the revealing self, we reveal ourselves."[22] The revelation is "ours" in the sense that we seek and find it; also in that it originates in our desire for clarity, so that any response revelation yields up springs from the source of our own need. Lentricchia writes of the "ironic consciousness which enables Frost to maintain his double vision, his skepticism, and his common sense." Emphasis on Frost's skepticism is justified, so long as it does not obscure the very unskeptical longing for response that motivates what Lentricchia calls "the act of the mind, the dynamic thrust of consciousness." We may visualize the thrust as inwardly or outwardly aimed; we may imagine the thing at the bottom of the well to be truth, a pebble, or nothing; what is important is that we not underestimate the force of the curiosity which causes all the craning and peering in Frost's poems.

In "An Unstamped Letter in Our Rural Letter Box," the longing for response is somewhat more focused and even satisfied, perhaps because the otherness is more exactly identified. Not that communion between the person and otherness is easy. "An Unstamped Letter," indeed, inhibits speech in two ways. The poem defines itself in its title as the missive of a (highly literate)

"tramp astrologer" who has used the addressee's pasture for a
camp. The poem begins chattily with explanations as to where
the writer has slept and ends with a thought for the tramp's
unwitting host as "farming well—or pretty well." What takes
place between these local, earthly details is a very unearthly
moment—an epiphany (or to use a more Frostian word, a revelation) which also comes as close as Frost does anywhere to evok-
ing a *déjà vu.*

> It may have been at two o'clock
> That under me a point of rock
> Developed in the grass and fern,
> And as I woke afraid to turn
> Or so much as uncross my feet,
> Lest having wasted precious heat
> I never should again be warmed,
> The largest firedrop ever formed
> From two stars' having coalesced
> Went streaking molten down the west.
> And then your tramp astrologer
> From seeing this undoubted stir
> In Heaven's firm-set firmament,
> Himself had the equivalent,
> Only within. Inside the brain
> Two memories that long had lain,
> Now quivered toward each other, lipped
> Together, and together slipped;
> And for a moment all was plain
> That men have thought about in vain.

The comet, a heavenly conjunction, triggers a conjunction in the
mind, a revelation which is described emphatically but ob-
scurely; the two memories and their combination remain obscure, the light of revelation falls obliquely.

If all has become "plain / That men have thought about in
vain," why does the poem not suit its action to the word and
reveal plainly what is plain? Such a revelation is prohibited, I
think, by the same decorum that prevents the star-gazing tramp
from addressing the farmer in person (or prevents the gazer at
well-curbs from dragging the pebble up to the light and verifying
his surmise). The tramp prefers to leave an indirect sign of his
own passage (he might after all have chosen not to leave any
letter, but he is a poet), thus communicating at a remove, re-

specting the double decorum of his own mysterious experience and of the separateness of another person's experience. The poem is quite explicit on the subject of this separateness:

> 'Tis possible you may have seen,
> Albeit through a rusty screen,
> The same sign Heaven showed your guest.
> Each knows his own discernment best.

An unstamped letter written by a departed traveler has the character, as utterance, of a poem or prayer or any words which are both directed outward from an impulse to share and also constrained by a sense of limits and respect for boundaries. Revelation seems to mean, especially here, a temporary dissolution of boundaries, both out in the heavens and "inside the brain." Whatever occurs inside the tramp-astrologer's brain, if it is "the equivalent . . . within" of the stir in the heavens, is an interior shock, a microcosmic catastrophe. It is in retreat from this inner shock, moreover, that the speaker has recourse to the gestures of social decorum and wry privacy that finish the poem—like the speaker's in "A Star in a Stone-Boat," who rarely lifts his gaze from walls after his experience with a star. The formal isolation of the poem's procedure is a way of conveying the privacy of revelation and even of protecting that privacy—yet the letter is written, is deposited and found in the rural letter box. In a sense, the fact of our reading it is a response; the act of reading this poem is part of a chain of communication that began with the stir in heaven.

"Take Something Like a Star" addresses itself to otherness directly, without the mediation of a letter to a neighbor, a tricky reflection in water, or a head "thrust in." Precisely because this poem is a straightforward address to a star, it shows with special poignance the act of seeking response.

> O Star (the fairest one in sight),
> We grant your loftiness the right
> To some obscurity of cloud—
> It will not do to say of night,
> Since dark is what brings out your light.
> Some mystery becomes the proud.
> But to be wholly taciturn
> In your reserve is not allowed.

> Say something to us we can learn
> By heart and when alone repeat.
> Say something!

The request for "something we can learn" is the same as the request in "The Most of It" for "counter-love, original response." But in that poem, or in "For Once, Then, Something," a quizzical acceptance of the unknowable nature of much of the universe is embodied in the pebble or the buck, the inscrutable apparitions of nature; *this* is the response that is given, unsatisfying though it may be. In "An Unstamped Letter" the fortuitous, miraculous conjunction of planets and memories comes unsought and almost wordlessly (at least in the laconic account the poem gives of it). Here, by contrast, the expressed need is for a less intuitive, more rational answer, something in words, a lesson "we can learn by heart." Is the lesson sought that of scientific facts about the universe? The second half of the poem, even while it requests talk of Fahrenheit and Centigrade from the star, doubts that such knowledge is what we need of otherness, or what it can give us.

> And it says, "I burn."
> But say with what degree of heat.
> Talk Fahrenheit, talk Centigrade,
> Use language we can comprehend.
> Tell us what elements you blend.
> It gives us strangely little aid,
> But does tell something in the end.
> And steadfast as Keats' Eremite,
> Not even stooping from its sphere,
> It asks a little of us here.
> It asks of us a certain height,
> So when at times the mob is swayed
> To carry praise or blame too far,
> We may take something like a star
> To stay our minds on and be staid.

The star's final message has nothing to do with words but everything to do with human imagination, with what we insist on making out of whatever seems to be out there. The end of the poem falls off in excitement from the beginning, but this slackening seems appropriate, for the poem traces and enacts a transition. From a desperate desire for response from the universe, we are thrown back to the expedient of (stoically, "staidly") finding some message in the star's very refusal to speak. The end of the poem, a kind of lecture on the virtues of moderation, has a Horatian elegance but is at variance with the radical isolation of the opening. The one consistent point about the star is the sense of its distance and loftiness, its refusal to stoop; we must stand on tiptoe instead. Stretching, we achieve "a certain height," but our urgent desire to *know* seems to get lost in the staidness recommended at the end.

In a very late poem, "Away!", that desire is satisfied, the connection with otherness is made—and perhaps found wanting.

> And I may return
> If dissatisfied
> With what I learn
> From having died.

What would "dissatisfy" Frost in death would be the blank nothingness of a region where there is nothing left to learn, no talk, no something to learn by heart. As long as life lasted, there was curiosity and uncertainty, the hope and fear familiar from the pacing bear. Speculating continually about death, Frost never quite convinced himself that the nature of the other side was knowable from here. "With so many ladders going up everywhere, there must be something for them to lean against."[23] Must there?

Frost's poems become clearer and starker as the wash of the world's colors drops off; and as this happens, there emerge the outlines of a vast but personal dialogue. Beyond the cycles of terrestrial weather, we are left with what Frost once called his lover's quarrel with the world—the black and white rhythm of question and (perhaps) answer. The bleak, or at least austere nature of the subject matter—stars, death, last things—is matched by an austerity of style which has little to do with Frost's superb ear for human speech or eye for landscape. It is an austerity which responds to a laconic cosmos in kind— Frost's own version of the imagination pressing against the pressure of reality.

Frost's pithy, often epigrammatic late poems have moved away from eclogue, drama, narrative, even lyric: almost nothing is left but thought which is also a wholly unsentimental kind of feeling. Frost is seldom regarded as a minimalist, but Wade Van

Dore's account of some of the poet's late remarks sheds a fascinating (if, alas, not wholly reliable) light on the bareness of expression so conspicuous in the star poems.

> At times I've felt like paring my writing down until nothing was left but an exclamation mark—which could be seen as the shortest poem ever written. Often I have scary doubts about words. Didn't Thoreau say "If words were invented to conceal thought, then printing is a great improvement on a bad invention"? Or something like that. Writing is a kind of weakness, and once you get along in it, I expect the greatest thing would be not to write at all. Then we could hope the act of *non*writing would be seen as the ultimate gesture—like that look a dying person can give instead of words. Maybe the best thing Eliot ever wrote was that about the world ending not with a bang but a whimper. Unless words are extensions of whimpers and terrifying screams they can't be taken too seriously.[24]

These words are cited by Van Dore in the trivializing context of Frost's subtlety and coyness ("Our poet went so far in cultivating a teasing kind of subtlety that he couldn't at times resist trying to assume another's identity; or if not that, then disappear altogether . . ."). But Frost's "scary doubts" about words are too consonant with his other scary doubts not to be taken seriously. Having been enthralled by the beauty of language all his writing life, Frost may finally have approached the point of the ineffable. He did not stop writing as did—to take two examples—Laura Riding or Ezra Pound; but his writing was progressively pared down until it approached the slimness of an exclamation point. Impatient with our insistent human requests for words, words, words, the star answers only by doing what it does, burning—an act, perhaps, of non-writing, that "ultimate gesture." We will see that in the case of Seferis too, there is something in the act of writing about a quality like light that pushes up against the limitations of language and forces a poet to question the importance of modes of writing—dramatic, lyrical, narrative—that had seemed more than adequate until late in his career.

2. Seferis on Light

Not all of Greece is full of ancient remains; not every region of the country is a coast or an island. But none of Greece is immune

to light. The insistent presence and consequent fame of Greek
light have made the very phrase into something of a cliché both
for travelers in the country and for Greek poets.[25] A poet like
Seferis, who wants to use traditional sources but also to make
them his own, is faced, when it comes to the important experience of light, with the problems of how to pay homage to the
extraordinary nature of the element, remain true to his own
sense of it, and at the same time to avoid repeating the worn-out
metaphors to which previous writers on the same topic have had
recourse.

We saw in Chapter II that a similar problem confronted Seferis
when he came to write about the sea. The solution there lay in
steering clear of the shoals of rhapsodic generalization and
rhetorical vagueness. But it is more difficult to find a new way of
writing about light. A poetic image must be identified—isolated,
as it were—before it can be put to use. Light is easy to see, to
talk about, to praise; not so easy to isolate in our perception.
Light is not simply a thing seen; it affects the way everything is
seen, and thus becomes, or appears to become, a part of everything.

Difficult to separate from the world it helps to define, light
plays a role analogous to the way we experience language—a
relation that can be illustrated by adducing such linkages of lan-
guage-perception and light as phrases like "transparent style,"
"the tyranny of lucidity," or even the old chestnuts "casts fresh
light on," "see in a new light."[26] Language, like light, illumines; it
is lightlike also in its propensity to inhere, or seem to inhere, in
the thing illumined without actually *being* that thing.

I think it is not too farfetched to say that Seferis's thinking and
writing about Greek light can be interpreted as an attempt to
abolish the transparency of the famous Greek sun, that tyran-
nous lucidity shining daily over the stones, sea, and people. The
tyranny of Greek light lies in its intensity combined with its
ubiquity, its unrelenting continuity.

> . . . for a northerner to understand [the sun's] full implications
> requires a considerable effort of the imagination. It is not
> merely that our sun is more pallid than [Seferis's] or that we in
> the north seek the sun in summer while Greeks seek the
> shade. Perhaps one can come closer to its meaning for Seferis
> if one recalls that the tragedies of English drama take place at
> midnight, whereas those of Greek drama reach their catas-

trophe at high noon: the bloodstained worlds of Macbeth and
Orestes exist at the antipodes of night and day. W. H. Auden
. . . says farewell to the island of Ischia; observing that the
"Greeks used to call the Sun/He-who-smites-from-afar," he
comments on the hopelessness of life under such an unchanging, inescapable source of heat and brightness. Auden, however, is writing about the Italian *mezzogiorno* and the despair
of its relentless sun; the intenser sun of the Greek *mesimeri*
[noon] brings, beyond despair, tragic terror.[27]

These observations of Walter Kaiser are useful; but, like Auden, he is writing as a foreigner, a "northerner." What his passage leaves out is that for those accustomed to that blazing sun,
its extraordinary quality is nearly blotted out by familiarity
(which, as Proust knew, breeds not contempt but insensibility).
Precisely because, for a Greek, the quality of Greek light is an
everyday experience, an imaginative effort is needed in order to
perceive the sun and its light freshly. Returning to our comparison of light and language, such an effort is like the constant,
counterintuitive mental adjustments which must be made by
anyone who struggles to realize that an apparently true statement "ain't necessarily so." The Saussurean attempt to tint that
deceptively pellucid pane of glass which is our daily experience
of language is an illuminating *(sic)* analogue to Seferis's various
modes of showing that Greek light is less clear and simple than
we have been led to assume. We have been dazzled, that is, not
only by the distinctive quality of strong sunlight but also by the
persuasive currents of a literary and popular cultural tradition
which has conventionally enshrined "Greek light."

Seferis's first way of tackling the ubiquity and hence the invisibility of light is to draw a veil over the sun.[28] Some poems
depict light or the sun itself as a covering for some ulterior form
of illumination—a kind of arras beyond which a, or the final,
truth lurks. In this phase of imagery, the light is usually equated
with the sun. Later, notably in *Thrush,* the preferred word is
simply *light*—a more abstract term, which is accompanied by a
more abstract solution to the problem of light's invisibility. Light
in *Thrush* is seen as dialectically inseparable from its black ob-
verse; the image becomes double, an "ultimate paradox, both
life-giver and death-bringer, desired and feared, 'angelic' and
'black' "[29]

Finally, in *Three Secret Poems,* light is associated with the
idea of expression; self-expression; literary creation. Light,

white, the white or blank page, the mirror, and the mind merge
into a composite symbol which clearly shows the connection
between light and language. Instead of being transparently familiar to the point of invisibility, this symbol is a strenuous, felt link
between inside and outside, the poet and the world. By the time
we reach the end of *Three Secret Poems,* we are far from the
usual sun-baked turf of poets on Greek light.

i   *Who's suffering behind the golden silk, who's dying?*

Light cannot be a simple radiance illumining the things of this
world if we conceive of it as concealing something. The notion of
beyondness, of a truth that is hard to get at, has already mani-
fested itself in Seferic phrases such as "beyond the statues"
(*Mythical History* 5) or in the sense of the sea as an inscrutable
depth to be plumbed rather than a pleasant blue end in itself. In
several poems including "Our Sun," "Interlude of Joy," "Morning," "The King of Asine," and "Agianapa I" (though I shall not
discuss them all in detail), Seferis perceives the sun as a shield or
veil which conceals rather than lights up a mystery.

Before considering these poems, we should pause briefly to
remember some of the traditional associations of light. In the
Christian tradition from the Gospels on, light is a constellation of
moral virtues which touch on both ethical and physical behav-
ior—a *topos* which flourished in secular terms in the love poetry
of Petrarch and his school and was protested against by Shakespeare when he objected that "My mistress' eyes are nothing
like the sun" (Sonnet 130). The radiance of the sun, moral purity,
and physical blondness were combined into a nexus of poetic
symbol which was still in full force in the nineteenth century—
consider the heroines of novels like *Ivanhoe, The Marble Faun,*
and *Pierre* (not to mention Shakespeare's own Dark Lady). Like
any Western writer, Seferis is acutely aware of this heritage of
symbol and idea associated with light. But he is also equally and
perhaps more immediately in touch with the ancient Greek associations of light, which tend to touch on life itself—not the ethical aspects of a life but life as opposed to death and hence
consciousness as opposed to the lack of it. Two critics who
consider the ancient Greek sense of light cite its reflection in
language in a way that may by now be expected. "In Greek
mythology," writes Ariana Pherentinou, "light is the form of
Apollo which is associated with life, death, fate, and harmony,"

adding that "light for Seferis gathers together all the elements of ancient faith" and noting in a footnote that "in the ancient language [Ancient Greek] 'I see light' means 'I live, I exist' (*Libation Bearers* 1646)."[30] And Emily Vermeule in a penetrating passage of her book *Aspects of Death in Early Greek Art and Poetry* discusses the connection between light and life, most specifically the intelligence that characterizes living beings.

> . . . darkness is the oldest metaphor for both stupidity and death, and always the most common. As one of America's popular philosophers, Woody Allen, put it, "The thing to remember is that each time of life has its appropriate rewards, whereas, when you're dead, it's hard to find the light-switch." This was a cliché already in the epics of Gilgamesh or in the sun-hymns of Egypt. The Greeks also felt that the sun was the external monitor and shape of intelligence even when it had the disadvantage of being born new each day, not storing wisdom. The intelligence which reveals itself through the eye as brightness, like the inter-change between *auge* "ray" and *augazomai* "see," *leusso* "look" and *leukos* "white (light)," is the miniature mortal counterpart to Helios, the eye of heaven who knows everything because he sees everything. It is within this convention that we are all still called bright or dim. As the sun sees because there is fire in him, the agent or fluid of sight, so the Greek eye is its own source of light, looking brilliantly or darkly at friends and enemies. The eye feeds information to the mind. . . .

And Vermeule cites the modern Greek phrase *tha sas skotóso*— "I'll murder (literally *darken*) you."[31]

Light then, as the mind's alertness, is a sign of life. But in some of the prophetically dark prewar poems in *Logbook I* (1940) and elsewhere, Seferis wrenches light out of its traditional guise as illuminating and life-giving, and works to make light visible in a world of opacity and death and puzzlement. The very title of "Our Sun" may mean "our traditional idea of the sun, the sun we thought we had." But traditional verities do not work in a world of bewildered violence.

> This sun was mine and yours; we shared it.
> Who's suffering behind the golden silk, who's dying?
> A woman beating her dry breasts cried out: "Cowards,
> they've taken my children and torn them to shreds,
>   you've killed them

gazing at the fire-flies at dusk with a strange look,
lost in blind thought."
The blood was drying on a hand that a tree made green,
a warrior was asleep clutching the lance that flared against
his side.

It was ours, this sun, we saw nothing behind the gold
    embroidery
then the messengers came, dirty and breathless,
stuttering unintelligible words
twenty days and nights on the barren earth with thorns
    only
twenty days and nights feeling the bellies of the
    horses bleeding
and not a moment's break to drink the rain water.
You told them to rest first and then to speak, the
    light had blinded you.
They died saying: "We don't have time," touching some
    rays of the sun.
You'd forgotten that no one rests.
. . . .

This sun was ours; you kept all of it, you didn't want
    to follow me.
And it was then I found out about those things behind
    the gold and the silk:
we don't have the time. The messengers were right.

The poem is full of unanswered questions and uninterpreted
emblems. Does the woman in line 3, for example, answer the
question posed in line 2? The woman's words contain, *en abîme,*
a smaller and more remote image of the abstracted contemplation of light (the gazing at the fireflies); and the dried blood and
sleeping warrior present further riddles. The second stanza
seems concerned to decipher some of these mysteries, but the
gold embroidery of the sun obstructs vision rather than aiding it.
Nor is language capable of the task of interpreting: the words of
the messengers are unintelligible.[32] The passage recalls two other
places in Seferis where words fail to communicate meaning, or
simply fail to appear when needed: a passage from *Mythical
History* 22 and Part 2 of "On Stage," the second of the *Three
Secret Poems.*

So very much having passed before our eyes
that our eyes in the end saw nothing. . . .

Searching in collapsed buildings that might have been
   our homes
trying to remember dates and heroic deeds:
will we be able?

                                        (Mythical History)

Gongs were heard
and the messengers arrived—
I wasn't expecting them,
even the way they spoke beyond recollection—

                                        ("On Stage")

But it is in "Our Sun" that the image of the unintelligible or
undelivered message is most closely associated with another
failure of enlightenment, a sun that hides instead of showing.
"The light had blinded you"; the speaker's companion has perhaps been too dazzled to see that the messengers are on the
point of death, to see an unbearable truth. Is that why the companion finally keeps the sun to him or herself, not wanting to go
beyond a present state of knowledge and penetrate the veils—
from a reluctance to learn the unpalatable truth "behind the gold
and the silk?"

   Opposites collide in this poem: vision and blindness, speech
and unintelligibility. (One can also discern contrasts between
wetness and dryness: drying blood, dry breasts, bleeding horses,
drinking rainwater, and a wet mouth.) These are not unrelated
qualities crammed together surrealistically; it is rather that the
usual bonds of symbol and meaning have reversed themselves,
so that messengers are unintelligible, the sun blinding, and so
on. The themes suggested by the mere mention of such a nexus
of images and ideas recall some of the world's great tragedies,
the stories of Oedipus and of King Lear. Misunderstood messengers and messages loom especially large in the Oedipus legend,
and blindness and insight are the subjects of both. Most relevant, in both these plays light and understanding have a particularly vivid importance. The putting out of eyes (Oedipus's,
Gloucester's) is either a cause or a result of a sudden access of
visionary power. Lear does not lose his eyesight, but the old king
does deliver obscure but penetrating "messages" and persist-
ently attempts to undress, to strip off the veils and layers which
interfere with naked truth ("Off, lendings!" he says). Other veils,
concealing silks and embroideries, in *King Lear* include the misleading garments worn by the disguised Kent, Edgar's fantas-

tical madman's rags, and even the metaphorical disguises worn
by the villainous hypocrites of the play before they, so to speak,
unmask themselves.

In its compressed, elliptical way, "Our Sun" manages to suggest virtually all these tragic themes. Light, like language, carries a truth which may not be understood (and thus may also be
said to conceal that truth). Like a piece of fabric, the light of the
sun seems to show something, but that something is merely
surface; one must find out about the things *behind* the gold and
silk, but even finding them out may not save one from the knowledge that it is too late (Oedipus's discovery of the truth is too
late, as is the sudden recollection of Cordelia in the last scene of
King Lear). And yet, in terms of absolute truth, enlightenment in
tragedy never really comes too late. Despite the cost in human
suffering, it is better to pierce the gold embroidery and face
whatever is there.

"Morning," like "Our Sun" in *Logbook I,* also deals with inner
and outer blindness and includes the image of an obscuring
fabric; in "The King of Asine" "a startled bat/hit the light as an
arrow hits a shield"; in "Interlude of Joy" a puzzled observer
concludes

>   inexplicable.
> I don't understand people:
> no matter how much they play with colors
> they are all black.

But it is in "Agianapa I," published in *Logbook III* (1955), that
the themes of light and vision arise in a tragic context once
again. This time the reference to tragedy is more explicit than
was the case in "Our Sun," and the play is Seferis's perennial
favorite, the *Agamemnon*.

> And you see the light of the sun, as the ancients
> used to say.
> And yet I thought I was seeing all these years
> walking between the mountains and the sea
> talking by chance with men in perfect armour;
> strange, I didn't notice that I saw their voices only.
> It was the blood that forced them to talk, the ram
> that I slaughtered and spread at their feet;
> but that red carpet was not the light.
> Whatever they told me I had to recognize by touch

as when they hide you at night, hunted, in a stable
or when you finally reach the body of a full-breasted
   woman
and the room is thick with suffocating odors;
whatever they told me: fur and silk.

Strange, here I see the light of the sun; the gold net
where things quiver like fish
that a huge angel draws in
along with the nets of the fisherman.

Different kinds of vision are at issue here. To see the light of the sun "as the ancients used to say" means simply being alive, but the poem tries to take the idiom literally and discovers the complicated messages received by the various senses: seeing voices, recognizing by touch, taking commands from others ("whatever they told me . . . whatever they told me") or trusting the evidence of one's own perceptions. The red carpet speaks the language of violence and blood; it seems to have a message to deliver, but its message cannot be the same as that of light, since the blood of slaughter says death and seeing light means life. Any such paraphrase of the poem sounds painfully obvious, but Seferis's achievement here is to try to get back to simplicity, back to a lost directness of perception, within the limits of everyday language. Phrases like "seeing the light of the sun" do sound banal, but their meaning is not really simple. The gulf the poem makes us feel between the first line of the first stanza and the first line of the second stanza—lines superficially so similar—is very difficult to describe in words; the verb *to see,* the noun *light,* recur, but in a transfigured sense. (Transfiguration, a fresh vision, is also the theme of "Engomi" which closes *Logbook III*—"Agianapa I" opens it.)

The red carpet mentioned in "Agianapa I" hints at Aeschylus's *Agamemnon,* but the slaughtered rams and voices which respond to blood recall equally strongly the Nekyia of the *Odyssey.* It is not until the net in the final stanza that we truly approach the tragic constraints of the world of the *Oresteia* (even though the angel and fisherman in the same stanza have a faintly Christian ring). We have already seen how the deceptive and obstructive nature of light makes it resemble a concealing fabric in "Our Sun"; we have noted that poem's affinities to tragedies of vision and blindness like *Oedipus the King* in which the approach to truth is also the tearing off of a veil. But in the

Agamemnon, unquestionably the most important ancient tragedy for Seferis, the protean symbol of the cloth (Aeschylus refers to it variously as a robe, cloak, and fishing net) has a somewhat different and quite particular force—a force for which we should be alert in Seferis as well.

> In the poetry of Seferis, [the] "net," like [the words] "cloth-fabric-sheet," is constantly reiterated with the meaning of unavoidable fate [*moira*] and simultaneously of every trick, snare, or deception which life stages. The memory of the *Oresteia* and the net of Clytemnestra are everywhere clear. According to tradition, Clytemnestra, after having led Agamemnon to the bath, wrapped him in a robe and killed him with a sword. In another version of the myth, Agamemnon was entangled in the net which Clytemnestra threw over him and, unable to escape, was murdered with a trident. In the *Agamemnon* of Aeschylus the same difficulties exist with regard to the manner of the murder. . . . But in any case, in the poetry of Seferis both versions are retained with about the same significance.[33]

The net, robe, sheet, or whatever it is (and Aeschylus's vagueness is probably intentional and certainly suggestive) is both the symbol of fate and one of its instruments. Even if we regard it as merely the tool of a malevolent will, it is a fearful device, none the less entangling for being visible. In "Our Sun" the speaker attempts to penetrate the embroidered draperies of the sun and see what is hidden. If the light of the sun is a "gold net / where things quiver like fish," light would seem not to conceal, or at least to offer countless openings to the curious eye. But the frisson one feels at the end of "Agianapa I" comes, I think, from the realization that we—"I," "things"—are all *inside* a great net, drawn in quivering like fish. We may not be destined for Agamemnon's end; the "full-breasted woman" is indoors, in darkness not light, and a stanza away. But we are certainly in the grip of a strong and mysterious power, feeling its complicated energy—not merely basking in banal sunlight.

By implicitly or explicitly comparing light to a cloth, these poems show that illumination itself can be stripped away—that behind one layer of vision lies another. In "Agianapa I," "Our Sun," and "Morning" (and also to some extent in "Interlude of Joy" and "The King of Asine"), the movement tends to be from emphasis on the mystery of light to some kind of unveiling and revelation—a revelation in turn which often serves to enhance the essentially enigmatic nature of things. Neither transparent nor invisible, light is still luminous, a rich source of meaning which the reader is encouraged to help supply. To attempt to define the meanings of light in these poems is to set forth a series of synonyms both for what the light illuminates and for what it is in itself. But again, such an attempt is also a way of avoiding *assuming* light, taking it for granted as pellucid ornamentation.

ii   *Angelic and black*

                    You say I am repeating
Something I have said before. I shall say it again.
Shall I say it again? In order to arrive there,
To arrive where you are, to get from where you are not,
    You must go by a way wherein there is no ecstasy.
In order to arrive at what you do not know
    You must go by a way which is the way of ignorance.
In order to possess what you do not possess
    You must go by the way of dispossession.
In order to arrive at what you are not
    You must go through the way in which you are not.
And what you do not know is the only thing you know
And what you own is what you do not own
And where you are is where you are not.

An avid student of *Four Quartets,* Seferis seems to have agreed with these lines from "East Coker" that one way to approach something difficult of access, even intangible, is through opposition. From light as a concealing cloth Seferis's poems move to the famous image in *Thrush,* light as its own antithesis. This dialectic of light and darkness is a natural extension of the vision in poems like "Our Sun" and "Agianapa I"; behind the silken veils and gold embroidery lies blackness. Already present at the close of "Interlude of Joy" (see page 185 above), this notion is set forth more fully—and dramatically—in the journal passages of 1946 both before and during Seferis's stay on the island of Poros, where *Thrush* was composed. Still in Athens, Seferis wrote in June 1946 of the

drama of the blood which is played out here around us between the light and the sea, and which few people are aware of . . . which perhaps one may begin to sense when he realizes that behind the grey and gold fabric of the Attic summer there is a *fearful black;* that we are all playthings of this black.[34]

In Poros itself, the sense of light comes out in the poem, which we will see in a moment (and in the later "Letter on *Thrush*"). The journal entries are not about a dialectic but try to convey an almost unbearable radiance.

> Crazy about the land. Every day carried away more and more by this drunkenness. The sea, the mountains that dance motionless; I found them the same in these rippled chitons . . . I know my whole life won't be long enough to express what I have been trying to say for so many days now: this union of nature with a simple human body, this worthless thing . . . As I'm writing now, I make desperate gestures in the void and express nothing.
>
> And yet I'm crazy about these things, in this light.
>
> "And you see the light of the sun"—
>
> as the ancients used to say. I could analyze this phrase and advance toward the most secret love. But to say what you want to say, you must create another language and nourish it for years and years with what you have loved, with what you have lost, with what you will never find again.
> . . . .
> This light, this landscape, these days start to threaten me seriously. I close the shutters so that I can work. I must protect myself from beauty, as the English from the rain and the Bedouins from the *chamsin*. You feel your brain emptying and lightening; the long day absorbs it. Today I understood why Homer was blind; if he had had eyes he wouldn't have written anything. He saw once, for a limited period of time, then saw no more.[35]

The dialectical sense of antithesis is stronger in the memory a few months later:

> I remember those days in Poros, and my impatience, when I heard "How beautiful! what a miracle! what magic!" In the evening, I used to read the newspaper as if uncovering an infected wound. That light and that wound: the back and forth between the light of day and the tragedy of man which you feel

in your gut: the marriage of heaven and hell, that was the suffering [or passion—*pathos*] of a beautiful day. You must be very much alive, you must have broken your ribs on many Symplegades, in order to hold onto that passion. You must have loved life like a man who has preserved inside, during every stage of his life, the child that he was.[36]

The third section of *Thrush,* part of which is entitled "The light," captures both the sense of a shuttling back and forth between beauty and horror, heaven and hell, recalled in the last-quoted passage, and the almost wordless calm and peace of the poet's surroundings. The motion and associations of the entire section are complex and have been partially discussed in earlier chapters. There is an underwater wreck, voices of an assemblage of ghosts, a further view of the penetration of dark water, and finally a combination of all these elements in a lyric crescendo.

> Light, angelic and black,
> laughter of waves on the sea's highways,
> tear-stained laughter,
> the old suppliant sees you
> as he moves to cross the invisible fields—
> light mirrored in his blood,
> the blood that gave birth to Eteocles and Polynices.
> Day, angelic and black;
> the brackish taste of woman that poisons the prisoner
> emerges from the wave a cool branch adorned with drops.
> Sing little Antigone, sing, O sing . . .
> I'm not speaking to you about things past, I'm speaking
>   about love;
> decorate your hair with the sun's thorns,
> dark girl;
> the heart of the Scorpion has set,
> the tyrant in man has fled,
> and all the daughters of the sea, Nereids, Graeae,
> hurry toward the shimmering of the rising goddess:
> whoever has never loved will love,
> in the light:
>
>   and you find yourself
> in a large house with many windows open
> running from room to room, not knowing from where to
>   look out first,
> because the pine-trees will vanish, and the mirrored

mountains, and the chirping of birds
the sea will drain dry, shattered glass, from north
    and south
your eyes will empty of daylight
the way the cicadas suddenly, all together, fall silent.

This passage frustrates attempts either to locate light beyond darkness or to discern darkness on the other side of light. With lyrical violence, Seferis juxtaposes images and lets the energy of contrasts and connections express the rhythm of opposition. The very disparate contents of the passage are somehow organized—not into a logical debate but into a counterpoint of contrasts epitomized in the repeated phrase *angelic and black.* Each image suggests its antithesis, and the passage progresses in a rapid zigzag that mimics a headlong narrative, though in fact there is nothing narrative about it. The slashing obliquity of the motion recalls the diagonal thrust earlier in *Thrush* of "the boys who dived from the bow-sprits," a kindred strip of white on black—an image which is reversed at the close of the poem when darkness enters and replaces the light of day in the house. As with some pieces of music, the finish of *Thrush* leaves an actively vibrating silence, as if the rhythms were still resolving themselves, the energy still at work.

The journal passages quoted on pages 188–90 are commonly cited in discussions of *Thrush* because they were written at about the same time and place as the poem and reflect not only themes akin to those of the poem but the actual sensations of literary creation. The journals do indeed make fascinating and valuable reading either in themselves or in connection with Seferis's poetry. For *Thrush* in particular, however, the much less frequently adduced essay on Delphi seems more directly relevant, for passages in this essay throw light *(sic)* on a habit of seeing a landscape rather than on a particular landscape. Seferis sketches a kind of moral, mythical, and etymological geography of the origins of Delphi, and in so doing emphasizes more graphically than the journal entries (or even *Thrush* itself) the intense and productive struggle he sees between the powers of light and those of darkness.

In the beginning was the wrath of the earth. Then Apollo came and killed the chthonic monster, the Python. They let it rot. The story goes that such is the source of the first name of

Delphi, Pytho [from root *pýtho,* to rot]. With such fertilizer there took root and flourished the power of the god of harmony, light, and prophecy. The myth may signify that dark powers are the leaven of light—that the more intense such powers are, the deeper will be the light whenever it prevails. And one ponders: if the landscape of Delphi throbs with such an inner scintillation, it is because there is perhaps no other corner of our country which has been more imbued with the chthonic powers and by absolute light.

Climbing towards Parnassus from the direction of the Stadium, one sees the great open wound which, like a blow of Hephaistos's ax, separates the two cliffs of the Phaidriades from their summit down to the Castalian spring, and even deeper down to the gorge of Pleistos; and one feels awe, as at the prospect of a wounded life which struggles to breathe, for as long as it still can, in the light, and rejoices that it is dawn and the sun is rising.

Or even, as night falls, when the cicadas wearily fall silent [compare last line of *Thrush*], a whisper may recall the stammering voice of the prophet Cassandra; perhaps it is the only sound in nature to resemble the, to us, unknown, I mean the unadorned outcry of the Pythia:
> *ótototoi, popoi dá*
> *ópollon ópollon*

(*Ag.* 1072)[37]

In this passage, Seferis perceives the cleft which splits light and darkness in two as a wound inflicted in the course of a contest which has not yet ended and will perhaps never end. To label the antagonists "good" and "evil" is to pose the terms of the struggle too simply. As Seferis's description of the physical site of Delphi makes clear, both sides are needed to contribute to and maintain the balance of the place. Neither chthonic power nor the strength of light is sufficient by itself.

Among other things, this meditation on Delphi may be read as a gloss on the play to which it refers in closing. Dark and light run too deeply through the *Oresteia* (as deep, in view of the Delphi passage, as a blow of Hephaestus's ax) for one to be able to call their alternation a pattern, theme, or motif. Rather, their struggle *makes* the plays, as the struggle between Apollo and the powers of earth has made the landscape of Delphi what it is. "We begin [the *Agamemnon*] in dark suspense; we are waiting for the light, and it no sooner dispels anxiety than a shadow falls again. The light and the darkness, hope and fear, triumph and defeat contend in all three plays, and the light will not prevail until the last."[38]

Some images of light in the *Agamemnon* are particularly germane to Seferis's dialectical sense of struggle. "A terrible brilliance smoulders in the night" (388) and "Justice shines in sooty hovels" (773) are two examples of the enhancement produced by setting brightness against a background of gloom. The creative struggle between light and darkness and the world each evokes means precisely that the two elements enhance and define each other.

The various versions of the dialectic of light merge in Seferis's "Letter on *Thrush*," a meditation (rather than an explication) which draws *Thrush,* the *Oresteia,* the pre-Socratic philosophers, and finally the *Odyssey* into a single strand, or rather a single pattern of opposition. Not that Seferis oversimplifies or claims that everything equals everything else; on the contrary, everything tends toward its own ineffability in his thought. But as we have seen in Chapter II, his intimate relation with all phases of Greek culture allows Seferis to move through and around thought and emotion by using, respectively, Aeschylus, Anaximander, Heraclitus, the Erinyes, Orestes, and the *Odyssey* to throw their several kinds of light on light.

. . . it is my belief that in the Greek light there is a kind of process of humanization; I think of Aeschylus not as the titan or the Cyclops that people sometimes want us to see him as, but as a man feeling and expressing himself close beside us, accepting or reacting to the natural elements just as we all do. I think of the mechanism of justice which he sets before us, this alternation of Hubris and Ate, which one will not find to be simply a moral law unless it is also a law of nature. A hundred years before him Anaximander of Miletus believed that "things" pay by deterioration for the "injustice" they have committed by going beyond the order of time. And later Heraclitus will declare: "The sun will not overstep his measures; if he does, the Erinyes, the handmaids of Justice, will find him out."

The Erinyes will hunt down the sun, just as they hunted down Orestes; just think of these cords which unite man with the elements of nature, this tragedy that is in nature and in man at the same time, this intimacy. Suppose the light were

suddenly to become Orestes? It is so easy, just think: if the
light of the day and the blood of man were one and the same
thing? How far can one stretch this feeling? "Just anthropomorphism," people say, and they pass on. I do not think
it is as simple as that. If anthropomorphism created the *Odyssey,* how far can one look into the *Odyssey?*

   We could go very far; but I shall stop here. We have arrived
at the light. And the light cannot be explained; it can only be
seen. The rest of this scenario [of *Thrush*] may be filled in by
the reader—after all, he has to do something too; but let me
first recall the last words of Anticleia to her son:

> The soul, like a dream, flutters away and is gone.
> But quickly turn your desire to the light
> And keep all this in your mind.
>
> (*Odyssey* 11.222–24)[39]

   Light cannot be explained, it can only be seen. This statement
is one more way of making light visible and problematic rather
than transparent and obvious. The referential richness of the
passage makes it a mine of metaphors for light, and if we add to
it visions of light from the poems, we see that light for Seferis
can be a veil to be pierced, a strange language, an antagonist in
an intense struggle, or the blood of man itself. All these versions
of what light is have in common that they make light a concrete
and positive force to be reckoned with, an element with the force
of law.

   To return to the close of *Thrush,* the images of light and darkness which so rapidly succeed one another have some of the
same synchronic unity as the passage about the Erinyes and the
pre-Socratics and Homer. Seferis draws, in the poem as a whole,
on an amazing array of sources; Vayenas names Homer, Heraclitus, Aeschylus, Hesiod, Sophocles, Plato, Mencius, Zen, *Per-
vigilium Veneris,* Dante, Cornaros, Calvos, Baudelaire, Laforgue, Pound, Eliot, Sikelianos, Cavafy.[40] Yet the poem does not
give—certainly the closing passage does not give—the sense of a
labored mosaic. It is as if Seferis felt instinctively that widely
differing periods, nationalities, and genres of literature and philosophy could freely participate in the debate between light and
darkness. By drawing so freely on other literatures and on the
Greek tradition, Seferis has cut a swathe through the past,
created a multifaceted yet in some ways simple work of art, and

in the process finally assembled a distinguished company of excellent ghosts, as Emily Vermeule says of *Odyssey* 11.[41]

The end of *Thrush,* packed though it is with references, is as simple and limpid in Greek as Seferis's carefully wrought style allows. If, as I tried to show in Chapter II, Seferis can wring from a single Aeschylean line a multiplicity of meanings, here he does the opposite magic, mixing the most disparate sources into harmony. The final draining of the sea and light at the end of *Thrush* seems to drain the rich pool of tradition, the possibilities of voices from the past. Yet the essay on Delphi may remind us what to listen for in the stillness that follows the cicadas' song. Will it be the uncanny shriek of a prophetic voice? Or is it also possible that, as in the Homeric Nekyuia, once messages to and from the dead have been given and received, there is no more to say? "The rest is silence," a tragic sentiment, would be at home in the world of blindness, vision, and struggle that Seferis creates around the idea of light.

iii   *In essence, I am a matter of light*

In Seferis's last published work, *Three Secret Poems,* light is again the subject of much meditation, and again it appears both as a concealing veil and as part of a dialectical struggle. But other traits of light are emphasized here for the first time: light's powers of renewal, of metamorphosis, and finally of silence (this last hinted at, as we have just seen, at the close of *Thrush*).

Silence plays an important role in all Seferis's mature poetry. *Mythical History,* for example, as a sequence of twenty-four separate poems, continually starts and stops, and the silence interspersed between sections affects both the pace and texture of the whole. This pattern of discontinuity is more marked in *Three Secret Poems.* The first poem of the three, "On a Ray of Winter Sun," is in seven sections; the second, "On Stage," also in seven; and the third, "Summer Solstice," is in fourteen, making twenty-eight sections in all. The periods of silence between utterances are thus more frequent here than in *Mythical History,* and the segments of poetry in general are shorter. Moreover, *Three Secret Poems* lacks the narrative cohesiveness that gives *Mythical History* what continuity it has. The lack of such narrative flow changes the status of the Seferic silences that form a considerable portion of *Three Secret Poems.* These silences have come to be more than mere blanks between patches of speech. They have entered the text itself—a text, too, which asks to be read with marked pauses within some sections as well as between sections. The slow, meditative pace of the voice leaves room for silence between words in a passage such as this:

> The sea: how did the sea get like this?
> I lingered for years in the mountains;
> the fireflies blinded me.
> Now, on this beach,
> I'm waiting for someone to land,
> or a piece of flotsam, a raft.
>
> But is it possible for the sea to fester?
> A dolphin once cut through it,
> as did once
> the tip of a gull's wing.
>
> ("On Stage," 4)

One senses a long pause between the first and second lines here, and probably also between the third and fourth lines, as well as the pause indicating the stanza break—and the longer pauses setting off this section from the surrounding ones.

It is partly the weight Seferis packs into his pauses which gives such a passage a portentousness which is characteristic but very difficult to describe. I agree with Peter Levi that "the economy and intense power of Seferis's style as it has developed have limited his range," and that the poet's tone of voice is "riveting . . . very serious and very complicated."[42] But how to measure this economy, gravity, and power is problematic. I believe the poet's use of silence is one key to the quality of the voice, particularly in *Three Secret Poems*.

Gérard Genette argues that the kind of intensity we conventionally attribute to lyric poetry results not so much from the words of the poem as from the *attitude de lecture* a poem imposes on the reader:

> . . . a motivating attitude which, beyond or prior to prosodic or semantic features, accords to the whole or part of the discourse that intransitive presence and absolute existence which Eluard calls "poetic prominence" . . . Here poetic language would seem to reveal its true "structure," which is not that of a particular *form* defined by its specific attributes but rather

that of a *state,* a degree of presence and intensity to which, as it were, any sequence can be brought, if only there is created around it that *margin of silence* which isolates it in the middle of ordinary speech.[43]

It is the proliferation of such silent margins in Seferis that helps to create the "presence and intensity" so marked in *Three Secret Poems.* (The phrase in quotes is Genette's, but note how closely it resembles Levi's description of Seferis's characteristic tone.)

Of course Genette ignores the nature of what is framed by his margins. Jonathan Culler writes that even a newspaper clipping can be made into a little lyric if properly spaced on the page;[44] how much more effective such spacing is when the words it borders are condensed and evocative to start with. If *Three Secret Poems* has silent margins, there are also many moments of silence within the text itself, and an impulse of condensation that approaches silence even where words are necessary. Isolated images are contracted to a laconic extreme of simplicity: sea, sun, fire, stage, light. By contrast, poems with narrative strands such as *Mythical History* or even *Thrush* are almost talky.

The desire for reduction to the most compact core of meaning and image offers itself in *Three Secret Poems* in several ways. It is the subject of the fourth section of the first poem, "On a Ray of Winter Light":

> Years ago you said:
> "Essentially I'm a matter of light."
> And still today when you lean
> on the broad shoulders of sleep
> or even when they anchor you
> to the sea's drowsy breast
> you look for crannies where the blackness
> has worn thin and has no resistance,
> groping you search for the lance—
> the lance destined to pierce your heart
> and lay it open to the light.

The Greek for "essentially" is *katá váthos,* a phrase rendered literally by the French *au fond,* "at bottom." As in "Our Sun" and "Agianapa I," light is depicted as something that must be actively sought out—here, dug down for. But now the speaker is not merely in pursuit of light; he is identified with it. Whether "you" is person or pure idea, it is presented dramatically, like a character uncloaking its true identity. (Compare the conclusion of "On Stage," Part 3: "Let anyone come and sleep with me who wants to:/am I not the sea?").

The "you" here is not the only thing in "On a Ray of Winter Light" to be stripped down to a fundamental form.

> The way the heart finds release
> the dancers turned into trees,
> into a huge forest of trees stripped bare.
>
> (1)

> White seaweed burns,
> gray-haired sea-nymphs, eyes lidless, rise from the
>   waves—
> shapes that once danced,
> flames now cristallized.
>
> (2)

> the voices
> under the chestnut trees turned into pebbles—
> pebbles that children throw.
>
> (5)

In short, metaphor here often takes the form of metamorphosis. But in general, *Three Secret Poems* are preoccupied not so much with the mythological or psychological aspects of metamorphosis as with the final attainment of some kind of stasis—a stability toward which all the transformations have been tending, and beyond which no more will be needed. It is not until "Summer Solstice," the last of the *Secret Poems,* that a resting place seems to be reached. The metamorphoses of "Winter Sun" with its dizzying transitions are replaced by suspension:

> On one side the sun at its grandest,
> on the other the new moon,
> distant in memory like those breasts.
> Between them the chasm of a night full of stars. . . .

> Eve of the longest day.

As the longest day (and longest of the *Secret Poems*) unfolds, the roamings of what has come before, not only in this sequence but in all Seferis's work up to this point, seem to arrive at a resting place—the garden of the poet's house in Athens. Notice the clarity and simplicity of the language, the way it stays close to home, avoiding the stretch of metaphor/metamorphosis. The language is not telescopic but introverted:

> The poplar's breathing in the little garden
> measures your time
> day and night—
> a water-clock filled by the sky. . . .
>
> In the little garden—this tiny patch—
> you can see the light of the sun
> striking two red carnations,
> an olive tree and a bit of honeysuckle.
> Accept who you are.
>   Don't
> drown the poem in deep plane trees;
> nurture it with what earth and rock you have.
> For things beyond this—
> to find them dig in this same place.
>
>   (7)

Because the garden is so small, any exploration has to be inward, downward, rather than superficial. After the kaleidoscopic transformations earlier in the poem, the little garden allows for only the most private and personal of metamorphoses: that of the poet into his own art. This passage follows the garden:

> The white sheet of paper, harsh mirror,
> gives back only what you were.
>
> The white sheet talks with your voice,
> your very own,
> not the voice you'd like to have;
> your music is life,
> the life you wasted.
> If you want to, you can regain it:
> concentrate on this blank object
> that throws you back
> to where you started.
>
> You travelled, saw many moons, many suns,
> touched dead and living,
> felt the pain young men know,

the moaning of woman,
a boy's bitterness—

what you've felt will fall away to nothing
unless you commit yourself to this void.
Maybe you'll find there what you thought was lost:
youth's burgeoning, the justified shipwreck of age.

Your life is what you gave,
this void is what you gave:
the white sheet of paper.

(8)

The white sheet is a very rich tabula rasa. It is a final manifestation of light in Seferis's work, if not the final one. As the
raw material of art, it is an agent of a special kind of metamorphosis. And it is a notable internalization of those margins of
silence that intersperse the entire oeuvre. That zone of stillness
which Genette says insulates a speech act and thereby enhances
its poetic effect is captured in this passage *within,* not on the
edge of, the words themselves. The spaces and phases of a
lifetime, of experience in life and letters, its "many moons, many
suns," its Tiresias-like comprehension of many lives—all this
can be expressed only if the blank page leaves room. Section 8 of
"Summer Solstice" functions as an *ars poetica:* it both explains
and exemplifies the technique whereby Seferis compresses an
epic range of prototypes and a variety of experience into the
austere boundaries of the little garden.

"Summer Solstice" continues beyond this section, but by doing so the poem to my mind dilutes the logic of its condensation.
Instead of coming to a halt inside the garden, the poem moves
on, as if by force of habit, to a mythological landscape ("to row
up the dark river. . . ," 9) which is familiar enough from Seferis's
previous work but which lacks the power and inevitability of
closure of the walled garden section. Finally, "Summer Solstice"
moves wholly away from any suggested landscape. It goes out to
sea, and also back to the dialectic of black and white (11). Again,
light is imaged as a veil behind which an ineffable newness or
final truth trembles:

The blood surges now
as heat swells
the veins of the inflamed sky.

> It is trying to go beyond death,
> to discover joy.
> The light is a pulse
> beating ever more slowly
> as though about to stop.

(12)

This is striking, but it lacks the gritty acknowledgment of limitation which make the seventh and eighth sections so honest, so "constricted but great," as Peter Levi says of another Seferis poem.

The image of the shut garden is triumphant not only because it rings so true. It also seems to resolve a persistent urge in Seferis's work—a longing for otherness. At various times in his poems we penetrate beyond the sun, behind the ruined marbles, toward the other world—and what is there? Finally there is "The white sheet of paper, harsh mirror, / [that] gives back only what you were." At the end of the mythologically buttressed journey out of the self, the self is what stares one in the face—"this blank object / that throws you back / to where you started."

The difficult mirror is another form of the challenge posed by the veil of light: both are images of the problematic approach to truth. Throughout his journals, Seferis complains of the difficulty of using words—dredging them up from the unconscious or the memory, lifting, shaping, carving, polishing them. These recalcitrant instruments are what fill the blank page if anything can, but still the vision and voice they express are difficult: "your very own voice,/not the voice you'd like to have." This is a tragic vision of art: creation is painful, difficult, and all one has.

Beyond the tragic vision of the page/mirror/garden, "Summer Solstice" offers only another version of the familiar dialectic. The terms of the contest have widened, to be sure; the opposition is no longer limited to light/dark. On the one hand now is the patience of the blank page, of harborage in the port of the self. On the other hand is motion, an orgasmic pulsing, shuddering, or throbbing. The octopus in 11 spurts out its ink; in 12 blood surges, heat swells, and light pulses; in 13 the dome of the sky opens for a birth-pang; in 14 we have a birth which is also a burning.[45]

The images, especially verbs, here are of contraction, constriction, release, spasm—transparently sexual in a way new for

Seferis. The rhythms of the dialectic reach a kind of climax which is at once an orgasm and a birth—but of what? The only answer that makes sense in terms of sections 7 and 8 is that the poem itself, the final product of opposing forces, has been painfully and gloriously born (or brought to light, another revealing cliché).

I would not insist that this is the sole significance of the birth at the end of *Three Secret Poems.* But "Summer Solstice" in particular and the poems generally gain in coherence if they are read as an extended meditation (*not* narrative or dramatization) whose subject is reflexive: the poetic process. The blank page into which all light can be received seems to be the newest and strongest image of a chief theme in *Three Secret Poems;* and that theme is the creative process.

Classifying Seferis's various works as "open" or "closed" poems, Nasos Vayenas understandably calls *Three Secret Poems* closed. Indeed, the poems are cryptic—as the Greek title *Kryphá* indicates. But so thoroughgoing has the late Seferis's dialectic become that these poems can be seen as accommodating both ends of the spectrum of openness and opacity. In the last section of the last secret poem, a final version of the familiar contrast is offered: the dark of the "lead melted for divination" against "the brilliance of the summer sea." Perhaps it is significant that this image incorporates the three principal elements in Seferis's vocabulary of images: stones (here, metal), sea, and light.

Three Secret Poems is a condensed version of much that Seferis had already seen or said. In his "Letter on *Thrush*" the poet calls himself "a monotonous and obstinate sort of man who, for the last twenty years, has gone on saying the same things over and over again—things that are not even his own."[46] Judging from the fact that the letter was written in 1949 and *Three Secret Poems* in the sixties, Seferis continued his "obstinate" path. But it is not true that the things he had to say were "not even his own." The "white sheet of paper, harsh mirror," reflected his own weary face, spoke with his own voice,

> your very own,
> not the voice you'd like to have.

If Seferis's images are not his own (and his ideas are inextricably associated with those images), then they are no other poet's either. They can only be attributed to the natural features, the lineaments of the world, he tried so long and hard to see, to see through, and to see beyond.

In *Three Secret Poems,* Seferis's dialectical oscillations are increasingly laconic and compressed; "margins of silence" not only intersperse the several sections of the sequence but also make their way into many portions of the poem. Frost's silence in his star poems is less of a physical fact, a white space on the page; rather it is an implicit feature of the nocturnal world which forms the logical setting for astral poems. The stargazers in Frost are usually solitaries (when they are not alone, as in "The Star-Splitter," they tend not to get much gazing done but to talk instead). The stars do not speak; the babble of voices is generally kept at a distance. The acute ear for talk that marks Frost's earlier work, especially in *North of Boston,* is still discernible in the star poems; what is missing is the give and take of human conversation. The writer of "An Unstamped Letter" goes out of his way to be a writer rather than a speaker; he does not want an answer to his letter. The speaker of "One More Brevity" evidently lives alone; he chats easily—to a dog.

And yet the unstamped letter is in "*our* rural letter box"; the absent landowner of the poem is also ourselves, the readers of the letter. The dog in "One More Brevity" is not just a dumb animal but a heavenly messenger—and also, again, the entity to whom the poem is addressed, or again ourselves. Thus these apparently stark and lonely poems are acutely aware of the fact that they are being read. In the absence of human chitchat in the foreground, language moves directly between poet, universe/star/sun—*and reader.* The same exclusion of human babble is evident in *Three Secret Poems,* particularly "Summer Solstice," in the poet's closed garden. The poet's mind moves within the circle of his own experiences; humanity is included in that experience of course, but remotely, as part of an incorporate past ("You travelled, saw many moons, many suns, / touched dead and living, / felt the pain young men know, / the moaning of woman, / a boy's bitterness . . ."). Yet in the midst of this intensely private communication, the poem presents itself as something written to be read, voiced to be heard: "The white sheet talks with your voice." This awareness of the eye and ear of a potential reader or listener is of a different quality in the late poems of both our poets from the active, talkier foregrounds of the earlier poems, where people talk and listen to each other and a third party is hardly thought of.

As Frost and Seferis approach the end of their words, they incorporate more silence into their work but also, paradoxically, write more *as writers* than ever before. Human talk may have ceased to interest them much, but they keep faith with the power of the word. We can dispense with the familiar pleasure of human interest or earthly detail in poems which continue to command our attention as pure utterance.

Notes

1. Santayana, in a letter, quoted by Iris Origo, *Images and Shadows* (London: Longmans, 1971), 268.

2. Robert Peterson, "It's Hard to Get into This World and Hard to Get Out of It," in *Interviews with Robert Frost,* ed. Edward Connery Lathem (New York: Holt, Rinehart & Winston, 1966), 295.

3. *Interviews,* 248–49.

4. Mark Harris, "I'm Modestly Satisfied. I've gotten my truth of feeling in," *Interviews,* 271.

5. For these two views, see Randall Jarrell, "The Other Frost," in *Poetry and the Age* (New York: rpt, Noonday Press, 1972) 33, and Nina Baym, "An Approach to Robert Frost's Nature Poetry," in Lewis P. Simpson, ed., *Profile of Robert Frost* (Columbus, Ohio: Charles E. Merrill Publishing Co., 1971), 90. Baym cites George Nitchie, *Human Values in the Poetry of Robert Frost,* as making the most extreme statements of the view that Frost, since he fails to answer ultimate questions about the universe, is a minor poet.

6. Samuel Taylor Coleridge, *Biographia Literaria.*

7. Alfred Kazin, "The Strength of Robert Frost," in *Profile,* 114.

8. *Profile,* 90.

9. *Interviews,* 250.

10. Robert Frost, "The Poetry of Amy Lowell," first published in *The Christian Science Monitor,* 16 May, 1925, reprinted in Elaine Barry, *Robert Frost on Writing* (New Brunswick, N.J.: Rutgers University Press, 1973), 136.

11. Marice C. Brown, "The Quest for 'all creatures great and small,' " in *Frost: Centennial Essays,* compiled by the Committee on the Frost Centennial of the University of Southern Mississippi (Jackson: University Press of Mississippi, 1974), 7.

12. *RF on Writing,* 136.

13. Frost, "Letter to the *Amherst Student,*" 25 March 1933, repr. in *RF on Writing,* 113–14.

14. Frost in a letter to Louis Untermeyer, 20 June, 1925, quoted in Peter J. Stanlis, *Robert Frost: The Individual and Society* (Washington, D.C.: Library of Congress, 1972), 49.

15. Robert M. Rechnitz, "The Tragic Vision of Robert Frost," in *Centennial Essays,* 138.

16. *RF: The Individual & Society,* 31.

17. Jarrell, "The Other Frost," in *Poetry and the Age,* 29–30.

18. Samuel Coale, "The Emblematic Encounter of Robert Frost," in *Centennial Essays,* 98.

19. For a stimulating discussion of "The Most of It," see Poirier, *Robert Frost: The Work of Knowing,* 159–69; 171–72.

20. *Work of Knowing,* 284.

21. *Work of Knowing,* 155.

22. Frank Lentricchia, "Robert Frost and Modern Literary Theory," in *Centennial Essays,* 318. Lentricchia's essay is perhaps the most stimulating in the volume.

23. Victor E. Reichert, "The Faith of Robert Frost," in *Centennial Essays,* 418.

24. Wade Van Dore, "The Subtlety of Robert Frost," in *Centennial Essays,* 537–38.

25. As witness such (Greek) titles of novels or volumes of poetry as *The Sun of Death, The Sovereign Sun,* etc.

26. The phrases are quoted or cited in Catherine Belsey, *Critical Practice* (London: Methuen, 1980), 4.

27. Walter Kaiser, trans., *Three Secret Poems by George Seferis,* (Cambridge: Harvard University Press, 1969), xi–xii.

28. Again, a cliché such as that in this sentence usefully demonstrates how automatically we link comprehension and clarity of vision.

29. *Three Secret Poems,* xii.

30. Ariana Pherentinou, *Aeschylus in The Poetry of Seferis* (Athens: ODEV, 1976), 40.

31. Emily Vermeule, *Aspects of Death in Early Greek Art and Poetry* (Berkeley: University of California Press, 1979), 24–25.

32. The dying messengers in "Our Sun" are startlingly like those in W. H. Auden's 1931 poem (from *The Orators*) "To My Pupils":

> Perfectly certain, all of us, but not from the records,
> Not from the unshaven agent who returned to the camp;
> The pillar dug from the desert recorded only
>   The sack of a city,
> The agent clutching his side collapsed at our feet,
> "Sorry! They got me!"

(W. H. Auden, *Selected Poems: New Edition,* ed. Edward Mendelson [New York: Vintage Books, 1979], 21.)

33. *Aeschylus in The Poetry of Seferis,* 17.

34. Seferis, *Days* (Journal) Vol. 5 (1945–1951) (Athens: Ikaros, 1977), 42.

35. Reginald Gibbons, ed., *The Poet's Work* (Boston: Houghton Mifflin, 1979), 70–73 (excerpts from Seferis's *Journals,* trans. Athan Anagnostopoulos).

36. *Days,* 92.

37. *Aeschylus in The Poetry of Seferis,* 40–41.

38. Robert Fagles, *The Oresteia of Aeschylus* (New York: Bantam Books, 1979), 15.

39. *George Seferis: On the Greek Style,* trans. Rex Warner (London: Bodley Head, 1966), 104–5 ("Letter on the [*sic*] *Thrush*").

40. Nasos Vayenas, *The Poet and The Dances* (Athens: Kedros, 1979), p. 296.

41. *Aspects of Death,* 28. The ghosts in *Thrush* tend to be unobtrusive and courteous; we can, for example, recognize approximations of King Lear or *The Golden Bough,* but the poem does not insist.

42. Peter Levi, S. J., "Seferis' Tone of Voice," in Edmund Keeley and Peter Bien, eds., *Modern Greek Writers* (Princeton, N.J.: Princeton University Press, 1972), 174.

43. Gérard Genette, *Figures II,* quoted in Jonathan Culler, *Structuralist Poetics* (Ithaca, N.Y.: Cornell University Press, 1975), 164.

44. *Structuralist Poetics,* 161.

45. The close of "Summer Solstice" strikingly recalls that of "Little Gidding," which is also the end of the last poem in a sequence, and also features children, fire, a rose, and an assurance that things are right or "well":

> And the children in the apple-tree
> Not known, because not looked for

But heard, half-heard, in the stillness
Between two waves of the sea.
Quick now, here, now, always—
A condition of complete simplicity
(Costing not less than everything)
And all shall be well and
All manner of thing shall be well
When the tongues of flame are in-folded
Into the crowned knot of fire
And the fire and the rose are one.

Compare Seferis:

As the pine tree at the stroke of noon
mastered by resin
strains to bring forth flame
and can't endure the pangs any longer—

summon the children to gather the ash
to sow it.
Everything that has passed has fittingly passed.

And even what has not yet passed
must burn
this noon when the sun is riveted
to the heart of the many-petalled rose.

46. Seferis, "Letter on *Thrush*," *On the Greek Style,* 105.

Conclusion

At the close of the Introduction, it was stated that "we shall probably find that studying [Frost's and Seferis's] major images tells us what we want to know about such poetic choices as form, the poet's relation to the past, or the matter of the personal voice." What, in brief, do the images which have been the subject of these pages have to tell us about such matters? I would conclude by giving—really, by recapitulating—answers that have in effect been provided already by the study of the images. The mode is repetitious, no doubt; but among the things Frost and Seferis have to teach us is that with each repetition we learn a little more, see further.

Stone, then, recalcitrant and indispensable, is of course an image common to the two poetic landscapes, and one which speaks not only of a sense of form as palpable but also of keen awareness of the presence of the past and pastness of the present. For the American poet, stone is the stuff of foundations, boundaries, signs of human definition. Mending a wall epitomizes the peaceful tasks of civilization—both the civic responsibilities of neighborliness and the aesthetic task of maintaining and/or renewing form and order. Even cellar holes and ruined foundations proclaim the tenacity of human life as it marks itself out on the landscape, distinguishing habitat from what Frost calls "the sameness of the wood."

For the Greek poet, stone is an even more ubiquitous signature of a geological and cultural inheritance. It is the stuff of the countryside; it is also the art that has engraved words on, or hewn shapes out of, a tough raw material. Stone is valuable enough to be worth being "brought back" from the past; in a reciprocal gesture, it is also thrown outward and down, to sink into the sea and beyond time like a message in a bottle. The poet's relation to the past? For Frost and Seferis, a time capsule designed both to withstand aeons and to show the most enduring and characteristic forms of our civilization might well be made of stone.

The images of gardens and the sea, examined in Chapter II, throw further light on both poets' relation to the poetry of the past, and thence to the importance each attributes to the development of a distinctive personal voice. For it is this class of images, venerable *topoi* in both Greek and English poetic tradition, that poses the challenge of originality more blatantly than do the image clusters of stone or of light. What fresh things can be said of the renewal of nature, of the Aegean—or how important, in fact, is freshness? It is a challenge that does not alarm Frost or Seferis. Both poets do work variations on these themes; but generally, both are less interested in somehow making the old themes new than in seeing them whole. For example, Frost approaches the natural cycle, or even a single tree, from various angles and stances; Seferis shows the protean quality of the sea by presenting it in different guises. Such variations become apparent, of course, only if we consider each poet's oeuvre as a whole. Often no one poem seems terribly ambitious in scope; yet the design formed by the sum of all Frost's seasonal pieces or Seferis's treatments of the sea turns out to be capacious indeed.

According to Barthes, as we saw in the Introduction, classical language is reducible to a "persuasive continuum which constantly postulates the possibility of dialogue." Such a continuum and hence such a possibility are especially detectable, I think, in Frost and Seferis poems that deal with the sea or with growing things. The continuum resides in the necessity of surveying each poet's whole oeuvre. No one work encapsulates the essence of what the sea or a tree means, but a fluctuating sense of such a larger meaning can be derived or extracted (Barthes's term is "reduced") from a reading of the entire oeuvre.

The possibility of a dialogue offers itself in two ways. First there is literal dialogue between speakers. Men are not alone in the poetic world of classical language, as Barthes points out; and the social context of poems which approach nature georgically or pastorally, or the sea through a crew of traveling companions, requires a good deal of human exchange in the form of spoken language. Secondly, and of great importance for these two poets, there is a continual dialogue with poets of the past. It is of this sort of atemporal exchange that Helen Bacon is thinking when she refers to "Frost's intimacy (and I mean *intimacy*, that sets up something like a dialogue outside of time and place) with classical authors in their own tongues."[1]

Some of Frost's more notable long-distance dialogues are with

Vergil, Catullus, Horace, Lucretius; Seferis's, with Homer, Aeschylus, Makriyannis. This continuum and its concomitant dialogues do not mean that Frost is rewriting Horace or Seferis Homer. Rather, the twentieth-century poets, by conducting an exchange with their predecessors, are incorporating poetry of the past into the present, and in the process extending that of the present into the past. Bacon puts it like this:

> Poets knew, Frost knew, there is only one tradition of literature. We scholars, locked in our specialties, tend to forget. . . . We cannot read Vergil unless we know Homer, but having read Vergil we will read Homer differently, and having read Milton, or Frost, we will read Vergil differently. We need to know the poets of the past to be good readers of modern poetry, but, just as important, to be good readers of ancient poetry we should read Frost and as many other modern poets as we can. "Progress is not the aim, but circulation." The great poets give us back our past by forcing us to circulate.[2]

There is another aspect of poetic voice—that whose province is personal feeling. The voice of feeling is relatively reticent in both Frost and Seferis, poets who find it easier to carry on an exchange with the past than to illuminate their conflicts and passions in the present. Still, to the extent that it makes itself heard at all, it is in the sea and tree images that the keenly personal voice is clearest in both poets. Richard Poirier has emphasized the sexual undercurrents of such Frostian flower pieces as "The Subverted Flower" and "Putting in the Seed," but Seferis's *Three Secret Poems* have apparently kept the secret of their use of wave imagery to suggest sexual spasm on a cosmic scale.

It is not that intimate experience and personal feeling are restricted, in either poet, to this particular category of imagery. Consider, for example, Seferis's "Erotikos Logos" with its intertwining serpents, or the conjugal quarrel occasioning Frost's "The Thatch." But it is generally the case that for both poets personal emotion is located in objects, tucked into the natural world rather than being given a conspicuous room of its own. If the result is a cautious and reticent voice, it is also, by the same token, an emotionally charged and suggestive landscape. Such displacement, as well as continual harkings back to the poetry of the past, is an indication of the essentially *balanced* quality shared by the two voices. The present is balanced by the past, the personal world by the natural world—perhaps overbalanced to some tastes, but the unadorned diction of both poets lends conviction to their forays in space and time, as it does to their personal choices of reticence.

The ability of Frost and Seferis to maintain a balance between extremes is probably subjected to its most searching test in the poems where images of stars and light predominate. In such poems both writers are less firmly buttressed than elsewhere by the solid structures of tradition. Rather than working quiet variations on traditional themes or conducting an exchange with past poetry—although they do both these things—Frost and Seferis seem in such poems to be especially isolated and vulnerable consciousnesses, alone—or close to it—in the universe. It is in this (often late) work that we hear at once the most distinctive and the least social voices of both poets. Concern with the historical or literary past as recorded on stone; care for natural cycles—these themes tend to fall away from poems whose subject has become the barrier that separates humanity from infinity.

In the absence of other, social voices, these poems have a special aura of solitude. Yet at the same time, their isolation seems to foster the development of a dialectical rhythm. In the stillness of some Frost star or Seferis light poems, an underlying pattern becomes discernible like a faint vibration—*men/de,* on the one hand/on the other hand, back and forth. Possibilities of a dialogue not personal but cosmic alternate with resounding silences. Is man a chained bear pacing helplessly back and forth, or can he actually commune with a star (Frost)? Is man a baffled and bedazzled gazer at a sun which, in turn, is merely a veil between him and further illumination, or can he see well enough to penetrate to the other side of the sun (Seferis)?

These questions have no final answer. Such answers as there are must be derived from the dialectical rhythms within the poems themselves, rhythms which also reverberate from one poem to another within each oeuvre. Moreover, in such dialectics an increasingly important part is played by silence. Near the end of each poet's life, the silence of the infinite spaces is frequently approximated or reflected by a more humanly scaled silence which comes to intersperse the poets' own voices—a silence expressed in Frost's unknowable skies or Seferis's sun, which becomes the "blank page, difficult mirror" of the poet's own work.

What do such silences portend? The contemplation of the cosmos is an imposing and isolating, finally almost a silencing, poetic theme. Frost and Seferis work by individual poems, not by heroically large epic renderings—that is, they grapple with immensity in small single utterances. No matter how traditionally buttressed, social, "horizontal" the matter of much of their work is, a certain verticality (in Barthes's sense, mentioned in the Introduction, of loneliness, abruptness, disconnectedness) necessarily affects poetic style when the poet is craning his neck to gaze upward.

Not to reflect this verticality in the poems would be a failure of honesty on the part of two poets who understood how the strength of a poetic voice was bound up with the poet's limitations. Frost and Seferis, accordingly, do not end their careers with anything like confident pronouncements. Still trusting to language, both increasingly ponder those areas that language cannot reach. The bare and austere, if also the splendid, nature of the subjects of stars and light is reflected in such late statements on poetic economy as the following:

> At times I've felt like paring my writing down until nothing was left but an exclamation mark—which could be seen as the shortest poem ever written.
>
> (Frost)[3]

and

> You remember Valéry said lyricism is, after all, the development of an exclamation, of an "Ah." For me "Ah" is quite enough. I never try to elaborate on the exclamation.
>
> (Seferis)[4]

But it is important to note that even when connections with the earthly landscape are stretched to a taut line, the exclamation point, or the simple "Ah," neither Frost nor Seferis ever quite despairs of perceiving or making connections. Neither poet lets go. The sense of dialectic is itself a kind of guard against disconnectedness: the impulse toward silence is balanced by the wish and habit of expression, of answering back, and for both

poets the impulse holds until the voice falls silent. The same kind
of decorum that makes Frost and Seferis so reticent about personal emotions in their poetry is, in a similar way, a kind of
shield against the despair or disintegration of a wholly pessimistic or hermetic or agèd-bardic voice.

   This balance is well illustrated by a passage from Frost's "One
More Brevity," a 1953 poem that ends by drawing a luminous
line between meaning and reticence, language and silence. The
poem is one of Frost's star-gazing pieces. Its opening couplet
reverberates with the lonely gaze beyond earthly horizons that
often characterizes the star poems:

> I opened the door so my last look
> Should be taken outside a house and book.

The poet wants to look up at Sirius, a star which is immediately
associated with a cosmic/canine watchfulness and comprehension:

> Before I gave up seeing and slept
> I said I would see how Sirius kept
> His watchdog eye on what remained
> To be gone into if not explained.

But as the door is opened, an earthly, rather than astral, dog slips
into the house. The poem is an account of what turns out to be
only a brief visit from this mysterious dog, and it ends with a
tantalizing speculation which leaves a door open to otherness by
balancing the earthly with the cosmic or mythological.[5]

> He might have been the dream of a ghost
> In spite of the way his tail had smacked
> My floor so hard and matter-of-fact.
> And things have been going so strangely since,
> I wouldn't be too hard to convince,
> I might even claim, he was Sirius
> (Think of presuming to call him Gus),
> The star itself—Heaven's greatest star,
> Not a meteorite, but an avatar—
> Who had made an overnight descent
> To show by deeds he didn't resent
> My having depended on him so long,
> And yet done nothing about it in song.
> A symbol was all he could hope to convey,

> An intimation, a shot of ray,
> A meaning I was supposed to seek,
> And finding, wasn't disposed to speak.

At the same time that the door is opened to enormous vistas, it is closed by the veil of wry but authoritative decorum that last line draws. Symbol, synecdoche, myth, anecdote, and reticence come together in a tantalizing "intimation, a shot of ray" couched in Frost's usual colloquial and unportentous diction. Although he may not be "disposed to speak," the poem does speak, to some extent, of a keen awareness of ultimate connections. If part of it closes a door, there is also in "One More Brevity" a strong wish to make and show connections. The dialectical impulses toward language and silence maintain a charged poise—a poise that is characteristic of many of Frost's star poems, and also of such late work of Seferis as *Three Secret Poems*. Of course, it is partly our temperament and awareness as readers which provide some of the impetus that opens a door or fails to open it, as Helen Bacon has beautifully shown.

If we must find a word applicable to both poets, a word which has not been used so often that it has lost all its meaning, "horizontality" may perhaps begin to express the way things connect in these poetic landscapes, their coherence, order, and suggestiveness as opposed to a rebarbative verticality. But even if it is intelligible, the notion of horizontality fails to convey the tension and aspiration that finally permeate both these poetic worlds—that outwardly radiating synecdochic energy that characterizes both poets' best work. Horizontality implies that the earthly landscape stretches out in a continuous gesture, even at a single level. But the progression we have been tracing from stones to gardens and the sea to stars and light moves from underfoot to overhead.

For these poets, the sense of being at home on earth carries little complacency with it. Crucial to both their visions of the world is a paradox of continuity and comprehensibility that accommodates continual oppositions: a classical care for form and proportion, allowing room for both learned allusions and colloquial simplicity; a loving attention to the world which also acknowledges emptiness; and an immersion in language and literature which makes a place for silence. No wonder these poets are hard to label: they fall between *men* and *de*. "Life," said Frost, "sways perilously at the confluence of opposing forces. Poetry in general plays perilously in the same wild place."⁶ Swaying and playing, these poets make the wild place into a familiar landscape, then suddenly open the door from familiarity back into strangeness. It is a deftly double accomplishment. The solidity of literary and earthly loyalties, combined with the eerie forays into silence and otherness, make it an accomplishment unlike other poetic projects of this century.

Notes

1. Helen Bacon, "Dialogue of Poets: *Mens Animi* and the Renewal of Words," *Massachusetts Review* 19, no. 2 (Summer 1978): 324.

2. Helen Bacon, "The Contemporary Reader and Robert Frost: The Heavenly Guest of 'One More Brevity' and *Aeneid* 8," *St. John's Review* 32 (Summer 1981): 10.

3. Robert Frost, quoted in Wade Van Dore, "The Subtlety of Robert Frost," *Frost: Centennial Essays,* 537.

4. Seferis, "The Art of Poetry," interview conducted by Edmund Keeley, *Paris Review,* no. 50 (Fall 1970): 88.

5. See Helen Bacon's penetrating analysis of "One More Brevity" in her article (note 2 above), to which I am greatly indebted.

6. Robert Frost, letter to R. P. Tristram Coffin, quoted in Helen Bacon, "In- and Outdoor Schooling: Robert Frost and the Classics," *American Scholar* 43, no. 4 (Autumn 1974): 641.

Bibliography

I Frost

Anderson, Margaret Bartlett, ed. *Robert Frost and John Bartlett: The Record of a Friendship.* New York: Holt, Rinehart & Winston, 1963.

Auden, W. H. "Robert Frost" and "American Poetry." *The Dyer's Hand.* New York: Vintage Books, 1968, pp. 337–53 and 354–68.

Bacon, Helen. "The Contemporary Reader and Robert Frost: The Heavenly Guest of 'One More Brevity' and *Aeneid* 8." *St. John's Review* 32 (Summer 1981): 3–10.

———. "Dialogue of Poets: *Mens Animi* and the Renewal of Words." *Massachusetts Review* 19, no. 2 (Summer 1978): 319–34.

———. "For Girls: from 'Birches' to 'Wild Grapes.'" *Yale Review* (Autumn 1977): 13–29.

———. "In- and Outdoor Schooling: Robert Frost and the Classics." *American Scholar* 43, no. 4 (Autumn 1974): 640–49.

Barry, Elaine, ed. *Robert Frost on Writing.* New Brunswick, N.J.: Rutgers University Press, 1973.

Brower, Reuben. *The Poetry of Robert Frost: Constellations of Intention.* New York: Oxford University Press, 1963.

Committee on the Frost Centennial of the University of Southern Mississippi, comp. *Frost: Centennial Essays.* Jackson: University Press of Mississippi, 1974.

Cook, Reginald L. *Robert Frost: The Living Voice.* Amherst: University of Massachusetts Press, 1974.

———. *The Dimensions of Robert Frost.* New York: Barnes and Noble, 1958.

Cox, Hyde, and Edward Connery Lathem, eds. *Selected Prose of Robert Frost.* New York: Collier Books, 1968.

Frost, Robert. *Collected Poems.* New York: Holt, Rinehart & Winston, 19th printing, 1967.

———. *Selected Letters.* Edited by Louis Untermeyer. New York: Holt, Rinehart & Winston, 1964.

———. *Letters to Louis Untermeyer.* New York: Holt, Rinehart & Winston, 1963.

————. Interviewed by Richard Poirier. In *Writers at Work Series: Paris Review,* 9–34. New York: Viking Press, 1963.

Gould, Jean. *The Aim Was Song.* New York: Dodd, Mead, 1964.

Grade, Arnold, ed. *Family Letters of Robert and Elinor Frost.* Albany: State University of New York Press, 1972.

Lathem, Edward Connery, ed. *Interviews with Robert Frost.* New York: Holt, Rinehart & Winston, 1966.

Mertins, Louis. *Robert Frost: Life and Talks—Walking.* Norman: University of Oklahoma Press, 1965.

Morrison, Kathleen. *Robert Frost: A Pictorial Chronical.* New York: Holt, Rinehart & Winston, 1974.

Munson, Gorham. *Robert Frost: A Study in Sensibility and Good Sense.* New York: George H. Doran Co., 1927.

Nitchie, George. *Human Values in the Poetry of Robert Frost.* Durham, N.C.: Duke University Press, 1960.

Poirier, Richard. *Robert Frost: The Work of Knowing.* New York: Oxford University Press, 1977.

Reeve, F. D. *Robert Frost in Russia.* Boston: Atlantic–Little, Brown, 1963.

Robert Frost: Lectures on the Centennial of His Birth. Washington, D.C.: The Library of Congress, 1975.

Simpson, Lewis P., comp. *Profile of Robert Frost.* Columbus, Ohio: Charles E. Merrill Publishing Co., 1971.

Squires, Radcliffe. *The Major Themes of Robert Frost.* Ann Arbor: University of Michigan Press, 1963.

Stanlis, Peter J. *Robert Frost: The Individual and Society.* Washington, D.C.: The Library of Congress, 1973.

Thompson, Lawrance. *Robert Frost, The Early Years: 1874–1915.* New York: Holt, Rinehart & Winston, 1966.

————. *Robert Frost, The Years of Triumph: 1915–1938.* New York: Holt, Rinehart & Winston, 1970.

————. *Fire and Ice.* New York: Russell and Russell, 1961.

Thompson, Lawrance, and R. H. Winnick. *Robert Frost, The Later Years: 1938–1963.* New York: Holt, Rinehart & Winston, 1976.

Vogel, Nancy. *Robert Frost, Teacher.* Bloomington, Ind.: Phi Delta Kappa, 1974.

II   Seferis

Antzaka, Sophia. *The Other Life in the Poetry of Seferis.* Athens, 1974.

Karantonis, Andreas. *The Poet George Seferis.* Athens: Hestia, 1957.

Keeley, Edmund, and Warren Wallace. "On Greek Poetry." Unpublished interview, 1979–80.

Lorentzatos, Zissimos. *The Lost Center and Other Essays.* Princeton, N.J.: Princeton University Press, 1980.

Pherentinou, Ariana. *Aeschylus in the Poetry of Seferis.* Athens: O.D.E.V., 1976.

Savidis, Giorgos, ed. *For Seferis: Festschrift.* Athens: Ikaros, 1961.

Seferis, George. *Six Nights on the Acropolis.* Athens: Hermes, 1978.

———. *Poems.* Athens: Ikaros, 11th printing, 1977.

———. *Days* (5 volumes):
Volume 1: 16 February 1925–17 August 1931. Athens: Ikaros, 1975.
Volume 2: 24 August 1931–12 February 1934. Athens: Ikaros, 1975.
Volume 3: 16 April 1934–14 December 1940. Athens: Ikaros, 1977.
Volume 4: 1 February 1941–31 December 1944. Athens: Ikaros, 1977.
Volume 5: 1 January 1945–19 April 1951. Athens: Ikaros, 1977.

———. "The Art of Poetry, XIII." *Paris Review,* no. 50 (Fall 1970): 56–93. (Interview by Edmund Keeley.)

———. *Three Secret Poems.* Translated by Walter Kaiser. Cambridge: Harvard University Press, 1969.

———. *Collected Poems* (expanded edition). Translated by Edmund Keeley and Philip Sherrard. Princeton, N.J.: Princeton University Press, 1981.

———. *Seferis on the Greek Style: Selected Essays on Poetry and Hellenism.* London: Bodley Head, 1966.

Thaniel, George. "George Seferis's 'Thrush' and T. S. Eliot's 'Four Quartets.'" *Neohelicon* 4, nos. 3–4 (1976): 261–82.

Tsatsou, Ioanna. *My Brother George Seferis.* Athens: Hestia, 1973.

Vayenas, Nasos. *The Poet and the Dancer: An Examination of the Poetics and Poetry of Seferis.* Athens: Kedros, 1979.

Vitti, Mario. *Corruption and the Logos: Introduction to the Poetry of George Seferis.* Athens: Hestia, 1978.

III General

Auden, W. H. *The Enchafèd Flood.* Charlottesville: University of Virginia Press, 1950. Reprint, 1979.

Bachelard, Gaston. *The Poetics of Space.* Translated by Maria Jolas. Boston: Beacon Press, 1964.

Belsey, Catherine. *Critical Practice.* London: Methuen, 1980.

Bodkin, Maud. *Archetypal Patterns in Poetry.* New York: Oxford University Press, 1934. Reprint, 1974.

H. D. *Tribute to Freud.* Introduction by Kenneth Fields. Boston: David R. Godine, Publisher, 1956. Reprint, 1974.

Fagles, Robert, and W. B. Stanford. *The Oresteia of Aeschylus.* New York: Bantam Books, 1979.

Frye, Northrop. *T. S. Eliot.* New York: Capricorn Books, 1978.

———. *Anatomy of Criticism.* Princeton, N.J.: Princeton University Press, 1957.

Gross, Harvey. *The Structure of Verse.* New York: Ecco Press, reprint, 1979.

Jarrall, Randall. *Kipling, Auden & Co.* New York: Farrar, Straus & Giroux, 1980.

———. *The Third Book of Criticism.* New York: Farrar, Straus & Giroux, 1969.

———. *Poetry and the Age.* New York: Noonday Press, 1970.

Perkins, David. *A History of Modern Poetry.* Cambridge: Harvard University Press, 1976.

Smith, Barbara Herrnstein. *Poetic Closure.* Chicago: University of Chicago Press, 1968. Reprint, 1974.

Vermeule, Emily. *Aspects of Death in Early Greek Art and Poetry.* Berkeley: University of California Press, 1979.

Index

Aeschylus, 39, 42, 92, 140, 142, 144–47, 193, 209. Works: *Agamemnon,* 39, 92, 122, 142–47, 185–87, 192–93; *The Libation Bearers,* 74, 146, 182
Auden, W. H., 160, 180

Bachelard, Gaston, 61, 65–67, 110, 114, 133
Bacon, Helen, 38–39, 208, 213
Barthes, Roland, 41–43, 208, 211

Calvos, Andreas, 25, 29, 38, 42, 140, 194
Caryotakis, Costas, 25, 29
Cavafy, Constantine, 25, 29, 42, 140, 194
Coleridge, Samuel Taylor, 157
Cook, Reginald L., 34–36
Corbière, Tristan, 36
Cornaros, Vintzentios, 25, 194
Crane, Hart, 8

De La Mare, Walter, 36
Delphi, 191–92
du Bellay, Joachim, 127

Eliot, T. S., 25, 31–32, 35, 38, 178, 194. Works: *Four Quartets,* 46, 188; *The Waste Land,* 123
Emerson, Ralph Waldo, 23

Frost, Robert, 7–12, 21–44, 46–68, 86–88, 90–120; as "antivocabularian," 8, 11; balance between inner and outer worlds, 12; education and associates, 23–24; growing things and cycle of seasons in imagery of, 90–120, 208–10; influences, 22–23; "literalness" an asset, 11; music and poetry, 26–27; poetic voice, 8; stars in imagery of, 152–78, 203–4, 210–14; stone and walls in imagery of, 46–68, 86–88, 207; and Wordsworth, 28–29. Works: "After Apple-Picking," 91–92, 94, 109, 118–20, 148; "Afterflakes," 165–66; "All Revelation," 171–73; "Any Size We Please," 153, 161–63, 165, 169–70; "Away!" 177; "Bear, The," 153, 159–60, 169; "Birches," 91, 93, 109–15, 118, 120, 161; "Black Cottage, The," 46, 57–61, 68, 87; "Bond and Free," 117; "Boundless Moment, A," 104–5; *Boy's Will, A,* 49; "Bravado," 168; "Carpe Diem," 90, 95–96, 98; "Census-Taker, The," 46, 57, 61–63, 87; "Cliff Dwelling, A," 46, 57, 67–68, 87; "Come In," 155–56; "Considerable Speck, A," 170; "Cow in Apple Time, The," 52–53; "Death of the Hired Man, The," 57, 169; "Desert Places," 168; "Drumlin Woodchuck, A," 52–53; "Education by Poetry," 119; "Encounter, An," 106–7; "Etherealizing," 170; "Fear, The," 57, 106; "Figure a Poem Makes, The," 100–1; "Figure in the Doorway, The," 50–51, 58; "Flower-Gathering," 93; "For Once, Then, Something," 171–73, 176; "Gathering Leaves," 102; "Good Hours," 65; "Goodbye and Keep Cold," 99; "Hardwood Groves, In," 95, 97–98, 102–3, 112; "Hill Wife, The," 106; "Home Burial," 169; "I Could Give All to Time," 105; "In Neglect," 52–53; "Into My Own," 68; "Leaf-Treader, A," 93, 102–4; "Letter to the Amherst *Student,*" 54–55, 161;

"Lost in Heaven," 168; "Mending Wall," 46, 48, 55–57, 87, 110; "Mood Apart, A," 50–51; "Most of It, The," 107–8, 170–71, 173, 176; *Mountain Interval,* 101; "Mowing," 118; "Need of Being Versed in Country Things, The," 57, 63–64; "Neither Far Out Nor In Deep," 165–66, 172; *North of Boston,* 59, 169, 203; "Nothing Gold Can Stay," 90; "Oft-Repeated Dream, The," 106; "On Looking Up by Chance at the Constellations," 162; "On the Heart's Beginning to Cloud the Mind," 172; "One More Brevity," 203, 212–13; "Pan with Us," 33; "Passing Glimpse, A," 58; "Pasture, The," 100; "Pea Brush," 98, 101–2; "Prayer in Spring, A," 98; "Putting in the Seed," 93, 99–100, 102, 105, 209; "Reluctance," 104; "Rose Pogonias," 93; "Servant to Servants, A," 169; "Skeptic," 153, 163–65, 169–70; "Sound of Trees, The," 106, 108–9; "Spring Pools," 95–98, 102, 105, 109, 120; "Star in a Stone-Boat, A," 168, 175; "Star-Splitter, The," 168, 203; "Stars," 166–67; *Steeple-Bush,* 156; "Stopping by Woods on a Snowy Evening," 105; "Strong are Saying Nothing, The," 98–100; "Subverted Flower, The," 209; "Take Something Like a Star," 158, 171, 175–77; "Thatch, The," 57, 65–67, 209; "There Are Roughly Zones," 105; "Time to Talk, A," 52, 87; "Too Anxious for Rivers," 160–61; "Tree at My Window," 106–7; "Trespass," 50–52; "Unstamped Letter in Our Rural Letter Box, An," 153, 171, 173–76, 203; "Why Wait for Science," 161; "Wild Grapes," 91–93, 109–10, 113–17, 120, 161; "Witch of Coös, The," 169

Garden of Eden, 90, 110

Homer, 38, 42, 70, 140, 147, 209. Works: *Odyssey,* 90, 122, 138, 141, 186, 193–95

Ivanhoe, 181

James, William, 23, 47
Jarrell, Randall, 37, 40, 165

Kaiser, Walter, 139, 180
Keats, John, 26
Keeley, Edmund, 21–22, 32–33, 70, 138–39

LaForgue, Jules, 31, 36, 122, 194
Lowell, Amy, 158
Lucretius, 161

Makriyannis, 25, 29, 30–31, 34, 38–39, 47, 72–73, 147, 209
Mangakis, G.-A., 121–22, 126, 141
Marble Faun, The, 181

Nabokov, Vladimir, 67
Narrative of Arthur Gordon Pym, The, 123

Oedipus the King, 184–86

Palamas, Costis, 29, 42, 140
Pierre, 181
Plato, 38, 194
Poirier, Richard, 21–22, 55, 124, 133, 218, 220, 274
Pound, Ezra, 8, 36, 38, 178, 194
Proteus, 138, 147
Proust, Marcel, 77–78, 180

Riding, Laura, 178
Rimbaud, Arthur, 70
Rossetti, Dante Gabriel, 36

Santayana, George, 23, 153
Seferis, George, 7–12, 21–44, 46–49, 69–88, 120–48; balance between inner and outer worlds, 12; cosmopolitan, 23; and demotic Greek, 29–30; influences, 22; light in imagery of, 152–55, 178–204, 210–14; loneliness, 24; "monotonous and obstinate," 8, 11; poetic voice, 8; sea in imagery of, 90–93, 120–48, 208–10; stone in imagery of, 46–49, 69–88, 207. Works: "Agianapa I,"

181, 185–88, 197; "Agianapa II," 153; "Cistern, The," 133–34; "Companions in Hades, The," 90; "Engomi," 33, 83–86, 146, 186; "Erotikos Logos," 209; "Fog," 122–23, 126; "Gymnopaidia," 79–83, 86, 134–35, 137; "Hampstead," 124, 144; "Interlude of Joy," 181, 185, 187; "In the Manner of G. S.," 126; "King of Asine, The," 33, 46–47, 71, 76, 87, 137, 181, 185, 187; "Last Stop," 39; "Mood of a Day," 123–24, 126–27; "Morning," 181, 185, 187; *Mythical History,* 33, 47, 70–76, 79, 82–83, 86–87, 91, 126, 128–34, 136, 138, 142, 145–46, 152, 181, 183–84, 195, 197; "Notes for a Week," 142, 144; "Our Sun," 153, 181–88, 197; "Piazza San Nicolo," 77–79; "Reflection on a Foreign Line of Verse," 90–91, 126–29, 138; "Return of the Exile, The," 76–77, 79; "Rocket," 124, 126; "Spring A.D.," 85; "Stratis Thalassinos among the Agapanthi," 125, 136, 140–42; "Stratis Thalassinos Describes a Man," 124–25; "Syngrou Avenue," 126–27; *Three Secret Poems,* 138–39, 146–47, 154, 180, 183–84, 195–204, 209, 213; *Thrush,* 38, 78–79, 91–92, 136–39, 142–43, 145–47, 154, 180, 188–89, 191–95, 197; *Turning Point,* 25, 122–24, 126

Shakespeare, William. Works: *King Lear,* 184–85; Sonnet 73, 104; Sonnet 130, 181

Sikelianos, Angelos, 8, 29, 42, 140, 194

Sisyphus, 48

Solomos, Dionysios, 25, 29, 38, 42, 140–42, 147

Squires, Radcliffe, 109, 114

Stevens, Wallace, 8–9, 95

Swinburne, Algernon Charles, 26–28

Tennyson, Alfred, 26–28, 94

Thomas, Edward, 24

Thoreau, Henry David, 23, 178

Untermeyer, Louis, 24, 26–27, 162–63

Valéry, Paul, 22, 31, 36

Vayenas, Nasos, 38, 77, 123, 194, 202

Vermeule, Emily, 135, 137, 147, 182, 195

Wordsworth, William, 22, 28–29

Yeats, William Butler, 117